Books should be returned or renewed by the last date above. Renew by phone **08458 247 200** or online *www.kent.gov.uk/libs*

Libraries & Archives

Shakespeare and Contemporary Theory

New historicism and cultural materialism

NEEMA PARVINI

B L O O M S B U R Y

LONDON • NEW DELHI • NEW YORK • SYDNEY

Bloomsbury Academic
An imprint of Bloomsbury Publishing Plc

50 Bedford Square
London
WC1B 3DP
UK

175 Fifth Avenue
New York
NY 10010
USA

www.bloomsbury.com

First published 2012

© Neema Parvini, 2012

British Library Cataloguing-in-Publication Data
A catalogue record for this book is available from the British Library.

ISBN: HB: 978-1-4411-1127-2
PB: 978-1-4411-9393-3

Library of Congress Cataloging-in-Publication Data
A catalog record for this book is available at the Library of Congress.

Typeset by Newgen Imaging Systems Pvt Ltd, Chennai, India
Printed and bound in India

CONTENTS

ACKNOWLEDGEMENTS

I would like to thank Robert Eaglestone, for his help and advice; Kiernan Ryan, my mentor, for his continued support; my friends who read drafts of chapters and sent me some useful comments, and my students at Richmond American International University for doing the same; David Avital for conceiving the original concept and making this book possible, and Laura Murray and the team at Bloomsbury for their assistance during the publication process; and my parents for making the effort to read and understand the manuscript, which meant a lot to me. Finally, I would like to thank my wife, Ria, for casting her journalistic eye on what I have written and making many useful suggestions – I think it is safe to say that she now understands Marxist theory very well.

A NOTE ON THE TEXTS

All references to Shakespeare's plays are to Jowett, John, William Montgomery, Gary Taylor and Stanley Wells (eds), *William Shakespeare: The Complete Works*, 2nd edn (New York and Oxford: Oxford University Press, 2005).

TIMELINE OF THEORETICAL AND CRITICAL DEVELOPMENTS

1904 – A. C. Bradley, one of the first professional literary critics, publishes *Shakespearean Tragedy* ushering in a period in which character analysis was the principal method of reading Shakespeare's plays.

1910 – Ernest Jones writes 'Hamlet and Oedipus' taking Bradley's approach to its logical conclusion by using the theories of Sigmund Freud to psychoanalyse Shakespeare's characters.

1916 – The Swiss linguist Ferdinand de Saussure's *Course in Structural Linguistics* is published posthumously; it would not have a serious impact on literary theory or Shakespeare criticism for several decades. It is also one of the most important books in the development of structuralism.

1924 – I. A. Richards publishes the enormously influential *Principles of Criticism*, a book that advocates a formalist approach to literature laying the foundation for 'practical criticism' and 'the Cambridge School' led by F. R. Leavis and L. C. Knights.

1928 – The Russian formalist Vladimir Propp writes *Morphology of the Folktale* in which he analyses the narrative functions of Russian folktales – his approach would prove to be very influential later in the century, especially in the development of narratology.

1930 – G. Wilson Knight takes a thematic approach to Shakespeare's plays in *The Wheel of Fire*.

1933 – L. C. Knights publishes 'How Many Children Has Lady Macbeth?' a blistering formalist attack on A. C. Bradley's mode of character analysis.

1935 – Caroline Spurgeon's *Shakespeare's Imagery and What It Tells Us* produces a taxonomy of images in Shakespeare's plays; formalism is now the dominant approach in Shakespeare studies.

1943 – E. M. W. Tillyard's *The Elizabethan World Picture*, in defiance of the formalist status quo, takes a much more historical view of Shakespeare's plays demonstrating how they reflect ideas that were typical of their time and place. In Britain, this approach vies with 'practical criticism' for dominance in the Shakespeare scholarship of the 1940s and 1950s.

1947 – Cleanth Brooks publishes *The Well Wrought Urn* signalling the dominance of 'The New Criticism' – another type of formalism – in North America.

1950s – dominance of formalism in North America and Europe; in Britain, while formalists following the Cambridge School are powerful they have rivals for hegemony in the form of historicists following Tillyard.

1961 – A. P. Rossiter's *Angel with Horns* is published posthumously. He takes issue with the way Tillyard assumes that Shakespeare accepted the supposed ideals of Tudor England without question and is followed in this endeavour later by, among others, Wilbur Sanders and Moody E. Prior.

1967 – Roland Barthes declares 'the death of the author' in an essay of the same name published in French. Authorial intention becomes severely discredited as a critical concept.

1969 – Louis Althusser writes his enormously influential essay 'Ideology and the Ideological State Apparatus'.

1970 – Michel Foucault's *The Order of Things* and *The Archaeology of Knowledge* are translated into English and become widely read by academics in the humanities in both the United Kingdom and United States of America.

1971 – Antonio Gramsci's *Prison Notebooks* written in the 1930s while the author was imprisoned in Italy by the Mussolini regime is translated into English and made available to British scholars.

1973 – The anthropologist Clifford Geertz publishes a collection of essays called *The Interpretation of Cultures* in which he introduces the concepts of 'thick description' and 'local knowledge', which would become key features of new historicism a decade later.

1977 – Michel Foucault refines his theory of power in *Discipline and Punish*; he establishes the concept of Panopticism that would become key for both new historicists and cultural materialists.

1977 – Raymond Williams publishes the seminal *Marxism and Literature* in which he first coins the phrase 'cultural materialism'.

1980 – Borrowing concepts and methodologies from Geertz and Foucault, Stephen Greenblatt introduces new historicism in *Renaissance Self-Fashioning*, which would prove to be one of the most influential books in the history of Shakespeare studies.

1983 – Jonathan Goldberg publishes *James I and the Politics of Literature*, in many ways the archetypical new historicist study.

1984 – Jonathan Dollimore's *Radical Tragedy* introduces cultural materialism borrowing many concepts from Althusser, Gramsci and Williams. This goes on to be one of the most important books written on early modern tragedy in decades.

1985 – Jonathan Dollimore and Alan Sinfield co-edit the landmark collection of essays *Political Shakespeare*, the book which first put cultural materialism on the map and which set the political agenda of Shakespeare studies for a generation. In the same year, Catherine Belsey publishes *The Subject of Tragedy*, and Graham Holderness publishes *Shakespeare's History*, both pioneering cultural materialist studies which demonstrate that this movement is not a flash in the pan. As if to underline the point, also in the same year, John Drakakis edits another very important collection of mostly new historicist and cultural materialist essays called *Alternative Shakespeares* – a book that proved to be so influential that it went on to receive two sequels (rare for academic books).

1986 – Leonard Tennenhouse writes *Power on Display* another archetypical work that perhaps best represents new historicism in its 'first wave'.

1987 – Jean E. Howard and Marion F. O'Connor co-edit *Shakespeare Reproduced*, a volume containing important essays from, among others, Don E. Wayne and Walter Cohen that does as much to highlight problems with new historicism as it does to champion it.

1988 – Stephen Greenblatt publishes *Shakespearean Negotiations*, perhaps his most famous book, in which he introduces several important theoretical concepts such as the circulation of energy and the idea of political 'containment'.

1991 – Ivo Kamps' *Shakespeare Left and Right* collects a number of important essays from the humanist opponents of new historicism and cultural materialism such as Richard Levin and Edward Pechter.

1992 – Alan Sinfield's *Faultlines* underlines the cultural materialist manifesto and further refines its theory. Contra-Greenblatt, it emphasizes political dissidence and subversion.

1993 – Graham Bradshaw publishes a sustained and viscous humanist attack on new historicism and cultural materialism in *Misrepresentations*. In the same year, Richard Wilson writes *Will Power*, a book full of exemplary Foucauldian and Althusserian cultural materialist readings typical of the period.

1994–9 – new historicism and cultural materialism are now firmly dominant in Shakespeare studies. As if to signal this, the market is almost flooded with a slew of anthologies such as H. Aram Veeser's *The New Historicism Reader* (1994), Kiernan Ryan's *New Historicism and Cultural Materialism: A Reader* (1996) and Terence Hawkes's *Alternative Shakespeares Volume 2*, and textbooks such as Scott Wilson's *Cultural Materialism* (1995), Jeremy Hawthorn's *Cunning Passages* (1996), Claire Colebrook's *New Literary Histories* (1997) and John Brannigan's *New Historicism and Cultural Materialism* (1998). In the same time frame, many new historicists and cultural materialists produce more important works including *The State and Social Struggle* (1994) by Jean E. Howard, *Big-time Shakespeare* (1996) by Michael Bristol, *Shakespeare's Universal Wolf* (1996) by Hugh Grady, *The Purpose of Playing* (1996) by Louis Montrose, *Engendering a Nation* (1997) by Jean E. Howard and Phyllis Rackin and *Shakespeare and the Loss of Eden* (1999) by Catherine Belsey.

2000 – Catherine Gallagher and Stephen Greenblatt restate their position in *Practising New Historicism*.

2002 – The evolutionary psychologist Stephen Pinker publishes *The Blank Slate* attacking 'the modern denial of human behaviour' in many humanities departments.

2003 – Terry Eagleton publishes *After Theory* in which he appears to call time on the period that saw the rise in influence of thinkers such as Althusser, Barthes, Derrida, Foucault and others.

2004 – Stephen Greenblatt publishes his biography of Shakespeare *Will in the World* in which he seems to move away from new historicism by humanizing Shakespeare.

2005 – Catherine Belsey also seems to move away from her earlier cultural materialist work in *Culture and the Real*.

2006 – Alan Sinfield restates and updates his cultural materialist manifesto in *Shakespeare, Authority, Sexuality*, although it feels more like a final throw of the dice.

2006–present – We see a general movement away from new historicism and cultural materialism. Several critics, including Hugh Grady, Terence Hawkes and Ewan Fernie advocate 'presentist' readings of Shakespeare's plays assessing how they might usefully be utilized to understand present-day issues; their positions are most usefully collected in *Presentist Shakespeares* (2007). Other critics such as Stephen Cohen seek a return to more formalist methods of reading; *Renaissance Literature and Its Formal Engagements* (2002) is a good older example of this work. Others still seek a return to the humanist idea of Shakespeare as an author and free-thinking individual; key works include Philip Davis' *Shakespeare Thinking* (2006), Andy Mousley's *Re-humanising Shakespeare* (2007), A. D. Nuttall's *Shakespeare the Thinker* (2007), Neema Parvini's *Shakespeare's History Plays: Rethinking Historicism* (2012), as well as works by critics who draw on theories from evolutionary biology and psychology such as Marcus Nordlund's *Shakespeare and the Nature of Love* (2007).

A WHO'S WHO OF NEW HISTORICISM AND CULTURAL MATERIALISM

Given the sheer number of scholars and thinkers covered in this book, this 'Who's Who' is far from exhaustive and will only cover the most important figures directly involved in the development of new historicism and cultural materialism. Earlier theories and critical positions are covered in some detail in Chapter 2 and alternative views in Chapters 6 and 7.

Althusser, Louis – French Marxist and structuralist thinker who was most prominent in Paris in the 1960s and early 1970s. His anti-humanist concept of ideology was to prove irresistible for a generation of cultural materialists in the 1980s. See Chapter 3 for his theory of ideology.

Belsey, Catherine – one of the foremost cultural materialists. Her work is strongly theoretical, nuanced and takes more from post-structuralism than most other cultural materialists. Her recent work has diverged from cultural materialism in several interesting ways. See Chapter 5 for her work as a cultural materialist, Chapter 6 for her book *Culture and the Real* (2005) and Chapter 7 for her views on evolutionary biology.

Bradshaw, Graham – one of the most vocal and passionate opponents of new historicism and cultural materialism. See Chapters 4 and 5 for the main features of his attack on cultural materialism.

Dollimore, Jonathan – along with Alan Sinfield, perhaps the most prominent among cultural materialists. Dollimore is committed to the anti-humanist idea of 'de-centring' the individual in both history and Shakespeare's plays. His *Radical Tragedy* (1984) is one of the most important works in cultural materialism. See Chapter 5 for his thought and practice.

Foucault, Michel – French post-structuralist and anti-humanist thinker, most prominent in the 1960s and 1970s, whose work on power and methods of discourse analysis have been more influential on new historicism than any other in the 1980s and beyond. For an account of his key theories see Chapter 3.

Gallagher, Catherine – new historicist and feminist scholar who has worked not only on Shakespeare and the early modern period but also on authors from the late-seventeenth, eighteenth and nineteenth centuries. In 2000, she co-wrote *Practicing New Historicism* (with Stephen Greenblatt) which is an important statement on new historicist thought and practice. For an account of her position see Chapter 4.

Geertz, Clifford – preeminent American cultural anthropologist who was active from the 1950s to the 1990s. He would be a key influence on the development of new historicism – arguably, in Stephen Greenblatt's case, he was more influential than even Michel Foucault. See Chapter 3 for an account of his methods.

Goldberg, Jonathan – one of the first new historicists and latterly a proponent of concepts and methods borrowed from deconstruction. His *James I and the Politics of Literature* (1983) is one of the best examples of the early new historicist tendency to view Shakespeare's plays as instruments of state power (see Chapter 4).

Gramsci, Antonio – Italian Marxist who wrote his *Prison Notebooks* sitting in prison in the 1930s. A key influence on both Louis Althusser and Raymond Williams his theories of hegemony were also a direct influence for cultural materialists, especially Alan Sinfield. For an outline of his most important ideas see Chapter 3.

Greenblatt, Stephen – the father of new historicism and its most important and influential practitioner. His *Renaissance Self-Fashioning* (1980) can be used as a marker that signals the start of the new historicism. *Shakespearean Negotiations* (1988) is the *example par excellence* of new historicism. For his theory and practice see Chapter 4.

Holderness, Graham – one of the original cultural materialists whose work, especially on the history plays, has proved influential.

Howard, Jean E. – important new historicist and feminist Shakespearean critic and editor.

Kastan, David Scott – one of the more erudite opponents of new historicism and cultural materialism whose *Shakespeare After Theory* (1999) can be seen as the start of a general turn in Shakespeare studies away from theory and towards more conventional historical research.

Levin, Richard – the most prolific and determined of opponents of new historicism and cultural materialism, Levin tirelessly attacked both approaches for over fifteen years. For a summary of some of these attacks see Chapters 4 and 5.

Monstrose, Louis – a first-generation new historicist whose work has always been marked by an independence of mind and a commitment to political agency that often puts him closer to the cultural materialists than to Stephen Greenblatt or the other new historicists. For a brief consideration of his work see Chapter 4.

Patterson, Annabel – broadly speaking a cultural materialist who always remained deeply sceptical of the anti-humanist theory to which her colleagues were in thrall in the 1980s and 1990s. Books such as *Shakespeare and the Popular Voice* (1989) and *Reading Holinshed's Chronicles* (1994) are atypical of cultural materialist work in their stubborn refusal to be drawn in by the theories of Althusser or Foucault.

Pechter, Edward – one of the early opponents of new historicism and cultural materialism whose essay 'The New Historicism and its Discontents: Politicizing Renaissance Drama' (1987) reflects the mood of the old establishment towards these emergent approaches in the 1980s.

Sinfield, Alan – alongside Jonathan Dollimore, the most important and vocal of the cultural materialists. Sinfield's work is almost stridently politically committed. His *Faultlines* (1992) perhaps best represents the dissident spirit and tone of cultural materialism as a form of political action. For an outline of his main theories, see Chapter 5.

Tennenhouse, Leonard – first-generation new historicist whose *Power on Display* (1986) sits with Jonathan Goldberg's *James I and the Politics of Literature* (1983) as the best example of the early new historicist obsession with Foucauldian power and tendency to view Shakespeare's plays as instruments of state power (see Chapter 4).

Tillyard, E. M. W. – the foremost 'old historicist' of the 1940s whose work was very often held up by new historicists and cultural materialists in the 1980s as good examples of an essentialist humanist using Shakespeare to reinforce the (patriarchal, imperialistic) status quo.

Williams, Raymond – Welsh literary theorist strongly associated with the 'New Left' movement whose ideas about culture proved to be enormously influential for cultural materialists. In fact the term 'cultural materialism' is taken from his work. Accordingly, it is not uncommon for him to be described as 'the godfather of cultural materialism'. For an account of his theory see Chapter 5.

Wilson, Richard – a cultural materialist whose work is more strongly influenced by Foucault than by Althusser or other Marxist writers, his recent work has moved towards other theorists such as Pierre Bourdieu. His *Will Power* (1993) is a very good example of how Foucault can be used to read Shakespeare's plays.

CHAPTER ONE

Introduction

Objective

To establish the purposes of and uses for this guide

Why this book and why now?

Summary

- Why is it still important and necessary to learn about new historicism and cultural materialism
- The aims of this guide
- How this book is structured

Some readers of this book may take a look at the title and perceive juxtaposition between the word 'contemporary' and the phrase 'new historicism and cultural materialism'. Stephen Cohen first claimed to be writing 'after new historicism' in 1996, so how can either of these movements be thought of as being 'contemporary'? Others may recoil in horror and trepidation at the word 'theory'. Around the turn of the twenty-first century, did not Terry Eagleton, among others, assure us that the Great Age of Theory is over?[1] Surely now at last, academics from literature departments everywhere could retreat to the relative safety of traditional, archival historical scholarship without the taint of such ghastly phrases as 'ideological state apparatus' or 'overdetermination' clouding our thinking and confusing our students?

Writing now, over a decade into the twenty-first century, it is difficult to remember a time when lecturers would not remind their students to 'provide historical context' in their essays. Fredric Jameson's endlessly repeated maxim 'always historicize' scarcely needs repeating anymore. It is the aim of this book to show university students and their teachers not only how we arrived at this point but also how new historicism and cultural materialism far from being 'over' are in fact still the overwhelmingly dominant approaches of Shakespeare scholars today – regardless of whether or not they identify themselves as being new historicists or cultural materialists and, perhaps more contentiously, whether or not they recoil in terror at the word 'theory' as described above.

In 1988, David Simpson bemoaned: 'there is no clear consensus that the task of literary criticism is to teach an analysis of the historical production of writing.'[2] It is not difficult to see how dramatically the critical climate has shifted since Simpson was writing. In 2000, Tamsin Spargo introduced *Reading the Past* by claiming that 'cultural materialism and new historicism seem to have become the new orthodoxy in many Literature departments'.[3] It is safe to say that in North America new historicism has replaced the New Criticism as the dominant *modus operandi* of literary criticism and that in Britain cultural materialism has the edge over 'the textual skills of Englit'[4] in all but the most resilient of English departments. The genesis of these critical modes has not been without controversy. As Peter Erikson notes, by the mid-1980s new historicism (and, by association, cultural materialism) had completed its 'initial phase of development . . . and entered a transitional stage marked by uncertainty, growing pains, internal disagreement, and reassessment'.[5] From this transitional stage the new historicist / cultural materialist approach to literature emerged reinvigorated and victorious in the 1990s, producing study after study in all periods across the discipline and establishing itself firmly as the new status quo.

Then, in the 2000s, something else happened. New historicism and cultural materialism had become so entrenched that critics felt they no longer needed to theorize to the extent they once did. 'Theory with a capital T' was so 'ubiquitous' that it became old hat.[6] The 'golden age of cultural theory' seemed like a moment that had passed.[7] It was once the case that new historicist and cultural materialist essays would include lengthy discussions of how they were defining 'ideology' and 'culture' and 'social dissidence' replete with suitably deferential references to Louis Althusser, Michel Foucault, Antonio Gramsci, Pierre Macherey, Raymond Williams and Pierre Bourdieu. But you would be hard-pressed to find a recent study of Shakespeare's plays that even mentions this cast of characters, let alone engages seriously with their respective theories. So does this mean that we have simply moved 'beyond' Foucault and friends? My deep suspicion is that nothing could be further from the truth. We might no longer be treated to 20-page tracts on the virtues of *Discipline and Punish*, indeed we might no longer get a reference to Foucault at all, but we will get a detailed historical essay establishing what the people in Shakespeare's time and place thought about whatever issue is at stake, most likely with the implication that Shakespeare's play is complicit with the status quo. There will be no mention of such old-fashioned terms as 'ideology critique' or 'discourse analysis', despite the fact that the essay is – consciously or not – plainly working within the same theoretical framework that produced those terms. I am saying that although the idea of 'Theory' is increasingly frowned upon by many within the academy, its influence endures hidden, disavowed and unquestioned. This is perhaps a little ironic considering that Althusser's ideology or Foucault's concept of power work in exactly the same way: they are systems that function invisibly – you do not realize that that you are caught up in them, they are assumptions that appear to be 'common sense'.

In some literature departments, theoretically engaged new historicism and cultural materialism have given way to a kind of old-fashioned antiquarianism in which the importance and primacy of historical contextual work is seen as little more than a matter of common sense and 'Theory' as little more than a distracting and confusing waste of time. It would not be difficult to find Shakespeare scholars in any of the world's leading universities today to support that position. My own view is that this 'anti-Theory' stance is conservative and profoundly lacking in self-awareness, two things of which it would have been unimaginable to accuse new historicists and cultural materialists in the fervour of the 1980s. It is one aim of this book to uncover and challenge some of the unspoken assumptions under which many scholars and their students operate in the modern literature department. In short, those who follow the 'status quo' may no longer refer to themselves as 'new historicists' or 'cultural materialists' but rather shrink from such obviously 'theoretical' labels to get on the 'real work' of literary history, no questions asked. I would argue that despite this tendency new historicism and cultural materialism still broadly represent the status quo, especially in their anti-humanist belief that individuals have few natural characteristics and are simply the products of their social conditions. The idea that human beings are as much products of their genetic makeup, their DNA, as they are of their social and cultural milieu would still very much be considered controversial in most English departments. If you do not believe me, why not test it out in your next postcolonial or feminist seminar group?

Just as with any status quo, the legacy of new historicism and cultural materialism must be contextualized and subjected to further assessment distinct from those found in their gestation period. From the vantage point of critical hindsight, we can dispassionately assess the true impact of these approaches on Shakespeare studies and in the discipline more widely. I am not alone in thinking that perhaps new historicism and cultural materialism have been rather too successful in their annexation of the discipline. I am also not alone in questioning their assumptions, theoretical foundations and overall worth to literary scholars. In order to come to such conclusions, it is first necessary to understand how new historicism and cultural materialism transformed literary studies in the 1980s, which theories they utilized and how, through these theories, they radically reread Shakespeare's plays.

I intend this book both as study aid and catalyst; my aim is not only to educate the students who read it but also to encourage them to think critically about the ideas at stake in new historicism and cultural materialism and to move *beyond* them in their own theory and practice. I would like as much as possible to demystify 'theory' from the jargon and perceived complication with which it is typically associated so that students can engage directly with the *ideas* at stake. I believe we are on the verge of a sea change in Shakespeare studies, at the punctuation mark between two eras of scholarship. I see two major turns on the horizon:

1 Towards evolutionary criticism following advances made in evolutionary psychology and neurobiology, advances that are starkly at odds with the anti-humanism of new historicists and cultural materialists. Broadly speaking, this is a turn from culture to the individual.

2 Towards a renewed concern with form and language. Again, broadly speaking, this is a turn from a concern with historical context to text.

This is an ideal time to look back at the legacy of the past 30 years of new historicist and cultural materialist criticism while thinking seriously about what is to come in the future. The lists of 'key questions for students' that follow each section are intended to facilitate this aim. This book is written as an accessible and concise entry point into a large and complex field, I encourage students to follow up on my recommendations in the 'further reading' lists, especially in areas that particularly interest them.

This book follows a clear chronological structure: in Chapter 2, I outline the most important positions in twentieth-century Shakespearean criticism before Stephen Greenblatt published *Renaissance Self-Fashioning* in 1980. This will help us assess the impact of new historicism and cultural materialism in the 1980s and 1990s later in the book. Chapter 3 establishes the key concepts that new historicists and cultural materialists have adapted from the theorists that influenced them most profoundly: Clifford Geertz, Antonio Gramsci, Louis Althusser and Michel Foucault (since the term 'cultural materialism' was coined by Raymond Williams, I will be dealing with his theory in the relevant chapter). Chapter 4 focuses on new historicism, its key ideas and methods, as well as criticisms of them and Chapters 5 does the same with cultural materialism. Chapter 6 delves into the many divergent positions that exist under the general umbrella of historicist and materialist work. And finally, in Chapter 7 I look at some of the emerging new alternatives and offer a few final thoughts on how we might move beyond new historicism and cultural materialism.[8]

Key questions for students

- Why is it important to establish the historical context of a text that you are reading?
- Is it possible to have a critical approach to literature without a theory?
- Why might some Shakespeare scholars dislike the study of literary theory?
- Is it best to follow the status quo or to find ways of challenging it?

Selected further reading

Cunningham, Valentine, *Reading After Theory* (Malden, MA and Oxford: Blackwell, 2002).

Docherty, Thomas, *After Theory: Postmodernism/Postmarxism* (New York and London: Routledge, 1990).

Eagleton, Terry, *After Theory* (London: Allen Lane, 2003).

Kastan, David Scott, *Shakespeare After Theory* (New York and London: Routledge, 1999).

Notes

1   Terry Eagleton, *After Theory* (London: Allen Lane, 2003); Valentine Cunningham, *Reading After Theory* (Malden, MA and Oxford: Blackwell, 2002); David Scott Kastan, *Shakespeare After Theory* (New York and London: Routledge, 1999) and, at least a decade ahead of the curve, Thomas Docherty, *After Theory: Postmodernism/Postmarxism* (New York and London: Routledge, 1990).

2   David Simpson, 'Literary Criticism and the Return to "History"', *Critical Inquiry*, 14(4) (Summer 1988), 723.

3   Tamsin Spargo, 'Introduction: Past, Present and Future Pasts', in *Reading the Past: Literature and History*, ed. Tamsin Spargo (London: Palgrave Macmillan, 2000), p. 11.

4   Scott Wilson, *Cultural Materialism: Theory and Practice* (Oxford: Blackwell, 1995), p. 19.

5   Peter Erikson, 'Rewriting the Renaissance, Rewriting Ourselves', *Shakespeare Quarterly*, 38(3) (Autumn 1987), 330.

6   Cunningham, *Reading After Theory*, p. 15.

7   Eagleton, *After Theory*, p. 1.

8   For a more polemical version of this, see Neema Parvini, *Shakespeare's History Plays: Rethinking Historicism* (Edinburgh: Edinburgh University Press, 2012).

CHAPTER TWO

Before new historicism and cultural materialism

Objective

To outline the state of literary studies before it was transformed by new historicism and cultural materialism in the 1980s

The first half of the twentieth century: Traditional scholarship from A. C. Bradley to Moody E. Prior

Summary

- The importance and centrality of Shakespeare criticism in literary studies
- A. C. Bradley's character analysis in the early 1900s
- The formalist criticism of L. C. Knights, Caroline Spurgeon and G. Wilson Knight in the 1930s
- The 'old historicism' of E. M. W. Tillyard, John Dover Wilson and Lily B. Campbell in the 1940s
- The liberal humanist 'ambivalent' Shakespeare of A. P. Rossiter, Wilbur Sanders and Moody E. Prior in the 1960s and early 1970s
- The legacies of those named above

Few writers have ever received as much critical attention as Shakespeare. A cursory search of available books on Amazon.com pulls up over 94,000 results and a search for any of the individual major plays over 9,000 results. Even if these figures are far from accurate, they give us an impression of the sheer amount of ink that has been committed to paper in discussing Shakespeare's plays. Given Shakespeare's stature in the canons of both English literature and literary studies more generally, his plays have long served as the testing ground for new methods of criticism. Although it is not always the case, the tendency is for critical debates to be fiercely contested in the realm of Shakespeare studies before filtering through to the rest of the discipline. Even as the concept of the literary canon has been steadily eroded since the 1980s, Shakespeare has remained central both to university courses and to leading literary critics. The most prominent new historicists and cultural materialists such as Stephen Greenblatt, Alan Sinfield and Jonathan Dollimore first made their names as critics of Shakespeare's plays. Certain works by Shakespeare act as a kind of litmus test for critical approaches. Here is Kiernan Ryan on the importance of *King Lear*, not only for new approaches in Shakespeare studies but also for literary criticism in general:

> As the touchstone of literary value and star witness in defence of the discipline, the tragedy is fated to be the target of every critical approach keen to stake its claim to priority. . . . *King Lear* has consequently become an exemplary site of contention between the leading schools of contemporary criticism; and to examine the most influential rival readings of *Lear* is to bring into focus not only the key disputes dividing Shakespeare studies today, but also the current predicament of criticism itself.[1]

Ryan's message is clear: *King Lear* affords innovative new readings a prominence and influence that few other texts can provide. In the overall scheme of literary studies, the same is true of most of Shakespeare's major canonical works. For example, had Stephen Greenblatt's famous essay about *Henry IV Parts 1 and 2*, 'Invisible Bullets' been about John Marston's *The Malcontent*, it seems unlikely to me that his theory of subversion and containment would have become a major source of debate in the late 1980s and early 1990s. Although some may not like it, the fact remains that Shakespeare criticism enjoys a visibility and therefore a certain prominence that criticism of works by other playwrights of the period do not. In fact, there are few writers from any period whose works have been so central in the history of critical approaches. Accordingly, the readings of individual plays have been important in the development of various critical schools. For example, *Hamlet* looms large over the history of psychoanalytical approaches to literature; as Rainer Emig says, 'the most fertile material for a Freudian reading [of literature] . . . has undoubtedly been Shakespeare's *Hamlet*'.[2] *The Tempest* occupies a similar position in the history of postcolonial approaches. In short, the reception history of Shakespeare's plays in many ways serves to illustrate the prevailing critical fashions of the past in microcosm.

The field of twentieth-century Shakespeare studies is vast, and I cannot provide anything approaching an exhaustive survey or even outline in the space afforded me here. As Gary Taylor said in 1990: 'Even for hard-core Shakespearians, lifers, it is impossible to digest the hundreds of books and thousands of articles published on the subject in any year.'[3] What I can do, however, is highlight the two key critical debates around which the study of Shakespeare's plays have revolved since at least the 1930s and note some of the major proponents on either sides of them:

1 Do Shakespeare's characters possess an interiority or psychological depth, or should Shakespeare's plays be read as being dramatic poems and their characters merely literary constructs?

2 Are Shakespeare's plays simply the product of their time and place, or do they have the capacity to transcend their cultural moment? Was Shakespeare able to see and think things most of his contemporaries could not?

The prevailing critical fashions have oscillated back and forth between the polar points of each of these two questions. And, broadly speaking, the same issues have been at stake in the years since the advent of new historicism in 1980. In the account that follows, it is important to remember that various positions often exist in parallel, and at any given time there are numerous things going on. If I may make a quick analogy to the world of popular music: what was the dominant genre of music in 1977? We might make cases for both punk and disco, some might even outline a case for progressive rock; important albums were also released that year by David Bowie, Iggy Pop, Talking Heads, Bob Marley and Kraftwerk, none of which fit into the three suggested categories above. The point is that we can only sensibly discuss general trends, the work produced in any given year of Shakespeare criticism will almost always exceed any tidy label we can put on it. For example, in the account of the 1960s below I find no place for the pioneering and influential work of Jan Kott, which set the template of Royal Shakespeare Company productions for at least a generation. For Kott, Shakespeare's plays provided a prototype to the Artaudian or Brechtian theatre of cruelty. Kott's darkly existential book *Shakespeare Our Contemporary* (1964) announces that '*King Lear* is the decay and fall of the world' and that *Macbeth* 'is the deepest of Shakespeare's tragedies' because it anticipates the 'Auschwitz experience'.[4] Outlines that discuss general trends have a hard time dealing with anomalies and are prone to exclude them.

I will start my consideration of Shakespeare criticism before new historicism and cultural materialism with A. C. Bradley's *Shakespearean Tragedy*, published in 1904. In some ways, Bradley can be viewed as the first modern Shakespeare scholar; his work is 'widely seen as inaugurating the modern age in criticism of early modern drama';[5] while in others he seems distinctly Victorian. As D. J. Palmer's now ageing *The Rise of English Studies* documents, he was among the first professional academic critics.[6] Criticism of Shakespeare's plays before 1900 was mostly the work of gentlemen amateurs, eccentrics such as Delia Bacon, essayists such as Samuel Johnson, William Hazlitt and Charles Dudley Warner and poets such as Samuel Taylor Coleridge or Algernon Charles Swinburne. E. M. W. Tillyard remarked that 'the dominant trend' before 1917 'was towards gossipy, and often highly metaphorical, description and unspecific praise'.[7] Although Bradley held a professorship at Oxford, as Katherine Cooke writes, he 'lived at the latest time when it was possible to write Shakespeare criticism without a heavy ballast of research material, or at the very least, a reputable record of research behind one'.[8] It is hardly surprising then that Bradley's criticism, with its easy, avuncular, conversational style retains an air of what A. D. Nuttall called the 'rambling, gentlemanly conversation' of Victorian criticism.[9] At times, however, such as in his refusal to accept Iago's motives at face value in *Othello*, Bradley 'strikes an authentically twentieth-century note'.[10] Bradley has always been famous, or perhaps more accurately notorious, for his strongly character-driven analyses of Shakespeare's plays, especially the tragedies and *Henry IV Parts 1 and 2*. Let us look briefly at a characteristically Bradleyan passage where he is discussing Iago's motives in *Othello*:

> What is the meaning of all this? Unless Shakespeare was out of his mind, it must have a meaning. And certainly this meaning cannot be found in any of the popular accounts of Iago. . . . What then were the real moving forces of Iago's action? Are we to fall back on the idea of 'motiveless malignity', that is to say, a disinterested love of evil or a delight in the pain of others as simple and direct as the delight in one's own pleasure? Surely not. I will not insist that this thing or these things are inconceivable, mere phrases, not ideas; for, even so, it would remain possible that Shakespeare had tried to represent an inconceivability. But there is not the slightest reason to suppose that he did so. Iago's action is intelligible; and indeed the popular view contains enough truth to refute this desperate theory. It greatly exaggerates his desire for advancement, and the ill-will caused by his disappointment, and it ignores other forces more important than these; but it is right in insisting on the presence of this desire and this ill-will, and their presence is enough to destroy Iago's claims to be more than a demi-devil. For love of the evil that advances my interest and hurts a person I dislike, is a very different thing from love of evil simply as evil; and pleasure in the pain of a person disliked or regarded as a competitor is quite distinct from pleasure in the pain of others simply as others. The first is intelligible, and we find it in Iago. The second, even if it were intelligible, we do not find in Iago.[11]

This has all of the classic traits of Bradley. First, note the absence of textual analysis. When Bradley quotes from Shakespeare it is usually in an illustrative capacity. Second, there is the tendency to treat Shakespeare's characters as if they were real people with proper psychological motives. Third, there is the assumption that everything we find in the plays was put there by Shakespeare very deliberately, with a specific purpose in mind. Finally, there is the tendency to put *himself* in the character's position and draw inferences from that.

In many ways, I think that Bradley's approach is one we can all recognize in ourselves. When we – we as normal, everyday people that is, rather than as literary critics – watch films and television dramas, or read novels, and discuss them with friends, we are drawn towards the sorts of questions Bradley asks. I would warrant that the modern casual theatre audiences watching performances of *Hamlet* and *Othello* are drawn to the same sorts of questions: why does Hamlet procrastinate so much before finally killing Claudius? Why does Iago act with such malice and spite towards Othello? Why does Hal reject Falstaff at the end of *Henry IV Part 2*? In many ways these are the 'obvious' questions to ask. But Bradley's way of reading is deficient in many areas: he neglects Shakespeare's language and wordplay; he is often guilty of anachronistically reading the plays according to the standards of his own time rather than of Shakespeare's; and finally, he commits what is for some, a grave error, in treating the characters of Shakespeare's plays as real people with implied lives outside of the text.

Nonetheless, Bradley's book proved to be very popular in the first two decades of the twentieth century and character analysis became the dominant method of criticism. There are grumblings about the Bradleyan approach as early as 1909, when Sir Walter Raleigh (the early twentieth-century scholar, not to be confused with his sixteenth-century namesake) said: 'our sin is not indifference, but superstition. . . . [Shakespeare's] poetry has been used like a wedding cake, not to eat but to dream upon . . . Let us make an end of this, and do justice to Shakespeare the craftsman.'[12] The inevitable backlash against Bradley started in earnest around 1930 when J. W. Mackail complained 'we have no right to invent a life-history of Autolycus's aunts'.[13] The real turning point came three years later when L. C. Knights published his seminal essay 'How Many Children had Lady Macbeth?', a blistering attack on Bradley's style of criticism. Knights was appalled at Bradley's emphasis on character and his sarcastic title pokes fun at Bradley's tendency to imagine the lives of characters outside the text. Knights was a member of 'the Cambridge School' associated with I. A. Richards and F. R. Leavis (see section below) which privileged above all else close reading and textual analysis. For Knights, Shakespeare's plays were long dramatic poems that should be analysed as such:

> A Shakespeare play is a dramatic poem. It uses action, gesture, formal grouping and symbols, and it relies upon the general conventions governing Elizabethan plays. But, we cannot too often remind ourselves, its end is to communicate a rich and controlled experience by means of words. . . . The total response to a Shakespeare play can only be obtained by an exact and sensitive study of the quality of verse, of the rhythm and imagery, of the controlled association of the words and their emotional and intellectual force, in short by an exact and sensitive study of Shakespeare's handling of language.[14]

One would assume then that Knights would produce readings of Shakespeare's plays that emphasize their verbal or linguistic qualities. This is not entirely the case. When one comes to read Knights' critical practice it is difficult not to be struck by his often moralizing tone: 'Macbeth is a state of evil', he tells us, 'it has a greater affinity with *The Waste Land* than with *The Doll's House*'.[15] This can be explained partly by the fact that Knights was as much influenced by his friend and colleague F. R. Leavis as he was by I. A. Richards. Leavis inherited from the influential nineteenth-century school inspector Matthew Arnold a belief that education is transformative and that Good literature is a force of moral good. Terry Eagleton even goes so far as to suggest that *Scrutiny*, the journal that Leavis edited (and that Knights often co-edited), was 'the focus of a moral and cultural crusade'. Michael Taylor concurs stating that Leavis and his followers launched the journal in 1932 'to celebrate the moral centrality of all great literature'. Leavis saw the mass culture of mechanized society as an abomination and thought that literature, as Eagleton puts it, 'could roll back the deadening effects of industrialized labour and philistinism of the media'.[16]

For more pure expressions of the formalist bent of much criticism of 1930s, it is perhaps best to turn from Knights to two other critics of the period: Caroline Spurgeon and the prolific G. Wilson Knight. Spurgeon's *Shakespeare's Imagery and What It Tells Us* published in 1935 is pioneering and peculiar in equal measure. She sets herself a unique task:

> I believe we can draw from the material of a poet's images definite information about his personality. In working out this line of thought, we are justified, I suggest, in assuming that a poet will, in the long run, naturally tend to draw the large proportion of his images from the objects he knows best, or thinks most about, or from the incidents, among myriads he has experienced, to which he is sensitive, and which therefore remain within his knowledge.[17]

What follows is a near-taxonomy of imagery in Shakespeare's plays compared and contrasted with the images found in the work of, among others, Francis Bacon and Christopher Marlowe. Let us consider some typical passages of Spurgeon's study:

> The images from sports and games form another sure indication of a writer's tastes and individuality. Shakespeare has a great many, chiefly from falconry, shooting with bow and arrow, deer hunting, bird-snaring, and fishing, and in games, chiefly from bowls, football and tennis, but his images from bowls, which he clearly knew and liked best, are about three times as many as from any other game. . . . It is characteristic that Dekker has nearly twice as many images from games as anybody else, including five from bowls, all showing a definite knowledge of the game. Shakespeare happens to have only two images from games in these five plays, although we know from his total number of game images that he was also well acquainted with bowls.[18]   .

This is the critic as trainspotter. Spurgeon notes down instances of particular image clusters and then produces statistics. Whatever one thinks of this approach, it would be churlish to deny the bald fact that someone whose work includes various images from bowls had some knowledge of the game. Although I am not sure what Spurgeon's answer would be to the reader who asks 'so what?'

If Spurgeon's meticulous concentration on imagery seems esoterically specific, then G. Wilson Knight gives us the opposite extreme. Often prone to flights of fancy which border on vagueness, he was interested not in particular images but, as he put it in 1932, in the 'groups of imaginative themes, poetical colourings . . . the symbols and symphonies of dramatic poetry' that make up the pervading atmosphere of the play under study.[19] Wilson Knight's key critical concept is the idea of reading the plays 'spatially', which he explained in the introduction to his landmark study of 1930, *The Wheel of Fire*:

> A Shakespearean tragedy is set spatially as well as temporally in the mind. By this I mean that there are throughout the play a set of correspondences which relate to each other independently of the time-sequence which is the story: such are the intuition-intelligence opposition active within and across *Troilus and Cressida*, the death-theme in *Hamlet*, the nightmare evil of *Macbeth*. This I have sometimes called the play's 'atmosphere'.[20]

In this way, Wilson Knight tends to read plays through the prism of a single set of images, which leads to some highly distinctive interpretations of Shakespeare's tragedies that, even today, can be strikingly original. Consider, for example, his famous reading of Hamlet that inverts the traditional (or at least Bradleyan) wisdom that Claudius is the villain of the piece and Hamlet is essentially a good man paralysed by doubt and fear:

> Claudius, as he appears in the play, is not a criminal. He is – strange as it may seem – a good and gentle king, enmeshed by a chain of causality linking him with his crime. . . . Hamlet is a danger to the state, even apart from his knowledge of Claudius' guilt. He is an inhuman – or superhuman – presence, whose consciousness . . . is centred on death. . . . He is feared by those around him. They are always trying in vain to find out what is wrong with him. They cannot understand him. He is a creature from another world. . . . The question of the relative morality of Hamlet and Claudius reflects the ultimate problem of this play.[21]

Nonetheless, this thematic approach has its drawbacks: in seeking for these unifying 'sets of correspondences' Wilson Knight has a priori (i.e. before even reading the play) assumed that one must be there and so he is almost certain to find it. It also means that he is likely to overlook other major aspects of the play, not least its characters and its internal contradictions. For example, his reading of *Hamlet*, drenched as it is in death, is nearly silent on the relationship between Hamlet and Gertrude, whom he offhandedly describes as 'the affectionate mother'.[22] And, as A. L. French points out, to make his reading work Wilson Knight swept 'the inconvenient aspects of Claudius under the carpet'.[23]

By the 1940s, just as the different variants of formalism practiced by Knights, Spurgeon, Wilson Knight and others had taken over from Bradleyan character analysis in becoming the new orthodoxy in Shakespeare studies, the critical pendulum was ready to swing again. The decade saw the publication of four landmark studies of what we might today call 'old historicism': *The Elizabethan World Picture* (1943) and *Shakespeare's History Plays* (1944) both by E. M. W. Tillyard, *The Fortunes of Falstaff* (1943) by John Dover Wilson and *Shakespeare's 'Histories': Mirrors of Elizabethan Policy* (1947) by Lily B. Campbell.[24] The two studies by Tillyard have been arguably as influential on the study of Shakespeare's plays as Bradley's *Shakespearean Tragedy*, if not more so. And like Bradley's, Tillyard's approach has been as notorious as it is famous. Tillyard's thesis is simple, perhaps crudely so: if he could establish 'the average beliefs of the well-educated Elizabethan',[25] then he held the key to understanding Shakespeare (being such an average well-educated Elizabethan) and therefore his plays. According to Tillyard, Elizabethan England was still in thrall to a set of medieval beliefs. The key concept is The Great Chain of Being, a strictly hierarchical universe ordained by God. Everyone and everything – God himself, the angels, human beings, animals, plants, the elements, the sun, moon and planets – has its allotted place in this cosmic order of things. In this hierarchy, men are above women, and kings, having been divinely ordained, are above their subjects. In such an order, dissidence is scarcely an option: to oppose the strictures of the Great Chain of Being is to oppose God Himself.

In addition, Tillyard argues that Elizabethans subscribed to a providential view of history he calls 'the Tudor myth':[26] God would punish those who disturbed his order and 'correct' history by re-establishing the order. For Tillyard, Shakespeare's history plays follow their chief source, Raphael Holinshed's *Chronicles*, in perpetuating this myth. The Wars of the Roses were seen by the Elizabethans as a punishment from God for Henry IV's murder of the divinely ordained monarch Richard II. Shortly after Henry's usurpation of the king in *Richard II*, the Bishop of Carlisle warns: 'if you crown him, let me prophesy/The blood of English shall manure the ground' (*Richard II*, 4.1.125–40). This is all the proof Tillyard needs to demonstrate that Shakespeare subscribed wholly to the prevalent ideas of his time. The historian Nigel Saul puts forward a neat version of this argument:

> To Shakespeare and his contemporaries the history of fifteenth-century England was a commentary on the bishop's prophetic utterance. All the ills that were to afflict the realm . . . flowed from Hereford's (Bolingbroke's) rebellion against Richard . . . [Henry Tudor] providentially healed the divisions by marrying Elizabeth of York . . . Underlying Shakespeare's preoccupation with civil strife was a deeper concern for social order. In the Elizabethan's world view civil discord imperilled the very existence of society. This was essentially the medieval view of the world. Everyone and everything was held to have its allotted place. From the bottom of society to the top, people were linked in a 'great chain of being', which duplicated the order of heaven.[27]

In the past six decades Tillyard's ideas have been widely discredited as being crudely reductive. It is not necessarily the case, for example, that *every* Elizabethan believed absolutely in the providential view of history he outlines. There were at least two alternative approaches that Shakespeare would have had some knowledge of: the humanist *Realpolitik* of Niccolò Machiavelli and the new anti-quarianism of William Camden.[28] And even if Shakespeare had no knowledge of either of those approaches, why did Shakespeare necessarily have to follow the status quo? Why could he not possess, as Wilbur Sanders put it in 1968, 'a mind which could read Holinshed and think otherwise'?[29]

Tillyard, Dover Wilson and to an extent Campbell (who was American), are perhaps best understood, ironically, if we historicize them. Britain was, of course, still very much at war in 1943 and in desperate need of both certainty and a solid national identity. This accounts partly for much of the patriotism one finds in Dover Wilson, but not entirely for the disconcerting implication in Tillyard that he himself sympathizes with the Elizabethan world picture. By the 1960s and early 1970s, when circumstances in both Britain and America had very much changed, Tillyard faced an almost inevitable backlash. Several critics, who we can broadly describe as liberal humanists, opposed Tillyard in a number of ways. These include A. P. Rossiter, the aforementioned Wilbur Sanders and Moody E. Prior. Plainly influenced by William Empson's *Seven Types of Ambiguity* (1930),[30] their Shakespeare was an ambivalent thinker who entertained multiple positions without feeling the need to come down on any one side. This Shakespeare resisted the glib moral and political lessons that the likes of Campbell saw in the histories. As Prior put it Shakespeare's history plays were 'exploratory rather than doctrinaire'.[31] And far from being Elizabethan state propaganda, they 'come to us clothed in their full human significance'.[32] Sanders agreed that where Tillyard saw Shakespeare's straightforward support for the ideas of his time he saw 'complexities':

> In choosing to treat this turbulent stretch of English history, Shakespeare has plunged into the very waters where the concept of kingship was fraught with the profoundest complexities. If he was planning to exemplify the simplified monarchic theory of Tudor propaganda, it was a singularly unhappy choice of subject.[33]

The supreme articulation of this ambivalent Shakespeare is undoubtedly found in Rossiter's *Angel with Horns* (1961). Rossiter talks about the 'the constant Doubleness of Shakespeare's vision in the Histories',[34] two contrasting alternatives held in dialectical tension. Back in 1904, Bradley – who, incidentally, enjoyed a period of critical rehabilitation in the 1960s[35] – had spotted a tendency in Shakespeare's work 'to show one set of forces advancing, in secret or open opposition to the other, to some decisive success, and then driven downward to defeat by the reaction it provokes'.[36] Rossiter's argument, unlike Bradley's, states that there is no eventual victor because the forces are held in a *dialectical* tension which constitutes an unresolved ambivalence. For Rossiter, the Tillyardian approach to the history plays is guilty of making 'simplifications which are in danger of diminishing the true complexity of Shakespearean History'. Rossiter argues that Shakespeare employs a kind of parody in the Histories that 'operates by juxtapositions of opposites; by contrasts so extreme as to seem irreconcilable'.

Rossiter continues: 'The parallelism is manifest. . . . The question of "Who is right, A or B?" is a no-question: the poem is *ambivalent*. It subsumes meanings which point to two opposite and irreconcilable systems of values.' And here is the crucial concept: 'I mean by "Ambivalence" that two opposed value-judgements are subsumed, and that both are valid. . . . The whole is only fully experienced when both opposites are held and included in a "two-eyed" view; and all "one-eyed" simplifications are not only falsifications; they amount to a denial of some fact of the mystery of things.'[37]

At this juncture, it is worth pausing. Sometime after the publication of Prior's *The Drama of Power* in 1973 Shakespeare criticism changed radically. As Annette Lavers puts it, there was a 'very rapid, almost violent, change in the language and assumptions of American literary criticism around this time'.[38] Presently, I think it would be useful to take stock of how the great critics whose work I have outlined above have left lasting impressions on the study of Shakespeare's plays. Bradley's character analysis would ultimately find its logical apotheosis in psychoanalysis. Ernest Jones's *Hamlet and Oedipus* (original essay 1910, expanded into a book in 1949), for example, arguably owes as much to Bradley as it does to Freud.[39] The work of Spurgeon, Knights and Wilson Knight can ultimately be viewed as precursors to the American 'New Critics' (see section below) who came to prominence in the 1940s and dominated mainstream Shakespeare scholarship and teaching methods for the next two decades. The sort of close attention to language that Knights promised, but never quite delivered himself, can be seen in M. M. Mahood's classic *Shakespeare's Wordplay* (1957) and Frank Kermode's late study *Shakespeare's Language* (2000), which he published at the age of 81. We can see the clear influence of Spurgeon in Wolfgang Clemen's *The Development of Shakespeare's Imagery* (1951). And something of Wilson Knight's 'spatial' method of reading in Helen Vendler's *The Art of Shakespeare's Sonnets* (1997). The legacy of Tillyard and the other exponents of 'old historicism' is found ultimately in the work of new historicists and cultural materialists, which even if they are staunchly opposed to Tillyard on many issues, must openly acknowledge the fact that his controversial studies set the political agenda in reading Shakespeare for the next seventy years. That said, it is worth mentioning C. L. Barber's *Shakespeare's Festive Comedy* (1959) – incidentally, much loved by Stephen Greenblatt, who provided a forward for the 2012 reprint – as a notable early attempt at moving historicism from the monolithic idea of 'the Elizabethan world picture' to individual social rituals and practices, although this book, well ahead of its time, probably owes more to Mikhail Bakhtin than it does to Tillyard.[40]

Before moving on to consider the theories that were instrumental in the development of new historicism and cultural materialism, it is necessary to expand further our understanding of formalism and its ancillary movement, structuralism. This is not least because an understanding of structuralism is vital to grasping the work of Louis Althusser and Michel Foucault and in turn the approaches that they so profoundly came to influence in the 1980s: new historicism and cultural materialism.

Key questions for students

- Do you think that it is right that Shakespeare still occupies such a central place in both literary criticism and literature courses at universities?
- What are the benefits and drawbacks of a character-based approach to Shakespeare's plays, such as A. C. Bradley's? Do you think that character is an important category of analysis when reading Shakespeare?
- Do you agree with L. C. Knights and F. R. Leavis that literature is inherently enriching, a force of moral good in society?
- How does Caroline Spurgeon's listing of image clusters in Shakespeare's plays help us understand them? Could this approach be usefully conjoined with other approaches?
- To what extent does G. Wilson Knight's theme-based reading of Shakespeare distort the plays? Do you think 'themes' are an important category of analysis when reading Shakespeare?
- Are there at all any positives to draw from E. M. W. Tillyard's 'old historicist' approach to Shakespeare's plays? And if not, why not?
- What do you think of A. P. Rossiter's 'two-eyed' Shakespeare, who can weigh up contradictory positions without taking sides? Do you agree with Rossiter that Shakespeare was always non-partisan in this way?

Selected further reading

Barber, C. L., *Shakespeare's Festive Comedy: A Study of Dramatic Form and Its Relation to Social Custom* (Princeton, NJ: Princeton University Press, 2012).

Bradley, A. C., *Shakespearean Tragedy: Lectures on Hamlet, Othello, King Lear, Macbeth*, 2nd edn (London: Macmillan, 1905).

Empson, William, *Seven Types of Ambiguity* (London: Chatto & Windas, 1930).

Jones, Ernest, *Hamlet and Oedipus* (New York: Norton, 1949).

Knight, G. Wilson, *The Wheel of Fire: Interpretations of Shakespearean Tragedy*, 4th edn (New York and London: Routledge, 2001).

—, *The Imperial Theme: Further Interpretations of Shakespeare's Tragedy* (New York and London: Routledge, 2002).

Knights, L. C., *Explorations: Essays in Criticism Mainly on the Literature of the Seventeenth Century* (London: Chatto & Windas, 1946).

Kott, Jan, *Shakespeare Our Contemporary*, 2nd edn (London: Routledge, 1991).

Mahood, M. M., *Shakespeare's Wordplay* (London: Methuen, 1957).

Nuttall, A. D., 'The Argument About Shakespeare's Characters', *Critical Quarterly*, 7(2) (1965), 107–20.

Prior, Moody E., *The Drama of Power: Studies in Shakespeare's History Plays* (Evanston, IL: Northwestern University Press, 1973).

Rossiter, A. P., *Angel with Horns: Fifteen Lectures on Shakespeare*, ed. Graham Storey (New York: Longman, 1989).

Sanders, Wilbur, *The Dramatist and the Received Idea: Studies in the Plays of Marlowe and Shakespeare* (Cambridge: Cambridge University Press, 1968).

Spurgeon, Caroline, *Shakespeare's Imagery and What It Tells Us* (Cambridge: Cambridge University Press, 2004).

Taylor, Michael, *Shakespeare Criticism in the Twentieth Century* (Oxford: Oxford University Press, 2001).

Tillyard, E. M. W., *Shakespeare's History Plays* (London: Chatto and Windus, 1944).

—, *The Elizabethan World Picture* (London: Vintage, 1959).

The 1950s to the 1970s: Formalism, structuralism and deconstruction

Summary

- Key general principles of Ferdinand de Saussure's *Course in General Linguistics*
- Practical criticism of the Cambridge School in Britain and the 'New Criticism' in America
- Formalism in practice: an assessment of a structuralist reading of 'Sonnet 129' by Roman Jakobson and L. G. Jones
- A brief look at Vladimir Propp's narrative functions
- The proposed method of reading narratives structurally in 'Introduction to the Structural Analysis of Narratives' and *S/Z* by Roland Barthes
- The emergence of deconstruction at Yale and its limited impact on Shakespeare studies

Jerome J. McGann complained in 1985 that he was working in 'an academic world . . . dominated by structuralist and post-structuralist theory and practice'.[41] Formalism dominated literary criticism in the 1950s and 1960s, and its successor, deconstruction (especially of the Yale school), had a period of dominance in the 1970s and early 1980s. In Europe, this manifested itself as structuralism, derived from the linguistics of Ferdinand de Saussure who 'attempted to provide a scientific basis for the study of language – and more generally of signs'[42] developed by the Russian and Prague Schools of the 1930s (Vladimir Propp, Roman Jakobson and Tzvetan Todorov) and then adapted, refined and radically re-theorized in Paris in the 1950s and 1960s (Claude Lévi-Strauss, Julien Algirdas Greimas and Roland Barthes). According to Terry Eagleton, literary criticism in the 1950s 'badly required the discipline of an objective system'.[43] Structuralism provided one such system. Structuralism was committed to the idea of the text as a functioning whole which could be analysed and picked apart to discover how it achieved its effects, as Roland Barthes states: 'the goal of all structuralist activity . . . is to "reconstitute" an object so as to manifest the rules of its functioning.'[44] Gerard Genette tells us that literature 'like any other activity of the mind is based on conventions of which, with some exceptions, it is not aware'.[45] In other words, literature itself is a system held together by 'certain objective laws'[46] which most people take for granted, and it is up to structuralists to uncover and define these laws – almost as if they were the seventeenth- and eighteenth-century physicists observing the universe and defining the scientific laws.

This is easiest to spot in the work of Saussure himself whose *Course in General Linguistics* published in 1916 sought to challenge the epistemological approach to linguistics that was dominant at the time with a new methodology that focused almost exclusively on the *function* of language. The epistemological approach to language tells us the origins of words; it traces their history until it finds an ultimate root. For example, an epistemological approach to the word 'stomach' would tell us that it is derived from the Latin 'stomachus' which itself is derived from the Greek word 'stomachos', and ultimately from 'stoma' which means 'mouth'. This approach is *diachronic* because it describes something that happens over time. Saussure was not interested in where words came from but how they functioned in everyday speech. He was interested in, for example, why when you or I hear the word 'stomach' – which if you think about it is just two arbitrary sounds – we understand it as being the big organ underneath our chests where all the food goes, and not as anything else in the world. Saussure's answer is twofold: first, it is necessary to recognize 'stomach', or indeed any utterance, as being 'the combination of a concept and a sound pattern', and that the relationship between the sound and the concept is completely arbitrary. Second, there is an overarching system governing all such utterances (or instances of '*parole*'), which he calls *la langue*, into which the members of a 'linguistic community' are born. We understand 'stomach' not because of the relationship between the utterance and the concept or because someone pointed to our stomach and told us 'this is called "stomach"', but because of its *structural relationship* to all of the other utterances in the language. Incidentally, this approach is *synchronic* because it analyses language at a given point in time. *La langue* is a vast system of interdependent differences through which we can distinguish words from each other: we understand 'stomach' because it is not 'cat' or 'horse' or 'head' or 'tree' (incidentally Saussure's own favourite example) or any other word. Saussure calls this 'a system of pure values' without which our view of the world would be a 'vague, shapeless mass'. Saussure goes as far as to suggest that individuals would be incapable of distinguishing between two ideas or sounds 'before the introduction of linguistic structure'.[47] It is important for us to note here that the structure *comes first* and conditions the individuals who happen to be caught in it. For Saussure, *la langue* is not a case of society developing organically and people devising a system for understanding things, but rather a prior condition for the possibility of individuals distinguishing between different concepts and different sounds. During the course of this book, we will see this tendency repeated time and again: a theorist defines general principles, typically involving an overarching structure like *la langue*, and then argues that those general principles are not only the way things are but also the way they *must* be and the way they have *always* been. When reading later chapters, especially the sections on Althusser and Foucault in Chapter 3, it will be useful to keep Saussure at the back of your mind.

It is possible to apply Saussure's terms of *la langue* and *parole* to a great many things and in a sense all modern structuralism and semiotics can be seen as the endeavour to do so. See, for example, Roland Barthes's *Mythologies* in which he performs structural analyses on, among other things, a professional wrestling match, soap detergent boxes, the face of the actress Greta Garbo, French red wine and a steak and chips dinner![48] For example, literature can be seen as a vast systematic body and takes the role of *la langue* and individual literary works can be seen as instances of *parole* (this would be something approaching T. S. Eliot's idea of 'tradition'[49]). Or perhaps more commonly, the individual text could be seen as *la langue* and all of the formal devices it employs as the instances of *parole*. Whatever the case, the structuralist study of literary texts typically concerns itself with form and structure. The content or 'meaning' of a text is of secondary concern because, in the final analysis, a text is:

> A construction of layers (or levels, or systems), whose body contains, finally, no heart, no kernel, no secret, no irreducible principal, nothing except the infinity of its own envelopes – which envelop nothing other than units of its own surfaces.[50]

The text then is a structure of smaller functioning units which 'projects the principle of equivalence from the axis of selection to the axis of combination':[51] words are constituted in a particular sequence not only for the 'meaning' that they seek to convey but also through sound, rhythm, prosody and so on, to create patterns of similarity, opposition and parallels. Accordingly, most structuralist criticism tends to focus on (formal) binary oppositions in texts and how poetic functions such as rhyme or metric stress serve to bind these oppositions symbiotically together.

The early structuralism which flourished in the semiotics of the Moscow Linguist Circle and the Prague School in the 1920s and 1930s found its British counterpart in I. A. Richards who wrote the seminal *Principles of Criticism* in 1924; his approach is known as Practical Criticism or, sometimes 'the Cambridge school' (see discussion of Knights and Leavis above). Like the Russian structuralists, Richards was concerned primarily with the form and linguistic functions of a text, but to this he added an important second dimension: the idea of aesthetic value in art. For Richards, 'the two pillars upon which a theory of criticism must rest are an account of value and an account of communication'; *bad* literature constitutes 'an instance of defective communication'. The critic's job is to identify and recognize how a literary text stimulates different 'mental events' in its reader *and* whether that literary text is of value, or, in other words, whether those mental events are events worth experiencing.[52] For Richards:

> The qualifications of a good critic are three. He must be adept at experiencing, without eccentricities, the state of mind relevant to the work of art he is judging. Secondly, he must be able to distinguish experiences from one another as regards their less superficial features. Thirdly, he must be a sound judge of values.[53]

Richards places the reader as subordinate to the text. The reader *experiences* the text and he or she should not let his or her own 'eccentricities' taint that experience. The critic's task is to record the important moments of that experience, how it affected them and then decide whether or not it has been a good experience. The goal here is to produce, to the highest possible degree, an *objective* reading of a text, so that even in moments of disagreement, 'when the attitude collapses the effect can be agreed upon'.[54]

In America, Richards' ideas found support in a movement that came to be known as New Criticism. One of its foremost practitioners, Cleanth Brooks, like Richards, believed:

> That literary criticism is a description and an evaluation of its object.
>
> That the primary concern of criticism is with the problem of unity . . .
>
> That in a successful work, form and content cannot be separated . . .
>
> That form is meaning . . .
>
> That the purpose of literature is not to point to a moral.[55]

Just as we saw in the work of G. Wilson Knight, New Criticism sought unity in texts above all else. A typical analysis would move from close reading to a conclusion praising how the work has achieved unity, often with open awe. Brooks' famous conclusion about Shakespeare's 'The Phoenix and the Turtle' might serve for *any* of New Criticism's reading of *any* ('good') poem:

> The urn to which we are summoned, the urn which holds the ashes of the phoenix, is like the well-wrought urn of Donne's 'Canonization' which holds the phoenix-lovers' ashes: it is the poem itself.[56]

This type of formalism gave rise to an inherent political conservatism. The text is an art-object studied almost in isolation; if anything is to be referred to outside of the text, it is invariably *another* text. A text produces its *own* poetics or structural system and therefore its relation to any other structural system, for example history or culture, is not relevant to the analysis. Thus, during the Cold War years, literary criticism managed to stave off controversy simply by disregarding politics in literature.

Let us consider Roman Jakobson and L. G. Jones's reading of Shakespeare's sonnet 129.

Sonnet 129

Th'expense of spirit in a waste of shame
Is lust in action; and till action, lust

Is perjured, murd'rous, bloody, full of blame,
Savage, extreme, rude, cruel, not to trust,
Enjoyed no sooner but despisèd straight,
Past reason hunted, and no sooner had
Past reason hated as a swallowed bait
On purpose laid to make the taker mad;
Mad in pursuit and in possession so,
Had, having, and in quest to have, extreme;
A bliss in proof and proved, a very woe;
Before, a joy proposed; behind, a dream.
All this the world knows, yet none knows well
To shun the heaven that leads men to this hell.[57]

When reading this sonnet, the majority of people might start
with the question 'what is it about?' On further consideration, we
might start drawing conclusions about the speaker's frustrated
sexual desire and whether or not his recommendation to 'shun the
heaven' of lust is a healthy one. Some readers may wonder about
what the prevailing attitudes to lust might have been in London in
the 1590s, when Shakespeare wrote these words. Is this view typical of the time or was Shakespeare doing something unusual here?
Such questions are not at stake for Jakobson and Jones; historical
context is explicitly not their concern. Although it is important for
them to note that the sonnet is the hundred and twenty ninth of a
sequence of one 144 sonnets, and that it is part of a longer tradition of sonnets that can be read diachronically from Petrarch to
the present, *who* wrote the text and *when* it was written are only
matters of trivia. The text is an individual structural unit made up
of smaller units; what exists outside of that, with the exception of
similar texts, is irrelevant.

Jakobson and Jones start their analysis by pointing out that the
sonnet consists of three quatrains with alternate masculine rhymes
and 'a terminal couplet with plain masculine rhyme'.[58] From here
on it starts to become slightly more complicated. First, they look at
the rhyme in closer detail:

Of the seven rhymes only the first, juxtaposing two nouns with
the same preposition (of shame – of blame), is grammatical. The
second rhyme again begins with a noun, but confronts it with a
different part of speech. The third rhyme and the last three rhymes

invert this order: a non-noun is followed by a noun, whereas the fourth, the central of the seven rhymes, has no noun at all and consists of the participle 'had' and the adjective 'mad'.[59]

Thus they succeed in taking the parts of the sonnet apart and describing the various nuances of the rhyme scheme. However, this is where they stop. The structuralist pursuit ends with the recognition that the first rhyme is grammatical and the second consists of a noun and a verb. Jakobson and Jones do not elaborate on the *effects* of these structural features either on the reader – because the reader, just as the author, is of trivial concern – or in the production of meaning.

They move on to the second part of their analysis: the interrelationship of strophic units (the three quatrains are the first three 'strophes' and the final couplet is the fourth):

> The first rhyming word within the second or only rhyme of each strophe is duplicated elsewhere in the sonnet: I, l.2 *lust – lust*; II, l.2 *had* – III, l.2 *had*; III, l.2 *extreme* – I, l.4 *extreme*; IV, l.1 *well – well*.[60]

Four strophic relationships are identified and these, we are told, 'exhibit three kinds of binary correspondences' to which the rhyme scheme's patterning can be applied. The *odd* strophes (I, III) are bound together by the rhyme of the first quatrain and they are opposed by the *even* strophes (II, IV). Why this is considered to be so significant is not entirely clear. The best we get is the rather cryptic: 'the lines themselves can display their own lucid binary correspondences'.[61] From here, Jakobson and Jones turn their attention to caesural breaks (i.e. pauses) and analyse where they occur in each line.

In a later segment entitled 'Interpretation', Jakobson and Jones begin by giving us an 'explanatory rewording' of each strophe 'literal as far as possible'. For example, strophe IV becomes: 'all this is well known to the world but nobody knows well enough to shun the heaven that leads men to this hell.' After rewriting the whole sonnet in this way, they pause to elaborate on puns and how to deal with ambiguous words. For instance, 'shame' has the dual meaning of chastity and of genitalia. We are reminded that 'the double entendre in the author's lexicon does not interfere . . . with the essentially homogenous and firm thematic construction of . . . this sonnet in particular'.[62] The 'Interpretation' section stops here. However, this laborious process goes on for another 15 pages or so, looking more and more closely at such topics as 'odd against even', 'outer against inner' and finally, anagrams.

So what does all this demonstrate? What have Jakobson and Jones said about this sonnet beyond describing its constituent parts? The answer is, of course, very little because they never set out to do more than that. To some readers this might appear to be somewhat arbitrary – an almost pointless practice, because it seems so detached from the sonnet's *meaning*. The structuralist disregard for historical context, for both the author and the reader can seem impersonal, almost excessively meticulous, and reductive. But during the years of the Cold War it was attractive for a number of reasons. This critical detachment and disregard for context and meaning ensured that, on both sides of the Iron Curtain, literary scholars remained apolitical. Since they were dealing with *forms* rather than *ideas*, there was little risk of, for example, a critic from Moscow such as Jakobson picking up a copy of *Macbeth* and drawing parallels between Shakespeare's tyrant and the Soviet Premier.

Our consideration of formalism in literary studies before 1980 would be incomplete without a brief look at the work of Roland Barthes. Where formalist critics such as Richards, Brooks or Jakobson tended to focus on poetry, Barthes followed Vladimir Propp in wishing to define an underlying grammar for narrative.

1   Functions of the characters serve as stable, constant elements in a tale, regardless of how and by whom they are fulfilled.

2   The number of functions known to the fairy tale is limited [precisely 31].

3   The sequence of functions is always identical.

4   All fairy tales are of one type in regard to their structure.[63]

This is how Propp concluded his landmark study of Russian folktales, *Morphology of the Folktale* (1928). The consequences of Propp's study were twofold: first, it facilitated a marked interest in narrative among structuralists the result of which is known as narratology, particularly influential in film studies; second, its findings have gained some prominence in the popular consciousness, to the point where Propp's 31 functions of narrative are commonly taught on media studies GCSE and A-Level course syllabi in the United Kingdom. However, 'Propp's discovery',[64] as John Holloway devotedly called it in 1979, is not without its flaws. As Shlomith Rimmon-Kenan demonstrates, Propp's conclusion is not only 'dictated by the material [he] analysed' but also subject to 'a bias caused by his method'.[65] In other words, Propp's approach facilitates a 'discovery' he was always going to find. And even if Propp's conclusions about Russian folktales are true, do they hold true for more diverse narrative forms such as novels, plays or films?

The narratologist Claude Bremond noted this limitation with Propp's method and devised a model which added an element of bifurcation at each stage of the story, essentially a set of binary choices to accommodate deviances between narratives. However, this too has its limitations. How would Bremond deal with, for example, a narrative that refuses to conform to the traditional notions of 'good' and 'evil'? How would he deal with a Shakespeare play that appears to subvert generic conventions? Rimmon-Kenan's illuminating investigation into structuralist attempts to categorize narrative tendencies stops at this realization: 'to my knowledge', he says, 'the situation has not changed significantly to date'.[66] This declaration seems to disregard the work of Roland Barthes, who of all the French structuralists of the 1960s was the most faithful proponent of the Saussurean linguistic mode of analysis. Where Althusser and Foucault, who are discussed in Chapter 2, took their cue from Lacan and Marxism, Barthes seems to take his directly from Saussure.

Let us evaluate briefly Barthes's proposed method of literary analysis as manifest in his 'Introduction to the Structural Analysis of Narratives' and developed in *S/Z*. As we have seen, the goal of structuralism is to uncover the hidden rules that constitute the object being studied. The object in Barthes's case is narrative (or narrative structures). Because narrative seems so diverse – literally every story ever told – the structuralist approach faces an immediate problem. How do you draw general principles from something that seemingly has endless possibilities and variations? This is complicated further by Tzvetan Todorov's realization that:

> Meaning does not exist before being articulated and perceived . . . there do not exist two utterances of identical meaning if their articulation has followed a different source.[67]

In other words, even two narratives that articulate the same story are far from being identical. Nonetheless, 'narrative structures present characteristics which are remarkably *recurrent*' and therefore we can record 'distinguishable *regularities*' and in doing so start 'the construction of a *narrative grammar*'.[68] Barthes would not reject either of these claims. From Todorov he takes the notion of 'discourse', the supposition that every text is essentially unique (an implicit rejection of a universal narrative model such as Propp's in which all narratives are more or less same). However, although narratives are distinct and unique entities individually they still collectively share the same genetic makeup and are governed by a narrative grammar. We can trace this idea directly from Saussure: each utterance is an individual and unique instance of *parole* but collectively all utterances are governed by the *langue*. From Greimas, Barthes takes the idea of 'actants', in which characters are stripped of their 'humanistic connotations' and employed purely at the level of agent: the doer of an action.[69] Barthes also modifies Propp's concept of 'functions' into a set of subclasses.

Barthes divides the text into functions, or, to avoid confusion with Propp, 'lexies'. Jonathan Culler provides a succinct definition of lexies: 'the basic elements of the novel abstracted from their narrative presentation and prior to their reorganization by the synthesising operations of reading', as manifest in 'a stretch of text'.[70] In effect, lexies operate on the level of the reader's primary contact with the text. Barthes goes on to divide lexies into four basic classes:

1   Nuclei or 'cardinal functions' (hinge points in the narrative)

2   Catalysers (functional units that fill in discursive actions but do not affect the plot)

3   Indices (units signifying metaphoric relata)

4   Informants (serve to locate objects/actions in time and space).[71]

These lexies form the basis of narrative syntax and combine to make a sequence; these sequences in turn form the basis of an arching, subrogating syntax (which in essence is the narrative), and hence a narrative is a sequence of such sequences. The main problem with the model offered here is that, just as with Jakobson and Jones's reading of Sonnet 129, it can only serve to identify the features of narrative structures on a purely descriptive basis. It is difficult to see how Culler's claim that 'structuralism promotes analysis of the reader's role in producing meaning and of the ways literary works achieve their effects by resisting or complying with reader's expectations' is borne out.[72] Barthes is not looking for similar trends shared between texts; rather he seeks only to identify the structures that underline them. How can the text resist or comply with a reader's expectations when the model undermines notions of universalism such as Propp's? If there are no universal rules is not the reader, in effect, removed from the position of expectation?

Barthes was to realize the limitations of this model when he came to write *S/Z*. While maintaining that it is impossible to produce narrative 'without reference to an implicit system of units and rules',[73] Barthes introduces two new elements to his method: first: 'a distinction between readable texts and unreadable texts';[74] and second, he devises his famed set of five codes with which to interpret the subclasses of lexia.[75] The former introduces for the first time an aesthetic of sorts, because it is the unreadable or, as he calls them, 'writerly' texts that Barthes favours: they escape the 'boring predictability' that comes with generic narrative plots.[76] What Barthes has in mind is similar to Jean François Lyotard's idea of the postmodern.

> Those who refuse to re-examine the rules of art will make careers in mass conformism, using 'correct rules' to bring the endemic desire for reality into communication.[77]

But where Lyotard's concerns are social, Barthes's are purely structural: where Lyotard advocates social reform via radical avant-garde art works, Barthes only wishes to keep a genre from becoming staid.

Of Barthes's five codes, two stand out as being rather vague: the 'symbolic code' and the 'referential code'. The symbolic code can be defined as the extrapolation from the text of functions that facilitate symbolic readings. It is difficult to see how, using the model Barthes proposes, it is possible to make 'a symbolic reading'. We could suggest that, implicitly, this code is an admission on Barthes's part that a text is something more than a set of structural effects. It is possible to see further evidence of this in Barthes's failure to adhere to his own system in *S/Z*'s reading of Balzac's *Sarasire*. The referential (or 'cultural code') exists in what Barthes calls 'an agglomerative space, [with] certain areas of the text correlating other meanings outside the material text and, with them, forming "nebulae" of signifieds'.[78] Barthes' examples of this are always very specific, down to the naming of a specific location or culture (such as 'The Greeks'); he seems to forget that all language is culturally gendered and coloured in this way. It is not only Greek statues that come with a set of culturally imposed signified meanings and associations, but all words and their objects. The word 'apple' not only signifies the concept of the fruit but also all of the things that the reader has come to associate with apples, and by extension all of the things that society associates with them (e.g. the story of Adam and Eve, the story of Snow White and the Seven Dwarves and the theme of temptation). I fail to see the real difference between the symbolic code and the referential code: in truth they are two sides of same coin. This seems to highlight structuralism's inability to handle the relationship between the text and the outside world. The impact of narratology on Shakespeare studies has been limited. 'One reason', as Helmut Bonheim explains, 'is that narratologists concentrate on narrative prose and largely ignore drama'.[79] But what attempts have been made to study the narrative and plots of Shakespeare's plays – for example, Rawdon Wilson's *Shakespearean Narrative* (1995), Barbara Hardy's *Shakespeare's Story Tellers: Dramatic Narration* (1997), J. Hillis Miller's *Reading Narrative* (1998) and the essays collected in *Shakespeare Survey 53: Shakespeare and Narrative* (2000) – all owe an avowed debt to Barthes.

Jacques Derrida is another thinker who was profoundly influenced by the work of Ferdinand de Saussure, as well as the work of the German philosophers Friedrich Nietzsche and Martin Heidegger. Derrida influenced a school of criticism called deconstruction, which became prominent at Yale during the 1970s. Few words make some literary academics, especially those of the 'anti-Theory' persuasion whom I described in Chapter 1, recoil in fear quite like 'Derrida' and 'deconstruction'. This is because, to put it frankly, Derrida's writing borders on being unreadable, especially for exponents of the Plain English Campaign. It is frustratingly abstract, dense, diffuse, loaded with esoteric jargon and demands a working knowledge of Plato, the development of Western philosophy, Nietzsche and Heidegger to understand that many students of literature plainly lack. This being the case, for our purposes, which are:

1 To establish what deconstruction is
2 To understand the significance of deconstruction in the history of Shakespeare studies
3 To understand how it contributed to the climate in which new historicism and cultural materialism eventually flourish

I do not think a direct and sustained engagement with Derrida is necessary. Partly because Derrida himself was not a literary critic but a philosopher, and although 'deconstruction' borrows many of his key concepts, its real founder was Paul De Man who became Professor of French and Comparative Literature at Yale in 1971. It is really De Man's interpretation of one of Derrida's key ideas that led to deconstruction becoming a force in literary studies.

Derrida saw himself principally as continuing 'a line of thought which begins with Friedrich Nietzsche and runs through Martin Heidegger . . . characterized by an ever more radical repudiation of Platonism'.[80] Derrida had in mind Plato's metaphysical Theory of Forms, in which there is a world of forms or shadows – the appearance of everyday objects that most people mistake for reality – and the World of Forms made up of ideal and perfect abstract objects, which are beyond human understanding. For Derrida this idea, which he criticized for being 'logocentric', would lock Western metaphysics into thinking in terms of reductive binaries (e.g. presence versus absence, truth versus falsehood) for the next two millennia. Derrida 'finds fault with a massive consensus characteristic of Western philosophical culture and opposes to it at various turns the disruptive differences flattened out by the reductive installation of logocentrism'.[81] For us, however, what it is important is that this endeavour led Derrida to his concept of *différance*, which was his key contribution to deconstruction. *Différance* is best understood in terms of how he critiqued and altered Saussure's logocentric model of word and concept, or to use the technical terms 'sign' and 'signified'. Keith Green and Jill LeBihan do a better job of explaining it than Derrida himself:

Reworking Saussure's theory of binary oppositions, Derrida shows that in each pair one element is suppressed and one privileged. Derrida tried to show how the privileged term depended for its meaning upon the suppressed one. Language is ultimately arbitrary, being a purely unstable differential system. Meaning is further suspended in the process of reading; and because language is subject to temporal processes something is always deferred – meaning is always 'in process' and not fixed. Every text is subject to a kind of generalised absence.[82]

Let us take, as an example, one seemingly simple binary opposition: good and evil. For Derrida, 'good' would be the 'privileged' term and 'evil' the suppressed one because 'evil' is defined as being a *lack* of 'good' (or at least this has generally been the case in Christian theology). It is not possible to think of 'evil' without some corresponding concept of 'good' against which it is defined. However, if you think about it further, the same is also true of 'good'. The concept of 'good' *necessitates* the concept of 'evil', because without it 'good' has nothing against which to define itself. The logocentric Christian move would be to dismiss this and argue that 'good' can be defined positively, as a property of God's grace. But the deconstructionist answer to that would be that even 'God' is defined by 'not-God'. There is no escape from this double bind. In fact any binary opposition – 'something' versus 'nothing', 'hot' versus 'cold', 'in' versus 'out', 'left' versus 'right' and so on – contains this reciprocal relationship, each word depending on its opposite for meaning.

If you recall Saussure's theory of differences, words do not only depend on their antonyms for meaning but on *every other word in the linguistic system*. So we recognize 'evil' not only because it is not 'good' but also because it is not 'cat', 'dog', 'nose', 'vacuum', 'disestablishmentarianism' or 'pipe' and so on until every single word in *la langue* is exhausted. This remains the case for Derrida and he calls this process 'deferral': the meaning of a given word is almost endlessly deferred because it is defined exclusively by its difference from all the other words. However, it is clear that not all words have the same relationship. As we have just seen, 'good' and 'evil' appear to come as a pair, and there are other words related to that pair whether directly (e.g. 'morality', 'ethics', 'sin', 'deeds', 'will') or symbolically (e.g. 'darkness', 'light', 'angels', 'devils'). Meaning is not only endlessly deferred a la Saussure's system of difference, but also endlessly slippery because words, whether their speakers or authors intend it or not, imply each other. Let us take a simple sentence paragraph:

It was a hot day. The good man turned left and lit his cigarette.

Although this seems like a straightforward statement, there are in fact many hidden words to which the meaning of any of the words in the sentence itself is intrinsically bound. For us to know that 'it was a hot day' we need to have some knowledge of both 'cold' and 'night'. The word 'was' has some ambiguity here. 'Was' is the past tense of 'is' or 'to be' and implies that this 'hot day' actually took place. Did this hot day *really* take place? 'It' is doing little in this sentence because it refers implicitly to 'day', in fact were it not for 'a' we could rewrite this sentence as 'the day was hot'. So why is this sentence written 'it was *a* hot day'? This implies the absence of 'the'. This is just one 'hot day' in any number of hot days, which may imply that this is summertime. Then again, if it is summertime, then would the narrator bother to point out the hotness of the day, is a hot day in summer time particularly remarkable? The sentence is uncertain on whether the hot day, which it takes the time to point out, is actually worth mentioning at all. We are not even sure if this hot day even happened. With all this uncertainty created by the first sentence, there are a lot of questions to ask about the second one. We have already established that this narrator, unsure as to whether or not this hot day is worth writing about, cannot be trusted. 'The good man' is a much more assertive statement because the definite article 'the' is giving us a specific man, whereas before we got any old 'hot day'. We also get a value judgement, he is 'good' – but that immediately puts us in mind of 'evil' people. Why is it worth mentioning that he is 'good'? Are there evil people lurking around the corner? Is this man some sort of hero? Is our unreliable narrator who cannot decide on which hot day this was to be trusted here? Maybe it does not mean 'good' as opposed to 'evil' but that the man is good *at something*, maybe he is a skilled golfer taking a cigarette place on a golf course surrounded by people who are 'bad' at golf. And so on and so forth *ad nauseum.* I have just carried out a deconstructive reading of my own simple statement. The point is that whatever I intended the sentence to mean, is far from the meaning that you construct when you read the words. My reading ended up with a man on a golf course, yours may well have ended up with a detective in a trench coat. These two sentences are inadequate vessels for whatever message I originally wished to convey. *That* message is endlessly deferred in the free play of association that its words produce. This is the point that deconstructionists wish to demonstrate time and again. As Eagleton says, 'the tactic of deconstructive criticism . . . is to show how texts come to embarrass their own ruling systems of logic'; or, as Leonard Jackson puts it, 'the rhetorical features of texts – the precise terms and metaphors used, for example – are examined and shown . . . to undermine the text's intended meaning and reference'.[83] In deconstruction the signifier becomes fundamentally unstable and is always so.

While for Derrida, this instability was something to be celebrated and an opportunity to be playful, for De Man it was tantamount to staring into the existential abyss. De Man's general approach can be summed up by a word he seems to use over and over again. In his *Blind and Insight* (1971) we witness texts and images from them 'dissolve into nothingness', 'collapse . . . into nothingness', become 'allegorized into nothingness'.[84] This perhaps sums up also the obvious limitation of deconstruction that it seems incapable of anything more than pointing out the same thing again and again, the proverbial one trick pony repeating the same trick with increasingly diminishing returns. Brian Vickers did not pull any punches in 1993 when he wrote:

> What use is deconstruction as a model for literary criticism? My answer, and the answer of other independent observers (we are not dealing here with assertions and counter-assertions of rival groupies, each bent on advancing their own school) has to be: not much. . . . deconstruction might be a useful propaedeutic exercise in philosophy classes. . . . but as a model for literary criticism it is seriously defective.[85]

It is important to note that De Man was not a Shakespeare scholar and wrote primarily about nineteenth-century French literature. Of the so-called Yale school, whose number typically include J. Hillis Miller, Geoffrey Hartmann and Harold Bloom, only Bloom – who himself cannot with any accuracy be described as a deconstructionist – has published significantly on Shakespeare. Since the base of deconstruction was elsewhere in the discipline, it never really established itself in Shakespeare studies as anything more than a minor or ancillary movement that seemed to peter out sometime in the late 1980s. As Russ McDonald says, 'although some of its vocabulary and principles have perforce made their way into other modes of critical reading, deconstruction *per se* made little impact on Shakespeare studies, few Shakespeareans identified themselves as "deconstructionists".'[86] In the landmark *Alternative Shakespeares* (1985), one of about half a dozen seminal works in the establishment of new historicism and cultural materialism as the new dominant methods of studying Shakespeare's plays, Malcolm Evans has an essay called 'Deconstructing Shakespeare' that looking back today seems oddly out of place. There was a collection published in 1988 called *Shakespeare and Deconstruction*, Howard Felperin's idiosyncratic *The Uses of the Canon* (1990) shares some sympathies with the deconstructionist approach, and the new historicist Jonathan Goldberg's famous reading of the Dover Cliff scene in *King Lear* is undoubtedly deconstructionist.[87] But all in all, there is not a lot to write home about. It is difficult to disagree with Stephen Wittek's withering assessment that

> The impact that the philosophy of Jacques Derrida had on Shakespeare criticism is comparable to the impact a round of fireworks has on the night sky: explosive, dramatic, even awe-inspiring – but ultimately ephemeral. . . . [The] 'Deconstructionist School of Shakespeare Studies' . . . never really existed.[88]

I have included the discussion of deconstruction here for two reasons. First, because it is important to be aware of it as a strain in new historicist and cultural materialist practice; and second, because it forms part of the formalist atmosphere in which Stephen Greenblatt and others were working in the 1970s. It is possible to draw a straight line from the New Criticism to deconstruction. Derrida's much quoted line 'there is no outside the text' might easily have been said by Cleanth Brooks.[89] It is worth remembering that in the 1960s Greenblatt himself studied at Yale – a stronghold for both the New Criticism and deconstruction – where Brooks was a professor from 1947 until his retirement in 1975, and Paul De Man from 1971 until his death in 1983. It is difficult for us to imagine now how all-pervasive formalism must have been during the era in which Greenblatt and other American critics of his generation grew up. This is worth keeping in mind when we come to consider new historicism later, not only to account for why they argued so passionately and vehemently for a different, more politically and historically aware criticism in the 1980s but also so we can trace the residue of formalist methods and thinking in their theory and practice.

Key questions for students

- Do you think Ferdinand de Saussure's conclusions about how language functions are correct? For example, is the connection between words and the concepts they signify really arbitrary as he suggests? What about his idea that we can only differentiate between different words or different concepts through *la langue*?
- Can I. A. Richards's goal of being an 'objective' reader be achieved? Do you think that there is Good art and Bad art? And if so, how can we judge art without the sort of objective standard Richards outlines?
- Do you agree with Cleanth Brooks that 'the primary concern of criticism is with the problem of unity'? Do all great literary texts move towards creating a unified whole?
- Can you see any benefits of the approach taken by Roman Jakobson and L. G. Jones in their reading of 'Sonnet 129'? If so, what are they?
- Is it possible to apply Vladimir Propp's theories about narrative in Russian folktales to Shakespeare's plays?
- Is Barthes's model for analysing narrative useful at all? And if so, is it useful for forms other than novels? Could Barthes read a Shakespeare play like he reads Balzac's *Sarasire*?
- Do you agree with Brian Vickers's assessment that 'as a model for literary criticism' deconstruction is 'seriously defective'? And if so, why? Can deconstruction offer us useful tools that could be utilized in conjunction with other approaches?

Selected further reading

Barthes, Roland, 'Style and Its Image', in *Literary Style: A Symposium*, ed. Seymour Chatman and Samuel R. Levin (Oxford: Oxford University Press, 1971), pp. 3–15.

—, *Mythologies*, trans. Annette Lavers (London: Paladin, 1973).

—, *S/Z*, trans. Richard Miller (London: Jonathan Cape, 1975).

—, *Essais Critique* (Paris: Seuil, 1977).

—, *Image-Music-Text*, trans. Stephen Heath (New York: Hill and Wang, 1978).

Brooks, Cleanth, 'The Formalist Critics' (1951), in *Literary Theory: An Anthology*, ed. Julie Rivkin and Michael Ryan (Oxford: Blackwell, 1998), pp. 52–7.

Culler, Jonathan, *Structuralist Poetics* (Ithaca, NY: Cornell University Press, 1975).

—, *Barthes* (London: Fontana Press, 1983).

Derrida, Jacques, *Of Grammatology*, trans. Gayatri Chakravorty Spivak (Baltimore, MD: John Hopkins University Press, 1976).

—, *Writing and Difference*, trans. Alan Bass (London: Routledge and Kegan Paul, 1978).

—, *Margins of Philosophy*, trans. Alan Bass (Hertfordshire: Harvester, 1982).

Eagleton, Terry, *Literary Theory: An Introduction* (Oxford: Blackwell, 1996).

Jackson, Leonard, *The Poverty of Structuralism* (New York and London: Longman, 1993).

Jakobson, Roman and L. G. Jones, 'Shakespeare's Verbal Art in "Th'expense of Spirit"', in *Language in Literature*, ed. Krystyna Pomorska and Stephen Rudy (Boston, MA: Harvard University Press, 1987), pp. 198–215.

Lavers, Annette, 'Deconstruction', in *The Cambridge History of Literary Crticism Volume 8: From Formalism to Poststructuralism*, ed. Ramen Selden (Cambridge: Cambridge University Press, 1995), pp. 166–96.

LeBihan, Jill and Keith Green, *Critical Theory & Practice: A Coursebook* (New York and London: Routledge, 1996).

Man, Paul De, *Blindness and Insight: Essays in the Rhetoric of Contemporary Criticism* (Oxford: Routledge, 1996).

Onega, Susana and José Ángel García Landa, *Narratology* (New York and London: Longman, 1996).

Propp, Vladimir, *Morphology of the Folktale*, trans. Laurence Scott (Austin, TX: University of Texas Press, 1968).

Richards, I. A., *Principles of Literary Criticism* (New York and London: Routledge, 2001).

Todorov, Tzvetan, *Litterature et Signification* (Paris: Larousse, 1967).

Notes

1 Kiernan Ryan, 'King Lear: A Retrospect, 1980–2000', in *Shakespeare Survey Volume 55: King Lear and its Afterlife*, ed. Peter Holland (Cambridge: Cambridge University Press, 2007), p. 1.

2 Rainer Emig, 'Literary Criticism and Psychoanalytical Positions', in *The Cambridge History of Literary Crticism Volume IX: Twentieth-Century Historical, Philosophical and Psychological Perspectives*, ed. Christina Knellwolf and Christopher Norris (New York and Cambridge: Cambridge University Press, 2001), p. 177.

3 Gary Taylor, *Reinventing Shakespeare: A Cultural History from the Restoration to the Present* (Oxford: Oxford University Press, 1990), p. 369.

4 Jan Kott, *Shakespeare Our Contemporary*, 2nd edn (London: Routledge, 1991), pp. 2, 3, 152.

5 Andrew Hiscock and Lisa Hopkins, 'Introduction', in *Teaching Shakespeare and Early Modern Dramatists*, ed. Andrew Hisckcok and Lisa Hopkins (New York and Basingstoke: Palgrave Macmillan, 2007), p. 8.

6 For an account of the professionalization of literary criticism and the development of English as an academic subject during the industrial era, see D. J. Palmer, *The rise of English studies: an account of the study of the English language and literature from its origins to the making of the Oxford English School* (Oxford: Oxford University Press for the University of Hull, 1965), although I would recommend supplementing Palmer's dated and sometimes esoterically narrow book with 'The Rise of English' in Terry Eagleton, *Literary Theory: An Introduction* (Oxford: Blackwell, 1996), pp. 15–46.

7 E. M. W. Tillyard, *The Muse Unchained; an Intimate Account of the Revolution in English Studies at Cambridge* (London: Bowes and Bowes, 1958), p. 84.

8 Katherine Cooke, *A. C. Bradley and his Influence in Twentieth-Century Shakespeare Criticism* (Oxford: Clarendon Press, 1972), pp. 78–9.

9 A. D. Nuttall, 'The Argument about Shakespeare's Characters', *Critical Quarterly*, 7(2) (1965), 107.

10 Michael Taylor, *Shakespeare Criticism in the Twentieth Century* (Oxford: Oxford University Press, 2001), p. 42.

11 A. C. Bradley, *Shakespearean Tragedy: Lectures on Hamlet, Othello, King Lear, Macbeth*, 2nd edn (London: Macmillan, 1905), pp. 123–4.

12 Quoted in Anne Bradbury, 'Introduction', in *Shakespeare Criticism 1919–1935*, ed. Anne Bradbury (London: Oxford University Press, 1936), p. vii.

13 J. W. Mackail, *The Approach to Shakespeare* (Oxford: Clarendon Press, 1930), p. 25.

14 L. C. Knights, *Explorations: Essays in Criticism mainly on the literature of the seventeenth century* (London: Chatto & Windus, 1946), pp. 4, 6.

15 Ibid., p. 5.

16 Eagleton, *Literary Theory*, pp. 29, 30; Taylor, *Shakespeare Criticism in the Twentieth Century*, p. 23.

17 Caroline Spurgeon, *Shakespeare's Imagery and What It Tells Us* (Cambridge: Cambridge University Press, 2004), p. 12.

18 Ibid., pp. 27, 33.

19 G. Wilson Knight, *The Imperial Theme: Further Interpretations of Shakespeare's Tragedy* (New York and London: Routledge, 2002), p. 22.

20 G. Wilson Knight, *The Wheel of Fire: Interpretations of Shakespearean Tragedy*, 4th edn (New York and London: Routledge, 2001), p. 3.

21 Ibid., pp. 38, 39.

22 Ibid., p. 47.

23 A. L. French, *Shakespeare and the Critics* (Cambridge: Cambridge University Press, 1972), p. 34.

24 E. M. W. Tillyard, *The Elizabethan World Picture* (London: Vintage, 1959); E. M. W. Tillyard, *Shakespeare's History Plays* (London: Chatto & Windus, 1944);

25 Tillyard, *The Elizabethan World Picture*, p. 43.

26 Tillyard, *Shakespeare's History Plays*, p. 321.

27 Nigel Saul, *Richard II* (New Haven, CT and London: Yale University Press, 1997), pp. 2–3.

28 See Niccolò Machiavelli, *The Prince*, trans. Geoffrey Bull, 4th edn (New York and London: Penguin, 2003); William Camden, *Annales the true and royall history of the famous empresse Elizabeth Queene of England France and Ireland &c. True faith's defendresse of diuine renowne and happy memory. Wherein all such memorable things as happened during hir blessed raigne . . . are exactly described.* (London: Printed [by George Purslowe, Humphrey Lownes, and Miles Flesher] for Beniamin Fisher and are to be sould at the Talbott in Pater Noster Rowe, 1625). For a detailed look at this topic see Neema Parvini,

Shakespeare's History Plays: Rethinking Historicism (Edinburgh: Edinburgh University Press, 2012), Chapter 6: 'Shakespeare's Historical and Political Thought in Context', pp. 120–73.

29 Wilbur Sanders, *The Dramatist and the Received Idea: Studies in the Plays of Marlowe and Shakespeare* (Cambridge: Cambridge University Press, 1968), p. 74.

30 See William Empson, *Seven Types of Ambiguity* (London: Chatto & Windus, 1930).

31 Moody E. Prior, *The Drama of Power: Studies in Shakespeare's History Plays* (Evanston, IL: Northwestern University Press, 1973), p. 9.

32 Prior, *The Drama of Power*, p. 12.

33 Sanders, *The Dramatist and the Received Idea*, p. 76.

34 A. P. Rossiter, *Angel with Horns: Fifteen Lectures on Shakespeare*, ed. Graham Storey (New York: Longman, 1989), p. 63.

35 '. . . it has again become respectable to direct attention to the psychological truth of [Shakespeare's] creations', Anne Ridler, 'Introduction', in *Shakespeare Criticism 1935–60*, ed. Anne Ridler (New York and London: Oxford University Press, 1963), p. vii. See also Cooke, *A. C. Bradley and His Influence in Twentieth-Century Shakespeare Criticism*, pp. 232–4, where she argues that 'the sixties . . . have seen the rehabilitation of Bradley the critic'.

36 Bradley, *Shakespearean Tragedy*, p. 55.

37 Rossiter, *Angel with Horns*, pp. 44, 46, 50, 51.

38 Annette Lavers, 'Deconstruction', in *The Cambridge History of Literary Crticism Volume 8: From formalism to poststructuralism*, ed. Ramen Selden (Cambridge: Cambridge University Press, 1995), p. 179.

39 See Ernest Jones, *Hamlet and Oedipus* (New York: Norton, 1949).

40 See M. M. Mahood, *Shakespeare's Wordplay* (London: Methuen, 1957); Frank Kermode, *Shakespeare's Language* (Harmondsworth: Penguin, 2000); Wolfgang Clemen, *The Development of Shakespeare's Imagery*, 2nd edn (Cambridge: Cambridge University Press, 1977); Helen Vendler, *The Art of Shakespeare's Sonnets* (Boston, MA: Harvard University Press, 1997); C. L. Barber, *Shakespeare's Festive Comedy: A Study of Dramatic Form and Its Relation to Social Custom* (Princeton, NJ: Princeton University Press, 2012).

41 Jerome J. McGann, *The Beauty of Inflections: Literary Investigations in Historical Method and Theory*, revised edn (Oxford: Clarendon Press, 1988), p. 90.

42 Leonard Jackson, *The Poverty of Structuralism* (New York and London: Longman, 1993), p. 3.

43 Eagleton, *Literary Theory*, p. 79.

44 Roland Barthes, *Essais Critique* (Paris: Seuil, 1977), p. 218.

45 Gerard Genette, *Figures 1* (Paris: Editions du Seuil, 1966), p. 258.

46 Eagleton, *Literary Theory*, p. 79.

47 Ferdinand de Saussure, *Course in General Linguistics*, trans. Roy Harris (Peru, IL: Open Court, 2006), pp. 67, 71, 155.

48 See Roland Barthes, *Mythologies*, trans. Annette Lavers (London: Paladin, 1973).

49 See T. S. Eliot, 'Tradition and the Individual Talent', in *Selected Essays* (London: Faber and Faber, 1999), pp. 13–22.

50 Roland Barthes, 'Style and Its Image', in *Literary Style: A Symposium*, ed. Seymour Chatman and Samuel R. Levin (Oxford: Oxford University Press, 1971), p. 10.

51 Roman Jakobson, 'Closing Statement: Linguistics and Poetics', in *Style in Language*, ed. Thomas A. Sebeok (Cambridge: Cambridge University Press, 1960), p. 358.

52 I. A. Richards, *Principles of Literary Criticism* (New York and London: Routledge, 2001), pp. 20, 186, 104.

53 Ibid., p. 104.

54 Ibid., p. 195.

55 Cleanth Brooks, 'The Formalist Critics', in *Literary Theory: An Anthology*, ed. Julie Rivkin and Michael Ryan (Oxford: Blackwell, 1998), p. 52.

56 Cleanth Brooks, 'The Language of Paradox' (1956), in ibid., p. 69.

57 All references to Shakespeare's works are to ed. John Jowett, William Montgomery, Gary Taylor and Stanley Wells, *William Shakespeare: The Complete Works*, 2nd edn (New York and Oxford: Oxford University Press, 2005).

58 Roman Jakobson and L. G. Jones, 'Shakespeare's Verbal Art in "Th'expense of Spirit"', in *Language in Literature*, ed. Krystyna Pomorska and Stephen Rudy (Boston, MA: Harvard University Press, 1987), p. 199.

59 Ibid.

60 Ibid.

61 Ibid.

62 Ibid., pp. 201–2.

63 Vladimir Propp, *Morphology of the Folktale*, trans. Laurence Scott (Austin, TX: University of Texas Press, 1968), pp. 21–3.

64 John Holloway, *Narrative and Structure: Exploratory Essays* (Cambridge: Cambridge University Press, 1979), p. 2.

65 Shlomith Rimmon-Kenan, *Narrative Fiction: Contemporary Poetics* (New York and London: Routledge, 1983), p. 21.

66 Ibid., p. 28.

67 Tzuetan Todorov, *Litterature et Signification* (Paris: Larousse, 1967), p. 20.

68 Julien Algirdas Greimas, *Modern Language Notes* (Paris: Le Seuil, 1971), p. 794.

69 Susana Onega and José Ángel García Landa, *Narratology* (New York and London: Longman, 1996), p. 45.

70 Jonathan Culler, *Structuralist Poetics* (Ithaca, NY: Cornell University Press, 1975), p. 202.

71 Roland Barthes, *Image-Music-Text*, trans. Stephen Heath (New York: Hill and Wang, 1978), p. 85.

72 Jonathan Culler, *Barthes* (London: Fontana Press, 1983), p. 81.

73 Barthes, *Image, Music, Text*, p. 81.

74 Culler, *Structuralist Poetics*, p. 190.

75 For a concise listing of these codes see ibid., p. 203.

76 Culler, *Barthes*, p. 87.

77 Jean-François Lyotard, *The Postmodern Explained to Children: Correspondence 1982–1985*, trans. Julian Pefanis and Morgan Thomas (London: Turnaround, 1992), p. 15.

78 Roland Barthes, *S/Z*, trans. Richard Miller (London: Jonathan Cape, 1975), p. 8.

79 Helmet Bonheim, 'Shakespeare's Narremes', in *Shakespeare Survey 53: Shakespeare and Narrative*, ed. Peter Holland (Cambridge: Cambridge University Press, 2000), p. 1.

80 Lavers, 'Deconstruction', p. 168.

81 Vincent B. Leitch, *Cultural Criticism, Literary Theory, Poststructuralism* (New York: Columbia University Press, 1992), p. 4.

82 Keith Green and Jill LeBihan, *Critical Theory & Practice: A Coursebook* (New York and London: Routledge, 1996), p. 215. For the philosopher's own attempts at a definition see Jacques Derrida, *Writing and Difference*, trans. Alan Bass (London: Routledge and Kegan Paul, 1978), pp. 280–1, and Jacques Derrida, *Margins of Philosophy*, trans. Alan Bass (Hertfordshire: Harvester, 1982), p. 27.

83 Eagleton, *Literary Theory*, p. 116.

84 Paul De Man, *Blindness and Insight: Essays in the Rhetoric of Contemporary Criticism* (Oxford: Routledge, 1996), pp. 73, 114, 160.

85 Brian Vickers, *Appropriating Shakespeare: Contemporary Critical Quarrels* (New Haven, CT: Yale University Press, 1993), p. 179.

86 Russ McDonald, 'Preface', in *Shakespeare: An Anthology of Criticism and Theory 1945–2000*, ed. Russ Mcdonald (Malden, MA and Oxford: Blackwell, 2004), pp. xii–xiii.

87 See Malcolm Evans, 'Deconstructing Shakespeare's Comedies', in *Alternative Shakespeares*, ed. John Drakakis (New York and London: Methuen, 1985); G. D. Atkins and D. M. Bergeron (eds), *Shakespeare and Deconstruction* (New York: Peter Lang, 1988); Howard Felperin, *The Uses of the Canon: Elizabethan Literature and Contemporary Theory* (Oxford: Clarendon Press, 1990); Jonathan Goldberg, 'Dover Cliff and the Condition of Representation', in *Shakespeare's Hand* (Minneapolis, MN: University of Minnesota Press, 2003), pp. 132–48.

88 Stephen Witteck, 'A Brief History of Deconstruction in Shakespeare Criticism', *The Birmingham Journal of Literature and Language*, 1(1) (2008), 3, 11.

89 Jacques Derrida, *Of Grammatology*, trans. Gayatri Chakravorty Spivak (Baltimore, MD: John Hopkins University Press, 1976), p. 158.

CHAPTER THREE

Theory in focus

Men make their own history, but they do not make it just as they please; they do not make it under circumstances chosen by themselves, but under circumstances directly encountered, given, and transmitted from the past.[1]

Objective

To establish and analyse the key theoretical concepts necessary for understanding new historicism and cultural materialism

Clifford Geertz: Culture, thick description and local knowledge

Summary

- Anti-humanism versus essentialist humanism
- Clifford Geertz's definition of culture
- 'Thick description'
- 'Local knowledge'
- Criticisms of Geertz
- Summary of Geertz's theory

In Chapter 2, I surveyed the main currents of Shakespeare criticism from 1904 to the 1970s. One of the most obvious differences between the critics we looked at in that chapter and the new historicists and cultural materialists is the latter group's engagement with theory, in particular the theory of Louis Althusser, Raymond Williams, Michel Foucault and, in Stephen Greenblatt's case, the anthropologist Clifford Geertz. Before looking at each of these in some closer detail, it is worth stating at the outset that these diverse thinkers are united by their commitment to anti-humanism. Anti-humanism can be broadly defined as the rejection of essentialist humanism: the belief that there is such a thing as a universal human nature and that individuals have innate traits and characteristics. Whether implicitly or explicitly, *all* of the Shakespeare critics we looked at in Chapter 2 were essentialist humanists.[2] Let us recap the list of names: A. C. Bradley, L. C. Knights, Caroline Spurgeon, G. Wilson Knight, E. M. W. Tillyard, John Dover Wilson, Lily B. Campbell, A. P. Rossiter, Wilbur Sanders and Moody E. Prior. As we have seen, these critics occupied extremely diverse positions and were often completely opposed to each other. Yet, whatever their differences, both Bradley and Knights would have baulked at the idea that there is no such thing as a universal human nature. The same is true of Tillyard and Rossiter, or any other pairing you wish to pick out. This is what distinguishes Stephen Greenblatt, Catherine Gallagher, Alan Sinfield, Jonathan Dollimore, Catherine Belsey and the other leading new historicists and cultural materialists from all previous generations of critics. It is the conviction that human beings have no essential nature and all behaviour is conditioned in the individual by his or her social environment.

This position is succinctly summarized by the anthropologist Clifford Geertz, a seminal influence on Greenblatt, in his collection of essays *The Interpretation of Cultures* (1973):

> There is no such thing as a human nature independent of culture. Men without culture would not be the clever savages of Golding's *Lord of the Flies* thrown back upon the cruel wisdom of the animal instincts. . . . They would be unworkable monstrosities with very few useful instincts.[3]

Therefore every individual is the product of his or her particular culture and, by extension, anything individuals produce themselves are *also* the product of that culture. This has profound implications for literary criticism because authors of literary texts are individuals and therefore, by extension, the texts they produce are the products of the culture from which he or she originated. Geertz also claims that 'culture' manifests itself in the material objects it produces:

> Chartres is made of stone and glass. But it is not just stone and glass; it is a cathedral but a particular cathedral built at a particular time by certain members of a particular society.[4]

The cathedral is a cultural product available for analysis. If you accept Geertz's statement, it is logical to assume that studying the cathedral will tell us something about the culture that produced it. Literary texts, like cathedrals, are cultural products and they too are available for analysis. By the same logic, analysing the literary text will tell us something about the culture that produced it. The process is clear to see:

1 Culture produces the individual.

2 The individual produces a literary text.

3 Because culture produced the individual, the literary text will be inscribed with that culture.

4 Later on, a critic can come along and gain at least partial access to that culture by tracing its inscription in the text.

For Geertz, the individual here is scarcely necessary. What happens if we remove the individual from this process? Remember that the critic is an individual too.

1 Culture produces a literary text.

2 Later on, another culture reads the literary text and learns about the culture that produced it.

As an anthropologist, Geertz is not interested in literary texts *per se*, but in understanding other cultures. He defines culture as:

> An historically transmitted pattern of meanings embodied in symbols, a system of inherited conceptions expressed in symbolic forms by means of which men communicate, perpetuate, and develop their knowledge about and their attitudes toward life.[5]

> The culture of a people is an ensemble of texts, themselves ensembles, which the anthropologist strains to read over the shoulders of those to whom they properly belong.[6]

For Geertz, an anthropologist such as himself can read and analyse these 'texts' in order to get closer to a true understanding of how it functions – in a manner not altogether dissimilar to that of Roland Barthes picking apart wrestling matches and steak and chips dinners in *Mythologies*. In reading these 'texts' of culture, Geertz advocated an approach called 'thick-description ethnography', which sought to understand the meaning of certain actions and symbols in a given culture as the people of that culture would understand them. To adapt the classic example he cites, 'thick description' is understanding the difference between the contraction of the right eyelid and a cheeky wink perhaps played by a wangler about to play a prank on a third party. The former is just a muscular movement with little symbolic significance, the latter is unmistakably *cultural*. An alien who had no concept of winking, would surely not understand that our joker is about to play a trick. For Geertz, the goal of the anthropologist, being in effect an alien outside of the culture, is to understand the wink. His aim is to identify 'structures of signification . . . Winks upon winks upon winks'.[7] The ultimate aim is 'the understanding of how people understand themselves'.[8]

Geertz's approach is not that far away from the structuralists we looked at in Chapter 2. Although he set himself up against structuralism and its chief exponent in anthropology, Claude Levi-Strauss, Geertz is undoubtedly indebted to semiotics, the study of signs, which we can ultimately trace back to Saussure. The chief difference between Geertz and a committed structuralist like Levi-Strauss is that Geertz was interested in meaning and making active interpretations, whereas Levi-Strauss cared only about structure. In practice, however, the task Geertz sets himself strikes a decidedly structuralist note:

> Our double task is to uncover the conceptual structures that inform our subjects' acts, the 'said' of social discourse, and to construct a system of analysis in whose terms what is generic to those structures, what belongs to them because they are what they are, will stand out against the other determinants of human behaviour.[9]

The 'text' will have a symbolic significance for the culture, and from an analysis of this, we can derive a sort of symbolic map of the culture.

In addition, he also insists that, as much as possible, the focus of the observation should be local and isolated: 'The aim is to draw large conclusions from small, but very densely textured facts'.[10] This technique is known as 'synecdoche': the part tells us about the whole. In a later collection of essays, *Local Knowledge* (1983), he elaborates on the importance of this further: 'sorting through the machinery of distant ideas, the shapes of knowledge are always ineluctably local, indivisible from their instruments and their encasements'.[11] It is not possible to separate knowledge from context since all meaning is generated *in situ*, that is in a particular time and place from which it cannot and should not be moved. So the anthropologist should, as far as possible, read the 'texts' of the culture under study *in situ*. In other words, he or she should try to recover the original context as much as possible because without it the true 'meaning' of the object under study is not possible. This insistence on 'local knowledge' of specific cultures is a key difference between Geertz and a structuralist, such as Levi-Strauss, whose aim was to attain 'global knowledge' by stripping society down to reveal universal structures.

Nonetheless, despite this apparent concern with context, it seems to me that Geertz's approach to analysing culture is still very much like the way a formalist would approach a poem. All of the material objects or as he calls them 'texts' are the formal devices, instances of rhyme, imagery and so on that go on to make the unified whole of the culture. This is a somewhat contentious claim given that Geertz is generally seen as marking a shift *away* from formalism, but let us dwell on this further. His insistence upon 'locality' mirrors formalism's insistence on textual isolation and replicates it at the level of culture. In his use of synecdoche, Geertz seems to treat specific cultures as if they are living, breathing organisms and the 'generic . . . structures [that] are what they are' as if they were strands of DNA in which the culture's unique genetic code is stored. But does this really work? Is culture really something from which you can take one part and draw inferences about the whole? Let us choose a highly specific locality: let's say a small town in England and then a specific 'text' to analyse from that town; let's say its local football club. Let us pretend also that we are aliens to this town who know nothing at all about British culture. How much can an analysis of the behaviours witnessed in this football club really tell us about this town and its culture? More to the point, does the football club have anything to do with the reading group meeting taking place between six middle-aged women in the Women's Institute a few streets away? Does it have anything to do with the group of boys playing video games a few doors down, or the couple enjoying an Indian takeaway next door, or the meeting taking place at the church, or the fight breaking out in the public house across town or the county's Member of Parliament being interviewed at the local radio station? Perhaps the anthropologist would have to give a 'thick description' of each of these instances to gain a fuller understanding of the culture, but it is not clear to me a) whether they are at all connected beyond the fact they are happening in the same time and place, and b) whether they tell us anything about each other. For me it seems absurd to jump from the 'thick description' of any one or even *all* of these activities – which are undoubtedly parts of this town's 'culture' – to drawing general conclusions about the town's culture. My point is that synecdoche does not seem like a useful analytical tool here because by its definition it *depends* on there being a unified whole, and it is not clear to me that the parts of culture really add up to any such coherent 'whole'.

In the interests of balance and fair play, let's explore this further. Here is Geertz's answer to the sorts of questions I have been putting forward. In this passage, he has been discussing Balinese cockfights in Indonesia:

> For the anthropologist, whose concern is with formulating sociological principles, not with promoting or appreciating cockfights, the question is, what does one learn about such principles from examining culture as an assemblage of texts? . . . to treat the cockfight as a text is to bring out a feature of it (in my opinion the central feature of it) that treating it as a right or a pastime, the two most obvious alternatives, would tend to obscure: its use of emotion for cognitive ends. What a cockfight says it says in a vocabulary of sentiment – the thrill of risk, the despair of loss, the pleasure of triumph . . . Attending cockfights and participating in them is, for the Balinese, a kind of sentimental education. What he learns there is what his culture's ethos and his private sensibility . . . look like when spelled out externally in a collective text.[12]

He follows this with a rather bizarre analogy to the experience of watching *Macbeth* to learn about a man who has gained a kingdom at the expense of his soul; the Balinese, he tells us, go to watch cockfights to learn about what happens when the proud, aloof and arrogant rooster is provoked to anger: it will either be brought low or triumph. So the cockfight reveals in microcosm the way that the people of the Balinese culture view themselves, just as *Macbeth* tells us something about the way we view ourselves. I am afraid that I am still not entirely convinced by this explanation, but I am willing to work through the ideas in practice to see if they work. Let us return to our imaginary English town and attempt to do what Geertz does with the Balinese cockfight. The football club tells us that this town appreciates sport, competition, perhaps even fair play. It has a trophy cabinet, so there is a great emphasis placed on winning and losing, and victory is seen as important, to the extent that the game around which this club is built produced strong emotions 'for cognitive ends'. When a player scores a goal he punches the air in celebration and elation, as his teammates gather round to congratulate him; meanwhile the opposition have their heads buried in their hands in agony. The same sort of things seem to be true of the group of boys playing video games, as the victor of the game shouts 'yes!' and his defeated foes shake their heads. The reading group's meeting at the Women's Institute tells us any number of things: that the people of this town value discussion and sharing each other's opinions, that reading books is seen as being an important activity and that gender is a valid category around which to base an 'institute'. And in each of these cases socializing – spending time with other people – is of such significance that games and buildings have been designed for this very purpose.

After examining it further, then, I am willing to accept that these 'thick descriptions' of the activities in question do in fact tell us *something* about the culture to which they belong, albeit in a rather general and unremarkable way. But I remain much less convinced of the extent to which these activities are connected to each either, or of the idea that culture is a unified whole. The people in the football club and the boys playing video games seem to value competition a lot, but there is little evidence of this in the group at the Women's Institute. Could it be that the analysis of these people in these places simply tell us about the *people* in question, rather than about their 'culture' more generally? I am also rather sceptical about the extent to which these general conclusions are unique or specific to this little town in England. I am minded of Donald E. Brown's *Human Universals* (1991):[13] which culture *doesn't* value competition, experience emotion in victory or defeat, build structures around socializing or differentiate between men and women? Since Geertz does not believe in human nature, perhaps the thought would not occur to him, but it is difficult to think of a society that has no games, attaches no importance to (or has no concept of) victory or defeat, has no structures in place for socializing and draws no distinction between males and females. I will return to this theme later in the book.

Vincent P. Pecora has also criticized Geertz's analysis of local structures but for a different reason: its narrowness. Geertz seems incapable of taking broader contexts into account. For example, his reading of Indonesian history appears blind to the wider context of global politics that invariably informs what goes on inside that country. After a long and impressive account of the Sukarno coup of 1965, Pecora demonstrates that in Geertz 'neither American involvement [in the coup] nor Indonesia's wholesale swing to a pro-Western orientation [afterwards] is ever mentioned'.[14] This is because, put simply, they were not under his microscope.

We can summarize the anthropology of Geertz as follows:

1   Culture governs human behaviour and without it we have few, if any, useful instincts.

2   Culture manifests itself by making symbols in the material objects it produces.

3   These symbols can be read, analysed and interpreted like texts.

4   The best method of reading, analysing and interpreting is 'thick description', which is the attempt to understand these 'texts' as if you were a member of the culture that produced them.

5   This 'thick description' should be carried out, as far as possible', in its original context, in order to produce 'local knowledge'.

6 By doing this, we can uncover the rules by which different cultures govern the behaviours of the people who are a part of them.

While it is far too crude and reductive, not to mention inaccurate, to suggest that Stephen Greenblatt is essentially just Geertz as Shakespeare scholar, it is possible to trace many of his ideas and practices to the anthropologist's work as we shall see in Chapter 4.

Key questions for students

- Do you agree with the anti-humanists that there is no such thing as a universal human nature and that individuals are *entirely* the cultural products of their time and place? Why?
- How useful is Clifford Geertz's method of 'thick description' for helping us understand other cultures? Do you think it could really help us explain to an alien the difference between the muscular twitch of an eyelid and a cheeky boy winking before he plays a trick?
- Why does Geertz insist on 'local knowledge'? And do you agree with him that to understand a given 'text' we need to recover its original context?
- What are the similarities and differences between Geertz and the formalists and structuralists we looked at in Chapter 2? How does he differ, for example, from Roland Barthes?
- How might Geertz's anthropological methods be usefully adapted for the study of Shakespeare's plays?

Selected further reading

Geertz, Clifford, *The Interpretation of Cultures: Sketched Essays* (New York: Basic Books, 1973).
—, *Local Knowledge: Further Essays in Interpretative Anthropology* (New York: Basic Books, 1983).
Rosaldo Jr, Renato I., 'A Note on Geertz as a Cultural Essayist', *Representations*, 59, Special Issue: The Fate of "Culture": Geertz and Beyond (1997), 30–4.

Antonio Gramsci: Intellectuals, the organization of production, hegemony and how he differs from T. S. Eliot

Summary

- Gramsci's three-tiered model of 'forces of relation'
- Similarities and differences between Gramsci and T. S. Eliot on ideology and culture
- Hegemony and the dominant group
- Class struggle
- Summary of Gramsci's theory

Before we discuss the work of Louis Althusser, I would like to establish a few of the key concepts of Antonio Gramsci's work, which is an important precursor to Althusser's theory of ideology. Gramsci was a committed member of the Italian Communist Party during Benito Mussolini's Fascist regime in the 1920s and 1930s. Unsurprisingly, he spent much of his time in prison where he wrote his *Prison Notebooks* (1929–35), which were smuggled out of Italy by his sister-in-law, Tatiana, and eventually published in the 1950s. Gramsci wanted to 'enlighten' the masses but rejected traditional notions of enlightenment:

> The formation of a unitary collective consciousness requires various initiatives and conditions. The diffusion of a homogenous mode of thinking and acting, on the basis of a homogenous leadership, is its principal condition, though it cannot be its only one. A very widespread error is the belief that every social stratum develops its scientific consciousness and culture in the same manner and with the same methods, i.e. with the methods of the professional intellectuals.[15]

For Gramsci, this 'widespread error' manifests itself in many areas of everyday life. Gramsci conceived of the organization of production – what Marx would call the 'division of labour'[16] (e.g. the workforce of a factory) – in a three-tier system. This system of production has 'intellectuals' at the top, 'semi-intellectuals' in the 'intermediate stratum' and (non-intellectual) workers at the 'base'. I should note here that Gramsci believed that 'all men are intellectuals . . . but not all men have in society the function of intellectuals'.[17] One of the problems Gramsci sees in bourgeois society is that it consistently privileges the 'intellectual' bourgeois who sits atop this system but does not understand how those below him or her thinks: 'the managing director of a firm, an army general and the spiritual head of a philosophical school must be considered as the purest representatives of the bourgeois'.[18] There is a fundamental disconnection between, for example, the army general and private, or between Karl Marx (as 'the spiritual head of a philosophical school') and a local factory worker who attends communist meetings because the former in each case assumes that the latter can work 'in the same manner and with the same methods' as he can. Gramsci rejected the prediction made in Karl Marx and Friedrich Engels's *Communist Manifesto* (1848) that the workers would eventually and *inevitably* rise up in revolution to enact the 'forcible overthrow' of their bourgeois capitalist oppressors.[19] Because of his superior understanding of social stratification, intellectual functions and the workings of ideology, he 'did not share the analysis of the capitalist crisis as one leading to a rapid break-up of the capitalist system'[20]. It is the combination of this 'widespread error' of bourgeois society and the rejection of Marx and Engels's prediction – somewhat, it must be said, underlined by Mussolini's Italy and the spread of Fascism across Europe, which were, if anything, the *opposite* of the communist revolution they had predicted – that led Gramsci to advance his famous concept of ideological *hegemony*.

Perhaps idiosyncratically, in order to explain the nuances of this concept, I will contrast Gramsci with a thinker who was certainly not a Marxist himself, T. S. Eliot. Eliot's *Notes Towards the Definition of Culture* (1948) – most often overlooked these days – is a good example of a right-wing (rather than a left-wing or Marxist account) of the issues with which we are dealing. It is worth pointing out also, as Roger Kojeckey does, that Eliot 'profoundly respected . . . Karl Mannheim', who was arguably the first serious theorist of ideology after Marx'; he 'fled from Nazism to England in 1933, and was a close associate [of Eliot] . . .

from 1938'.[21] Eliot was strongly influenced by the ideas found in Mannheim's *Ideology and Utopia* (1936),[22] which was much more widely read and better known than Gramsci's work (not even published at the time); but his *Notes* serve as a much more accessible introduction to this complex field. I hope that in reading Gramsci against Eliot, through the process of comparing and contrasting, a very clear picture of his thought will unfold.

Eliot wonders 'whether what we call the culture, and what we call the religion, of a people are not different aspects of the same thing'.[23] Kenneth Asher notes that 'Eliot has arrived here at what, from a radically different perspective, Marx would have called pure ideology'.[24] Eliot's view of culture is strikingly materialist and not altogether dissimilar from what we saw in Geertz:

> It [culture] includes all the characteristic activities and interests of people: Derby Day, Henley Regatta, Cowes, the twelfth of August, a cup final, the dog races, the pin table, the dart board, Wensley-dale cheese, boiled cabbage cut into slices, beetroot vinegar, nineteenth-century Gothic churches and the music of Elgar.[25]

Here Asher dismissively quips that Eliot leaves himself 'open to the potential embarrassment of having to demonstrate how Christianity is embodied in "boiled cabbage"'.[26] But this would not be funny for some Marxists, for whom, as we shall see later with Althusser, culture or ideology is inextricably material. We can see that while the Marxists and Eliot are at opposite ends of the political spectrum, their analytical faculties lead them into similar conceptual areas.

Eliot predicates his view of society in *Notes* on a triple-tier system of class:

> The term culture has different associations to whether we have in mind the development of an *individual*, of a *group* or *class*, or of a *whole society*. It is a part of my thesis that the culture of the individual is dependent on the culture of a group or class, and that the culture of the group or class is dependent on the culture of the whole society to which that group or class belongs. . . . The culture of the group also, has a definite meaning in contrast to the less developed culture of the mass of society.[27]

This has important implications. It asserts that the individual is inextricably bound to a particular social group which itself is bound to the whole society. However, the 'whole society' is broad and indistinct, not fully 'developed', whereas individuals and the groups to which they belong have 'definite' meanings. Gramsci has a similar, though distinct, three-tier view of what he calls 'relations of force' in 'The Modern Prince' section of *Prison Notebooks*:

1 Individual philosophies generated by philosophers
2 Broader philosophical cultures articulated by leading groups
3 Popular 'religions' or faiths[28]

We can see how these strata roughly correspond to Eliot's 'individual', 'group or class' and 'whole society'. The difference is that whereas Eliot's categories are universal and general in that it seems that *all* people belong to all three levels of society (i.e. everyone is an individual who belongs to a group which is part of the whole society), Gramsci's are specific and hierarchical. These 'relations of force' correspond with his three-tier description of the 'organisation of production'. The first stratum is the 'intellectual' bourgeois of the ruling class: the managing director of the firm or the army general. The second stratum is the 'sub-intellectual' level of the petty bourgeois official: the managers, the petty officials and middle-ranking officers. The third stratum exists, as Michael Freedman describes, 'in [an] embryonic form among the masses'.[29] Gramsci's threefold structure is rigidly hierarchical: the higher up you go, the closer you get to ideological hegemony and 'philosophical sophistication'; the lower you go, the broader and less fully formed the philosophy gets.

Things had not always been organized in this way. Gramsci saw that with the advent of industrialization 'the old land-owning aristocracy [were now] joined to the industrialists', a move which united 'the traditional intellectuals with the new dominant class'.[30] Hence, Gramsci's great call is for the proletariat to get their hands on the reigns of knowledge, overthrow this alliance between industrialists and aristocrats (in other words the intellectual bourgeois ruling class), and strive for an autonomous and 'superior' culture led by the workers. This is obviously where he and Eliot differ considerably. For Eliot the commercialization of the traditional intellectual realms too has negative connotations but, unlike Gramsci, he wants a return to the old order rather than for the masses to rise and revolutionize knowledge. In fact, the rise of the masses is impossible in Eliot's philosophy as he maintains that it is impossible to 'educate' the masses; quite rightly, he has been accused – by Terry Eagleton, among others – of 'deeply emotional snobbery'.[31] However, this 'snobbery' is based on theoretical assumptions that are as present in the Marxists as it is in Eliot.

> People are unconscious of both their culture and their religion. . . . Anyone with even the slightest religious consciousness must be afflicted from time to time by the contrast between his religious faith and his behaviour; anyone with the taste that *individual* or *group* culture confers must be aware of values which he cannot call religious.[32]

In the same way, for Gramsci, ideology is a conscious creation for its producers (the bourgeois intellectuals) and an unconscious force for its consumers (the masses) that determines and controls their lives. Note, however, that though the masses are passive and not conscious of what is going on, they are implicitly *willing* consumers who allow themselves to be controlled. To use Gramsci's terms: this is 'the "spontaneous" consent given by the great masses. . . . to the general direction imposed on social life by the dominant fundamental group'.[33] The implication is that were they to wake up and snap out of it, they could see they were being coerced and taken advantage of, and stop giving this 'consent'.

Another feature that Eliot and Gramsci have in common is in the notion of constant and conscious struggle between competing ideologies. Eliot states: 'religion, politics, science and art reach a point at which there is conscious struggle between them for autonomy or dominance'.[34] This is similar to Gramsci's most famous concept of hegemony. For Gramsci, 'hegemony' is the predominance of one social class over another by means of coercion and what he calls 'intellectual and moral leadership'.[35] However, this 'hegemony' *subsumes* the other classes or groups over which it has dominion: for Gramsci '"hegemony" . . . constitutes a "historical bloc", that is unity between nature and spirit (unity between structure and superstructure), unity of opposites and of distincts'.[36] Therefore, Gramsci's 'hegemony' functions in a similar way to Georg W. F. Hegel's dialectics in which thesis and antithesis converge to form *synthesis*.

The key difference is that where dialectics seek to achieve theoretical balance through mutual inter-dependence, hegemony seeks to achieve *dominance* through mutual inter-dependence. As Joseph V. Femia puts it, 'the dominant ideology in modern capitalist societies is highly institutionalised and widely internalised. It follows that a ... direct attack on the bourgeois state ... can only result in disappointment'.[37] For Gramsci, it is clear that cultural or ideological hegemony – as manifest in the Western democracies – is a negative force that needs to be overturned. Hegemony *can* also be a positive force for Gramsci because it forms a vital part of his revolutionary 'solution'. 'Freedom' is the privilege of the 'intellectuals' who are canny enough to recognize their position in ideology and to use this realization as the basis for the domination of the 'less enlightened'. Therefore, freedom is *already* being enjoyed by the ruling class and becomes for the masses a 'radical possibility'. Gramsci is seeking to supplant the bourgeoisie with the masses: he wants for them to hold the reigns of ideological hegemony rather than to escape it altogether. This radical possibility amounts to 'a war of position' with revolutionary aims.[38]

Such a war is only made possible by the fact that in Gramsci's system, hegemony never has a total or secure grip on power, because the dominant group only comes to its position by means of struggle and is always subject to the competing forces that it suppresses:

> Germinated ideologies become 'party', come into confrontation and conflict, until only one of them tends to prevail, to gain the upper hand, to propagate itself throughout society – bringing about not only a unison of economic and political aims, but also intellectual and moral unity, posing all questions around which the struggle rages not on a corporate but on a 'universal' plane, and thus creating the hegemony of a fundamental social group over a series of subordinate groups.[39]

Despite appearances, these 'subordinate groups' have not lost everything and maintain some bargaining power. 'The general interests of the subordinate groups' hold the dominant group in perpetual states of 'equilibria'; hegemony prevails but 'only up to a certain point'.[40] For Gramsci, power is always kept in check by the prospect of rebellion, which will *necessarily* occur if the dominant group oversteps the mark. As an Italian political theorist, Gramsci saw himself writing in the tradition of Niccolò Machiavelli (ergo 'The Modern Prince' section of *Prison Notebooks*) and this is one idea that he inherited from the sixteenth-century Florentine master: 'the prince should . . . determine to avoid anything which will make him hated and despised', lest he risk the prospect of 'internal subversion from his subjects'.[41] While this may seem like an obvious point, as we shall see, it is one that seems to escape later thinkers such as Althusser or Michel Foucault, who often write as if power and the dominant ideology are absolute and almost impossible to challenge in this way. Somewhere along the line, the idea of checks and balances seems to go missing.

We can summarize Gramsci's theory as follows:

1   In any given society, there will be one group who through struggle achieve dominance and hegemony over all of the other groups in that society.

2   However, the dominant group's position is not totally secure and it is accountable to the other groups and liable to lose its position by losing the sort of struggle described above.

3   In capitalist society, it is the intellectual bourgeoisie, an alliance between the land-owning old aristocracy and the industrialists, who have hegemony over their sub-intellectual petty officials and the non-intellectual masses.

4   The intellectual bourgeoisie use their superior knowledge to control the masses who, unconsciously, give them their consent to do so.

5   The masses should become conscious of this situation, stop giving their consent to be controlled, and gain their own knowledge in order to become the new dominant group.

The main difference between Gramsci and what we find in Marx and Engels is in the fact that the latter assumed that this process would happen automatically, and of course, as a matter of historical inevitability. In stressing the specifically *intellectual* nature of the ruling class' dominion over the other groups in society, Gramsci moves beyond the purely materialist and technological account provided in *The Communist Manifesto*. Workers are not simply exploited because of disparity in wealth and private property or by the dehumanizing mechanization and de-specialization of skilled job functions, but actively coerced by the dominant group who use their social function 'as intellectuals' to create and exploit a knowledge deficit in the masses. Although he has not been as pervasive an influence over new historicists and cultural materialists as either Althusser or Foucault, Gramsci is generally regarded as a thinker who was ahead of his time and who is often more nuanced and flexible than some of his successors.

Key questions for students

- In the account given above, who did you find yourself agreeing with more, T. S. Eliot or Antonio Gramsci? Why?
- What do you think of Gramsci's idea that the dominant group has 'the function of intellectuals' in society?
- Why does the proletariat give its 'spontaneous consent' to live under the hegemony of the dominant group?
- Do you think there really is a single ideology in society that achieves hegemony over the others? What would that ideology be now in the 2010s?
- What would a Gramscian reading of Elizabethan England in the 1590s look like? See if you can produce one using what you know about the period.

Selected further reading

Asher, Kenneth, *T.S. Eliot and Ideology* (Cambridge: Cambridge University Press, 1998).

Athos, Lisa, *In Carcere con Gramsci* (Milan: Terracini, 1973).

Buci-Glucksmann, Christine, *Gramsci and the State*, trans. David Fernbach (Southampton: Lawrence and Wishart, 1980).

Eagleton, Terry, 'Eliot and a Common Culture', in *Eliot in Perspective* (London: Macmillan, 1970).

Eliot, T. S., *Notes Towards a Definition of Culture* (London: Faber and Faber, 1948).

Fernia, Joseph V., *Gramsci's Political Thought: Hegemony, Consciousness, and the Revolutionary Process* (Oxford: Clarendon Press, 1987).

Freedman, Michael, *Ideology: A Very Short Introduction* (New York and Oxford: Oxford University Press, 2003).

Gramsci, Antonio, *Selections from the Prison Notebooks*, ed. Quintin Hoare and Geoffrey Nowell Smith, trans. Quintin Hoare and Geoffrey Nowell Smith (London: Lawrence and Wishart, 1973).

Hawkes, David, *Ideology* (New York and London: Routledge, 1996).

Kojeckey, Roger, *T.S. Eliot's Social Criticism* (London: Faber and Faber, 1971).

Laclau, Ernesto and Chantal Mouffe, *Hegemony and Socialist Strategy: Towards a Radical Democratic Politics*, 2nd edn (New York and London: Verso, 2001).

Machiavelli, Niccolò, *The Historical, Political, and Diplomatic Writings of Niccolò Machiavelli, Volume 2*, trans. Christian E. Detmold (Boston: J. R. Osgood and Company, 1882).

—, *The Prince*, trans. Geoffrey Bull, 4th edn (New York and London: Penguin, 2003).

Mannheim, Karl, *Ideology and Utopia* (London: Kegan Paul & Co., 1936).

Louis Althusser: Into the matrix of ideological interpellation

Summary

- Ideology and the ideological state apparatus
- On 'priests and despots' as 'professional ideologists'
- Criticisms of Althusser's monolithic and static model of ideology
- Contradiction and overdetermination
- Spatializing history: 'ruptures' or 'epistemic breaks'
- No escape: Althusser and individual agency
- Summary of Althusser's theory

While Geertz was influential for Greenblatt personally, many scholars of his generation, especially in Britain, were seduced by Louis Althusser's concept of ideology. It is best to think of the new historicist / cultural materialist approach, as Edward Pechter does, as being 'at its cutting edge – a kind of "Marxist criticism"'.[42] In some ways, cultural materialism can be seen as continuing the project that Althusser outlines in his classic essay 'Ideology and the

Ideological State Apparatus' (1969). Cultural materialism has been characterized as writing explicitly 'under the sway of Althusser'.[43] When Walter Cohen considered cultural materialism he concluded that, of its theoretical sources, 'perhaps Althusser has exercised the greatest influence'.[44] Incidentally, in what follows, where Althusser talks about 'ideology' he means almost exactly the same thing as 'culture' as used by T. S. Eliot or Clifford Geertz: as he puts it, ' "culture" is the ordinary name for the Marxist concept of the *ideological*'.[45]

Althusser was a French Marxist philosopher and professor at the École Normale Supérieure in Paris, who came to prominence in the 1960s. It is worth noting here that as well as being a Marxist, Althusser was also working within the framework of French structuralism from which he borrowed many concepts. For example, his analysis of ideology is almost exclusively synchronic, much like Ferdinand de Saussure's analysis of language. He views history as a series of ruptures between discontinuous synchronic moments.[46] It is possible to see the ghost of Saussure – refracted through the mirror of the French psychoanalyst Jacques Lacan – in his theory of ideology: 'ideology' is *la langue* and its individual subjects are instances of *parole*. As with Gramsci, Althusser's work on ideology can be seen as answering the fundamental question as to why the uprising that Karl Marx predicted in *The Communist Manifesto* did not happen. Marx had predicted that it was only a matter of time before the exploited proletariat workers of the industrialized West would rise up in revolutions against the bourgeois ruling class: 'the victory of the proletariat . . . [is] . . . inevitable'.[47] What went wrong? Althusser's answer is that the workers did not rise up because they were completely in thrall to capitalist 'ideology', which sold them the illusion of being free and autonomous individuals who perform their social functions out of choice. Althusser defines 'ideology' as a *representation* of 'the imaginary relationship of individuals to their real conditions of existence'. This relationship 'has the function . . . of "constituting" concrete individuals as subjects' via a process of what he calls 'interpellation': individuals are interpellated as concrete subjects so that they can recognize themselves as 'concrete, individual, distinguishable and (naturally) irreplaceable subjects'. It is mainly through ideology that the state is able to keep its subjects subordinate and therefore prevent them from rising up in rebellion.[48]

Althusser makes a distinction between what he calls the Repressive State Apparatus (RSA), when the state is forced into action physically to apprehend or subdue its subjects, and the Ideological State Apparatus (ISA), which is far more insidious in that it dominates its subjects through their own thought processes, making natural or 'second nature' that which has been learnt. As with Geertz and his cathedral, for Althusser, ideology has a material existence: the ISAs take the form of 'Churches, Parties, Trade Unions, families, some schools, most newspapers, cultural ventures'. He talks about the religious ISA, the educational ISA, the family ISA, the legal ISA and so on. His general observation is that capitalist society has moved from the point where the religious ISA was key in maintaining order to one where it is chiefly the educational ISA and the family ISA that is producing 'labour power'. Which if you think about it is true: families raise their children to have the capacity to perform necessary social functions and schools and universities equip them with the necessary skills. In fact, the effects of these ISAs are so all-encompassing that 'an individual is always already a subject, even before he is born': in that a child will 'always already' have a name, a social context, an identity, a gender and a spectrum of social roles he or she will be expected to fill in the future. In the 1950s and 1960s when Althusser was writing, for some this range of roles would be rather narrow: it would be expected for men to take the same job as his father in the same coalmine or factory or dockyard. Thus, the state is able to reproduce the conditions of its own reproduction in its subject, and as long as this process takes place successfully, and it is difficult to see how or why it would not, its overthrow is virtually impossible. Ideology both constitutes political or cultural discourse and is its product: ideology begets ideology. Its chief function is to ensure 'the reproduction of labour power' so that the subjects 'work all by themselves' to maintain the conditions of the state.[49]

To use a 'real life' example, take yourself. Presumably, if you are reading this book, you are someone who has chosen to go to university. Why did you make that choice? Maybe you think that by getting a degree, you will further your chances in the job market. Why do you want to get a good job? Is it so you can have more money to be able to buy more things? The more money you have, the more choices you get, correct? Someone on a high salary can afford to choose between a great many things: different houses, different cars, different television sets, and so on. But for

Althusser, all such choices are necessarily illusory – there is no real freedom in your choices. In each instance you have merely rein-forced the ISA, merely replicated your ideologically-induced role as a Good Capitalist Citizen performing their social function. Your choice to go to university is scarcely a real choice but something that has been wholly determined. An economist, just by looking at the income of your parents could probably make a prediction on whether you would be someone who ended up at university or not. In a different set of circumstances you might not have gone on to university, but instead become a bin man, or a pub landlord, or a supermarket assistant or a hairdresser. 'But I'd never *want* to do any of those things!' You protest. But what of the people who fill those roles? Each of these roles exists, and each is always-already filled by someone who has supposedly chosen to fill that role. The hairdresser has convinced himself that he always wanted to be a hairdresser and that the other available roles – of doctor, lawyer, teacher, clerk, university student and so on – were not for him. For Althusser, this illusion of choice, the illusion that we have freedom, is ideology's foremost tool of containment. Individuals do not rebel because they live in the belief that they are free and autonomous rather than subject and exploited – they 'work by themselves' with-out apparent coercion – and, as Terry Eagleton says, 'unless we did so we would be incapable of playing our parts in social life'.[50] This might seem mild and inconsequential when considering how you ended up becoming a university student and how the hairdresser became a hairdresser, but it is the same general principle that drives people to pick up guns in the name of a war that they had no part in starting, to support a government that routinely exploits them or to worship a god that would deny them pleasure. Think of the moment in the film *The Matrix* (1999) when Neo first wakes up in the vat and realizes that life as he has known it thus far has been a simulated reality: the matrix is an Althusserian ISA.[51]

The final stage of Althusser's so-called quadruple system of ide-ological interpellation depends upon both individuals' recognition of themselves 'in ideology' and their subsequent vocalization of it. This is a complex but nonetheless straightforward idea; it is worth quoting Althusser verbatim:

We observe that the structure of all ideology, interpellating individuals as subjects in the name of a Unique and Absolute Subject is *speculary*, that is a mirror-structure, and *doubly* speculary: this mirror duplication is constitutive of ideology and ensures its functioning . . . The duplicate mirror-structure of ideology ensures simultaneously:

- the interpellation of 'individuals' as subjects;
- their subjection to the Subject;
- the mutual recognition of subjects and Subject, the subjects' recognition of each other and finally, the subject's recognition of himself;
- the absolute guarantee that everything really is so, and that on condition that subjects recognize what they are and behave accordingly, everything will be all right: Amen – 'So be it.'[52]

Althusser has borrowed the idea of the 'mirror phase', in which an infant first recognizes its own reflection in a mirror, from Jacques Lacan.[53] The important concept to grasp is that in order to be fully interpellated individuals have to identify themselves fully as being part of the ideology. This is not to say that they recognize that they are *in* ideology but that they recognize that they have become one with their role as ideological subject – so not 'I am a capitalist lackey', but 'I am a university student. Amen. So be it', or 'I am a hairdresser. Amen. So be it'.

This theory is explicitly anti-humanist. Althusser saw himself as cleansing Marx from the taint of the humanist ideology he had inherited from the German idealist philosopher Georg W. F. Hegel. He saw Hegel's project as:

The reduction of *all* the elements that make up the concrete life of a historical epoch . . . to *one principle* of internal unity, is itself only possible on the *absolute condition* of taking the whole of concrete life of a people for the externalization-alienation of an *internal spiritual principle*, which can *never definitely be anything but the most abstract form of that epoch's consciousness of itself . . . its own ideology . . . its most abstract ideology.*[54]

For Althusser this is unsatisfactory; it is too close to the 'crude' eighteenth-century 'simple solution' that 'Priests or Despots . . .

"forged" the Beautiful Lies that so that, in the belief that they obeying God, men would in fact obey the Priests and Despots'. He also rejects the position of Ludwig Feuerbach, another German philosopher ('taken over word by word by Marx'), which posits the existence of men in terms of material alienation. In fact, Althusser's whole project is set up to demonstrate how 'the reproduction of labour power requires . . . a reproduction of submission to the ruling ideology for the workers'. This ideology manifests itself in a way that specifically *doesn't* alienate the workers who must be content (or at least have the illusion of being so) to 'work all by themselves'. This might appear to be a more sophisticated version of the 'Priests and Despots' argument, but what Althusser adds (which, note, is missing in Gramsci) is that the ruling class are *themselves* the subjects of the ruling ideology. It is not only labour power that needs to be reproduced but also 'the ability to manipulate the ruling ideology correctly for the agents of exploitation and repression'.[55] He elaborates on this idea in greater detail later on in the essay:

> Somewhere around the age of sixteen, a huge mass of children is ejected 'into production': these are workers or small peasants. Another portion of scholastically adapted youth carries on . . . until it falls by the wayside and fills the posts of small and middle technicians, white-collar workers, small and middle executives, petty bourgeois of all kinds. A last portion reaches the summit, either to fall into the intellectual semi-employment, or to provide, as well as the 'intellectuals of the collective labour', the agents of exploitation (capitalists, managers), the agents of repression (soldiers, policemen, politicians, administrators, etc.) and the professional ideologists (priests of all sorts, most of whom are convinced 'laymen' [the mass media, spin doctors, those in public relations, those in advertising etc.].[56]

The sharper readers among you will immediately note the similarity here with Gramsci's three-tiered model of society. However, the distinction between Althusser and Gramsci is clear: in Althusser even the top tier of society, 'the agents of exploitation' et al., are ideological subjects; they are merely performing a social function, a role that is 'always-already' there, that has to be there. In Gramsci, the people in the same position are 'philosophers' and 'intellectuals' rather than 'professional ideologists'. Think of the Ministry of Truth in George Orwell's *1984*: Winston is a 'professional ideologist' who is paid to write and disseminate propaganda and to alter the historical record according to the Party's interests; he is certainly not paid to be a philosopher or an intellectual.[57] The point is that while Gramsci's 'priests and despots' are free and consciously producing ideology with which to control the masses, Althusser's are not free and not conscious of the fact that *they too* are caught in this ideological matrix.

In many ways, Althusser simplifies Gramsci's notion of hegemony by referring all ideologies back to the state. We could see it as an inherent problem of Althusser's theory that his model seemingly cannot account for ideologies that *don't* work for the state. All ideologies have a material existence and further some end, almost always the state. He would account for ideologies that do not work for the current state as being those of bygone epochs (or old states), as being ultimately outmoded ideologies. This is an argument Althusser never makes but it is implicit in his system. For example, a man living in modern-day New York who still believes in and carries out the rituals of ancient paganism is a subject of an outmoded ideology (i.e. one that cannot be classed as an ISA). It is because the principal function of ideology in Althusser is to 'reproduce the conditions of labour power' (rather than to posit some ideal) that it is possible for an ideology to become 'outmoded' in this way. Unlike in Gramsci's model, in which various ideologies compete for hegemony, Althusser sees them all working in the same direction. For Gramsci, achieving hegemony is the ultimate goal of the class struggle. Althusser, on the other hand, sees this idea as being tainted by Hegel and a dangerous path towards totalitarianism: 'the hegemonic Stalinist philosophy [was] very precisely Hegelian . . . [I thus] sought to cleanse the Marxist tradition of any remnants of that 'flirtation' with the Hegelian dialectic'.[58] In any case, for Althusser, the 'struggle' for which Gramsci fights is only ever illusionary because all the ISAs are all working for the same cause. Those ideologies that have become 'outmoded' have no clear function and therefore cannot tangibly affect anything. In this instance, it would appear that Gramsci's model has more 'common sense'; Althusser's claim that we find *apparently* differing ideologies, which 'in reality' work towards the same ends, appears to be self-defeating, because it means nothing can be changed. John Fiske makes a similar point:

> Indeed, [Gramsci's] theory of hegemony foregrounds the notion of ideological struggle much more than does Althusser's ideological theory, which at times tends to imply that the power of ideology and the ISAs to form the subject in ways that suit the interests of the dominant class is almost irresistible. Hegemony, on the other hand, posits a constant contradiction between ideology and the social experience of the subordinate that makes this interface into an inevitable site of ideological struggle.[59]

If all ideology has the function of reproducing 'the state' (i.e. the dominant ideology), it is impossible to see how its subjects – as the products of that state – can enact change. However, if all ideologies are constantly competing for hegemony and the dominant ideology is held accountable to them through checks and balances, as in Gramsci, then it is easy to see how tangible change can be brought about. Althusser's model seems very static on this point. This echoes the critique of Althusser's great rival, the socialist of the British New Left, E. P. Thompson, who famously attacked and dismissed the Althusser's theory of ideology as 'a structuralism of *stasis*', which has 'no adequate categories to explain contradiction or change – or class struggle'.[60]

To be kinder to Althusser, this is simply not true if one looks outside 'Ideology and the Ideological State Apparatus'. In *For Marx* (1965), there is an essay – admittedly, at times, a rather confusing one, strewn as it is with the liberal doses of italics and anti-Hegelian rhetorical typical of Althusser's style – called 'Contradiction and Overdeterminiation'. In this, he tackles the question of why the Russian Revolution of 1917 took place and Lenin's explanation of Russia being the 'weakest link' in the imperialist chain.

> . . . [T]he whole Marxist experience shows that, if the general contradiction . . . between the forces of production and the relations of production . . . is sufficient to define the situation when revolution is the 'task of the day', it cannot of its own simple, direct power induce a 'revolutionary situation', nor *a fortiori* a situation of revolutionary rupture and the triumph

of the revolution. If this contradiction is to become 'active' in the strongest sense, to become a ruptural principle, there must be an accumulation of 'circumstances' and 'currents' . . . [that] 'fuse' into a *ruptural unity* . . . [to launch] an assault on a regime [against] which its ruling classes are *unable to defend* . . . an accumulation of contradictions. How else could the class-divided popular masses (proletariats, peasants, petty bourgeois) throw themselves *together*, consciously or unconsciously, into a general assault on the existing regime? And how else could the ruling classes (aristocrats, big bourgeois, industrial bourgeois, finance bourgeois, etc.), who have learnt by long experience and sure instinct to seal between themselves, despite their class differences, a holy alliance against the exploited, find themselves reduced to impotence, divided at the decisive moment . . . disarmed in the very citadel of their State machine, and suddenly overwhelmed by the people they had so long kept in leash and respectful by exploitation, violence and deceit?[61]

One can almost hear the Soviet national anthem playing as Althusser becomes more and more excited here. When 'contradictions' converge into this unstoppable maelstrom they are said to be 'overdetermined'. A single contradiction, or even multiple contradictions, alone are not enough to create these big moments of historical change or 'ruptures'; there needs to be 'a vast accumulation of "contradictions" . . . [at] play *in the same court*, some of which are radically heterogeneous'.[62] Althusser then makes the move of saying that *all* contradictions are in fact 'overdetermined' at any given time. William S. Lewis provides a marginally more lucid definition: 'overdetermination . . . can be said to be the point at which the ensemble of contradictions that make up a "whole" system are reflected on an individual contradiction.'[63] As far as I can make out (this is Althusser at his most abstract and obtuse), under normal circumstances contradictions are 'overdetermined' into being neutralized and displaced, effectively lulled into banal 'non-antagonism', by the dominant ideology. The key is whether or not they are 'fused' together and activated – overdetermined by an exceptional set of historical circumstances – to become antagonistic towards the dominant power. While this seems a rather long-winded and complicated way to describe radical social change,

E. P. Thompson's charge that Althusser has 'no categories' for doing so is surely unfounded.

Elsewhere, in *Reading Capital* (1968), Althusser analysed 'the currently widespread distinction between synchrony and diachrony' and challenged the concept of 'historical time as continuous and contemporaneous with itself'. Althusser posited an idea of history as a series of 'presents', 'merely successive contingent presents in the time continuum'.[64] For Althusser, history is fundamentally disjunctive; notions of the diachronic and synchronic become redundant in the face of a perpetual present that is consistently formed via a process of interpellation by ideology. In effect what he has done is dispensed with the idea of the diachronic and replaced it with a purely synchronic model that 'has no history'. He has spatialized time. For the literary theorist Richard Lehan this move 'drains meaning from history'. To 'spatialize time' is to 'rob it of sequence, direction, and agency'. He thinks this locks history into 'part of a tropological frieze', which begs the question of 'how . . . we get from frieze to frieze, or from what Foucault would call episteme to episteme'. Lehan argues ultimately for the recovery of 'the diachronic nature' of history and insists upon 'the belief that meaning is built into time' upon the fundamental logic of cause and effect. His solution is to re-establish 'the idea of historical process' by retracing 'the connection' between epistemes.[65] It is important to grasp this idea of 'ruptural' or 'epistemic' breaks in history to understand both Foucault, who takes it almost wholesale from Althusser, and the new historicists and cultural materialists who follow him.

Another problem that many commentators have seen in Althusser is that he seems to afford individuals very little autonomy: they are simply passive sponges who once interpellated by ideology have no choice but to fulfil their ideological function – hardly surprising for a militant anti-humanist. John Higgins offers a typical reading:

> Althusser's subject is a subject without an unconscious. He sees the moment of repression, that castrating moment of transition from pre-social to social existence, as one of successful and complete repression, inaugurating a homogenous and unbroken process of interpellation.[66]

Paul Smith puts it more succinctly: the individual subject 'seems to exist as a unity which is dependent upon a supposed unity of interpellative effects'.[67] Literary critics have inherited this view. Stephen Cohen notes that Althusser's 'Lacanian model of interpellation . . . has been critiqued as excessively totalizing and pessimistically inescapable'.[68] It is difficult to defend Althusser against these arguments since his model is explicitly one of containment and not freedom, although some have tried.[69] The most generous reading involves seeing 'ideology' not as an insidious tool of coercion but as a necessary (because there is no 'outside' of ideology) enabler through which to achieve social change. But this is a stretch because the status of ideologies outside of the state apparatus remains ambivalent at best in his works; it is underdeveloped. A further problem is that, even making allowances for the multiplicity of ideologies, the state and its ISAs in Althusser's analysis are almost always repressive in character. The state is never a force of positive change. Nicos Poulantzas touches on this matter in *State, Power, Socialism* by positing the necessity of the political obligation of those in power to the people they rule and the prospect of 'genuinely positive action by the State'.[70] As we saw with Gramsci's notion that the dominant power is always accountable, this is an idea that has its origins in Machiavelli: 'In fact, when there is combined under the same constitution a prince, a nobility, and the power of the people, then these three powers will watch and keep each other reciprocally in check'.[71] This prospect of a 'positive', socially obliged ruling class is also glimpsed in Gramsci, who speaks of 'the entire positive, civilizing activity undertaken by the State'.[72] In his later work, through his own reading of Machiavelli, Althusser does come to recognize some notion of political obligation in 'a state rooted in the people, a *popular state*'.[73] For this to happen, however, ideology would have to be sometimes not repressive in character and 'non-state' ideologies (e.g. those of 'the people') would have to both be possible and able to affect the state and the actions of the ruling class. If this follows, non-state ideologies must produce subjects who can recognize and assess the actions of the state and also, by extension, become openly critical of it to the extent where they are in a position to enact change. As Judith Butler argues: 'the radicalization of the subject or its gendering or its social abjection more generally is performatively induced from various diffuse quarters that do not always operate as "official" discourse'.[74] My feeling is that Althusser does not provide us with such a model.

We can summarize Althusser's theory as follows:

1   Ideology is the representation of the imagined relationship between individuals and the world around them, which serves to reproduce the 'means of production', that is the workforce required to keep the economy and the statue running in an orderly manner.

2   Ideology has always already interpellated the individual, even from before the moment they are born, insomuch as they already have an ideological role.

3   However, to be truly interpellated, the individual must accept their ideological role consciously and willingly. 'Amen. So be it'.

4   Ideologies have a material existence in 'state apparatuses' such as schools, families, churches, the media and so on; these are called ISAs.

5   These ISAs help to interpellate individuals fully and maintain the illusion that individuals are free and autonomous persons actively choosing their own roles in life.

6   In fact, they are not free, but as per 2, always already interpellated by ideology. This illusion of freedom means that individuals 'work by themselves' to perform their ideological function. For example, a coal miner goes to work every day believing he is doing it of his own accord and for reasons with which he agrees, probably for his own benefit or the benefit of his family.

7   Between ISAs there are many contradictions that are typically 'overdetermined' by being displaced as if they were trivial and of little consequence.

8   History is not continuous, but a series of 'ruptures'.

9   In order for one of these ruptures to take place, the many contradictions between ISAs and in ideology must be 'overdetermined' by becoming 'fused' together to create

an irresistible force against which the ruling class has no defence.

Althusser has suffered a decline in reputation since his heyday. Partly, this is because he murdered his wife in 1980 and spent the last decade of his life in and out of a mental asylum. Partly, this is because he has never shaken off Thompson's accusation of being 'on the theoretical production line of Stalinist ideology'; not at all helped by Althusser's coldly inhuman and theoretical account of Stalin, which as Tony Judt quips, is of a 'man whose main crime was to pervert the course of Marxism (which is rather like saying that Hitler's sin was to give physical anthropology a bad name)'.[75] And partly, it is because his theory of ideology is seen as too rigid and static to serve.

Nonetheless, apart from Michel Foucault, no figure has been more influential to Shakespeare studies and perhaps even literary studies more generally in the past thirty years. His statements on art are confined to two very short letters to André Daspre which call for a science of art,[76] and contain one of his more famous lines: 'I believe that a peculiarity of art is to "make us see", "make us perceive", "make us feel" something which *alludes* to reality!'[77] Althusser's influence in criticism stretches beyond new historicism and cultural materialism. The early work of both Terry Eagleton and Fredric Jameson,[78] for example, owes much to Althusser and, more directly, to his student Pierre Macherey, 'known primarily as [Althusser's] . . . student or "disciple"'.[79] Althusser and Macherey are also the principal starting points for Stuart Hall and the Birmingham Centre for Contemporary Cultural Studies, as well as Ernesto Laclau and Chantal Mouffe, who were influential in their own right in the 1980s and Slavoj Žižek in the 1990s and 2000s.[80] Much of this criticism was interested in the way literary and cultural discourse 'gives an implicit critique of its ideological content, if only because it resists being incorporated into the flow of ideology in order to give a determinate representation of it'.[81] My feeling is that it is absolutely vital to read at least Althusser's seminal essay on ideology to understand the cultural materialist project.

Key questions for students

- Have the choices in your life been free ones or have you been entirely conditioned by ideology at every turn, as Althusser describes? If you believe that they are free, with what argument do you counter his claims?
- Can you identify five ISAs from the world around you? List them.
- Why do you think it is important for Althusser that ideology has a specifically *material* existence?
- Who do you think offers us the best model for political resistance and change, Althusser or Antonio Gramsci? Why?
- What implications does Althusser's theory of ideology have for the study of Shakespeare's plays?

Selected further reading

Althusser, Louis, 'Ideology and the Ideological State Apparatus' (1969), in *Lenin and Philosophy and Other Essays*, ed. Fredric Jameson, trans. Ben Brewster (New York: Monthly Review Press, 2001), pp. 85–126.

—, *For Marx*, trans. Ben Brewster (1969; New York and London: Verso, 2005).

Althusser, Louis and Etienne Balibar, *Reading Capital*, trans. Ben Brewster (London: New Left Books, 1986).

Assiter, Alison, *Althusser and Feminism* (London: Pluto Press, 1990).

CCCS, *On Ideology* (London: Hutchinson, 1978).

Clarke, Simon, Terry Lovell, Kevin McDonnel, Kevin Robins and Victor Jeleniewski Seidler, *One-Dimensional Marxism: Althusser and the Politics of Culture* (New York and London: Allison & Busby, 1980).

Dews, Peter, 'Althusser, Structuralism, and the French Epistemological Tradition', in *Althusser: A Critical Reader*, ed. Gregory Elliott (Cambridge, MA and Oxford: Blackwell, 1994), pp. 104–41.

Eagleton, Terry, *Criticism and Ideology* (London: Verso, 1978).

Gerratana, Valentino, 'Althusser and Stalinism', *New Left Review*, 101–2 (January–April 1977), 110–24.

Jameson, Fredric, *The Political Unconscious: Narrative as a Socially Symbolic Act* (Ithaca, NY: Cornell University Press, 1981).

Judt, Tony, *Marxism and the French Left: Studies on Labour and Politics in France, 1830–1981* (New York and London: New York University Press, 2011).

Lacan, Jacques, 'The Mirror Stage as Formative of the Function of the I as revealed in Psychoanalytic Experience', in *Écrits: a Selection*, trans. Alan Sheridan (London: Tavistock, 1977), pp. 1–7.

Lewis, William S., *Louis Althusser and the Traditions of French Marxism* (Oxford: Lexington Books, 2005).

Macherey, Pierre, *A Theory of Literary Production*, trans. Geoffrey Wall (London: Routledge and Kegan Paul, 1978).

Marx, Karl, 'The Eighteenth Brumaire of Louis Bonaparte' (1869), in *Karl Marx: Selected Writings*, ed. David McLellan (New York and Oxford: Oxford University Press, 1977), pp. 300–25.

—, *Capital*, ed. David McLennan (New York and Oxford: Oxford University Press, 1995).

Marx, Karl and Friedrich Engels, *The Communist Manifesto*, ed. Gareth Stedman Jones, trans. Samuel Moore (New York and London: Penguin, 2002).

—, *The German Ideology*, ed. C. J. Arthur (1970; rpr. London: Lawrence and Wishart, 2004).

Mulhern, Francis, 'Althusser in Literary Studies', in *Althusser: A Critical Reader*, ed. Gregory Elliott (Cambridge, MA and Oxford: Blackwell, 1994), pp. 159–76.

Nelson, Cary and Lawrence Grossberg (eds), *Marxism and the Interpretation of Culture* (Urbana and Chicago: University of Illinois Press, 1988).

Poulantzas, Nicos, *State, Power, Socialism* (London: Verso, 1980).

Resch, Robert Paul, *Althusser and the Renewal of Marxist Social Theory* (Berkley, CA: University of California Press, 1992).

Smith, Paul, *Discerning the Subject* (Minneapolis, MN: University of Minnesota Press, 1989).

Thompson, E. P., *The Poverty of Theory* (London: Merlin Press, 1978).

Michel Foucault: Power relations and discourse analysis

Summary

- Power relations and power-knowledge
- Discursive formations and epistemic history
- Key differences between Foucault's power and Althusser's ideology
- How Foucault collapses traditional Marxist notions of base and superstructure by eschewing the economic base
- Bentham's Panopticon
- Criticisms of Foucault
- Summary of Foucault's theory

Much of Althusser's thought prefigures that of his former student, Michel Foucault. Foucault ultimately proved to be more palatable for the new historicists, who may have found Althusser's theory too centred on the State and, above all, *too Marxist* for Cold War-era American tastes. Although Foucault studied under Althusser at the the École Normale Supérieure and joined the French Communist Party, unlike his mentor, he was never a committed Marxist. He was also openly homosexual and something of a celebrity, making regular appearances on French television, once in a debate with Noam Chomsky on Dutch television, and in the 1970s delivered guest lectures at the University of California, Berkeley, which were attended by the young Stephen Greenblatt and Catherine Gallagher. His death of an AIDS-related illness in 1984 was well publicized.

Althusser and Foucault can be seen as two very different elaborations of the same theme. They wrestle with the same problematic, what Peter Dews describes as 'the problem of the relation between the individual subject and the overarching structures of history'.[82] Robert Paul Resch even goes so far as to call Foucault 'something of a renegade Althusserian'.[83] Like Althusser, Foucault owed much of his thinking and methodology to Saussurean structuralism in that, at least in his early years, he was still committed to the idea of a readily analysable and finite structural system. Rather than talking about 'culture' or 'ideology', Foucault is primarily concerned with 'power relations' that are held together by 'fields of discursive events'.[84] For Foucault all discourse necessarily entails a power-relation, which should 'take as its model a perpetual battle' rather like dialogue in a play by Harold Pinter where one party is always dominating the other.[85] Like Althusser's ideology, for Foucault, as he states in *The Order of Things* (1966), these various discourses constitute

> The fundamental codes of a culture – those governing its language, its schemes of perception, its exchanges, its techniques, its values, the hierarchy of its practices – establish for every man, from the very first, the empirical orders with which he will be at home.[86]

However, unlike Althusser's static and state-centric notion of ideologies that emanates from ISAs onto hapless individuals, for Foucault, as he outlines in *Discipline and Punish* (1975), discourses:

> Cannot be localized in a particular type of institution or state apparatus . . . these relations go right down into the depths of society . . . they are not localized in the relations between state and its citizens . . . they do not merely reproduce at the level of individuals, bodies, gestures, and behaviour, the general form of the law or government . . . there is neither analogy nor homology, but a specificity of mechanism and modality. . . . They are not univocal; they define innumerable points of confrontation, focuses of instability, each of which has its own risks of conflict, of struggles, and of an at least temporary inversion of power relations.[87]

It is clear that Foucault is in some form of dialogue with Althusser here. Whereas Althusser's theory is homogeneous, unitary and watertight, Foucault's is heterogeneous, fractured and bursting with sites of conflict. Althusser makes a distinction between what he calls 'scientific knowledge' and 'ideological knowledge'. For him, most common knowledge, the knowledge of common sense for example, is ideological; but he reserves a special category of knowledge for 'science', which is somehow able to observe 'the truth' objectively, free of the taint of ideology. Marx's critique of capitalism, Freud's 'discourse of the unconscious' or Lacan's conception of the 'mirror-phase' would all fall into this category.[88] Foucault implicitly rejects this model of knowledge with his claim that 'power produces knowledge . . . power and knowledge directly imply one another . . . there is no power relation without the correlative constitution of a field of knowledge, nor any knowledge that does not presuppose and constitute at the same time power relations'.[89] So it is impossible for an individual to know anything at all without being subject to a power relation or to the effects of a power relation. In this way, individuals can be said to be *always-already* in the grip of power-knowledge.

It is not only this last idea of Foucault's that has proved influential for new historicists and cultural materialists, but also his refutation of traditional history and its assumptions. In *The Archaeology of Knowledge* (1969), he follows Althusser in proposing a radical new way of approaching history by switching the historian's gaze from the ideology of continuity – with its assumptions of tradition, influence, development, evolution and 'spirit', all of which merely serve to obfuscate the complex and disparate nature of historical moments – to 'discontinuity, rupture, limit, series, and transformation'.[90] Rather than focusing on the exploits of individuals, Foucault finds it more valuable to analyse discourses and their 'complex relations with one another'.[91] He also, in what some might call a *post-structuralist* move, seeks to collapse the notion of the unified literary or historical text. For Foucault:

> The frontiers of a book are never clear-cut: beyond the title, the first lines, and the last full-stop, beyond its internal configuration and its autonomous form, it is caught up in a system of references to other books, other texts, other sentences: it is a node within a network . . . The book is not simply the object that one holds in one's hands . . . it constructs itself, only on the basis of a complex field of discourse.[92]

The book is one 'discursive event' in a *field* of discursive events, which form a 'discursive formation'. After making this move, Foucault reiterates his structuralist method by stating that such a discursive formation is 'a grouping that is always finite and limited at any moment' (and therefore open for analysis). So the historian's task is now to describe discursive events within particular discursive formations by trying to find an answer for the question of 'how is it that one particular statement appeared rather than another?' in order to unveil 'the emergence of a group of rules proper to the discursive practice' that serve to define 'the ordering of objects'.[93] By analysing individual discursive events the historian will be able to come to an understanding of 'its conditions of possibility'.[94]

To give an example of this rather abstract formulation, if I were to take Shakespeare's *Richard II* and ask myself how it came to be that Shakespeare wrote this play at the moment he did in the late 1590s, and not any other play, my search through the traceable discursive formation of 1590s England might throw up some interesting results – not least Elizabeth II's famous declaration that 'I am Richard II . . . know you not that', a wider debate about the extent of monarchical power and the nature of royal authority, the subsequent rebellion of Essex in 1601, and the 'urgent contemporary task of defining the nation state'.[95] So Shakespeare's

Richard II ceases to be an individual act of genius but rather reflects the contemporary concerns that produced it in the first place. The 'conditions of its possibility' (a play about a weak, ineffectual and eventually usurped monarch) might be said to be Elizabeth's own weakening grip on power and Shakespeare captured, in this discursive event, a moment of 'discontinuity, rupture, limit, series, or transformation'.

This way of thinking about *Richard II* is largely based on existing new historicist accounts of the play. It is thus clear how crucial an influence Foucault has been for new historicists as though they are continuing to do the work, the 'archaeology', that Foucault himself had sought to do. The relationship between new historicism and Foucault is indeed a close one, so much so that critics of new historicism like Terry Eagleton have suggested that:

> The new historicism, for all its occasional brilliance, is theoretically speaking a set of footnotes to Foucault. It is as though the theory is all in place, and all that remains to be done is run yet more texts through it.[96]

While Eagleton's claim is amusing, it is unfair to suggest that new historicism is simply Foucault *redux* and nothing else. The typical leftist criticism of new historicism, that it is 'apolitically tame and quietistic', can hardly be levelled at the culturally rebellious Foucault.[97] H. Aram Veeser's point that 'new historicism inherited nineteenth and twentieth century North American pragmatism and twisted it to fit Foucault's microphysics of power' is a key recognition.[98] Indeed, as Veeser goes on to suggest:

> Foucault and new historicism emphasise very different logics of capitalism. Foucault studies the individual dissolved in advancing microstructures of power and represents (in Edward Said's words) 'an irresistible colonizing movement that paradoxically fortifies the prestige of the both the individual scholar and the system that contains him'. New historicism emphasises by contrast the self-disrupting logics of capitalism.[99]

There is an implied criticism of Foucault himself here, who all too often, as Said says elsewhere, harbours a 'kind of fascination with the techniques of domination. Foucault ultimately becomes the scribe of domination' and forgets his commitment to the points of stress, ruptures and possible transformations he promised to focus on.[100]

If there seemed to be no escape from Althusser's ISAs, the dark and endless web of Foucault's power relations is arguably even *more* all-consuming and even more terrifying. I wish to spend some time to show the ways in which Foucault's concept of power-knowledge differs from Althusser's ideology, because it is not always made clear in the available accounts. In both Britain and America, literary critics appropriated both Althusser and Foucault as post-structuralist thinkers. I think this is a mistake. I regard Althusser as, strictly speaking, one of the last structuralists and, conversely, Foucault as one of the first post-structuralists. The other key difference is that Althusser was a Marxist who never truly abandons in his work the base / superstructure model that he insists on, in his famously enigmatic phrase, 'in the last instance'.[101] The 'base' in this model simply means the material economic base, which includes all goods, people, their labour, money and so on, whereas 'superstructure' is all of the abstract or conceptual entities on top of all that: politics, religion, philosophy, what Althusser would call the 'ideological'. The 'economic' is understood here in the traditional Marxist sense: it refers to the mode of production and to the distribution and consumption of goods, as well as their exchange in a value system. This is an inextricably *material* process. Marx and Engels insisted on the economy as the ultimate determining factor in *The German Ideology*: 'As individuals express their life, so they are. What they are, therefore, coincides with their production, both with *what* they produce and with *how* they produce. The nature of individuals thus depends on the material conditions determining their production'. This point is repeated and elaborated upon a few pages later:

> Life is not determined by consciousness but consciousness by life . . . the active life process . . . Life involves before everything else eating and drinking, a habitation, clothing and many other things. The first historical act is thus the production of the means to satisfy those needs, the production of material life itself.[102]

Later, in *Capital*, Marx extends this thesis to include money and the entire system of exchange-value implicit in any economy, which he calls 'the materialisation of human labour in the abstract'.[103] Thus, in the classic Marxist models, ideologies, such as 'morality, religion, metaphysics',[104] always spring from the material processes of human labour and the economic base and thus are regarded as 'super-structural' effects. Foucault, as a true post-structuralist thinker, dispenses with this model altogether and, in fact, sweeps aside 'the economic base' to make it a part of the superstructure. Althusser does the opposite: by making ideology 'material' he makes it part of the economic base and follows Marx at least 'in the last instance'.

Althusser defines ideology as the *imagined* relations between material objects; therefore, ideology exists only in so far as there are material objects. Foucault's power is rooted in discourse and relations of discourse, not materiality – discourse is not only written, it can be spoken or even contained in a thought. This ensures the ubiquity of power even in the absence of 'apparatus'. Whereas Althusser's ISAs *need* institutions and other material objects in which to manifest, Foucault 'power relations' only need as a bare minimum two people. As Foucault argues in *The History of Sexuality, Volume 1* (1984): 'there is no absolute outside where [power] is concerned'. In Althusser there is also no 'absolute outside' of ideology, but where power is necessarily repressive (in the sense that it is at the very least, to use Foucault's phrase, 'an extortion of truth'),[105] ideology is simply the condition of sociality; where power depends only on the disembodied realm of discourse, ideology is tied to material conditions. These are key differences. In Althusser, and in Marxism more generally, there can be material objects without ideology, but in Foucault there can be no discourse without power.

It is difficult to see how one could realistically call Foucault a materialist. His theorization of power conflates the category of power with that of knowledge, hence his neologism 'power-knowledge': there is no knowledge that does not exist as a power-relation and vice versa. This means that power is always at a super-structural remove from physicality in Foucault: 'it is a perpetual victory that avoids any physical confrontation and which is always decided in advance'.[106] For the Althusser and his followers, power depends, 'in the last instance', on repression – that is, on physical violence, *action* – to maintain hegemony, *not* knowledge. The idea of the RSA (repressive state apparatus) is totally missing in Foucault because power, even external power ('the sphere of force relations') must always be internalized.[107] Power in Foucault is almost always 'soft power', violence is not necessary: it is the power to compel people, without apparent coercion, to say and do things that are not necessarily in their own best interests but in the interests of the dominant power. Foucault is very clear on this point in his famous description of Bentham's Panopticon found in *Discipline and Punish*:

> . . . the major effect of the Panopticon [is] to induce in the inmate a state of conscious and permanent visibility that assures the automatic functioning of power. . . . [T]he perfection of power should tend to render its actual exercise unnecessary . . . He who is subjected to the field of [the Panopticon's] visibility, and who knows it, assumes responsibility for the constraints of power . . . he becomes the principle of his own subjection. By this very fact, the external power may throw off its physical weight . . .[108]

The Panopticon is a prison designed by the English political philosopher Jeremy Bentham in the 1790s. The prison is circular; there is a tower in the middle and cells around its perimeter with windows facing the tower. From the tower a guard can view every cell. With the use of backlighting, the guard is able to see the shadows of each prisoner in his or her cell: there is constant visibility. For Foucault, the genius of Bentham's design lies in the fact that the guard need not be present; 'what matters is that the [prisoner] *knows himself* to be observed'.[109] In effect, the prisoners 'work by themselves'; they know not to try anything because they believe they are being watched, regardless of whether or not they *are* being watched. Belief of this kind is enough to regulate behaviour, and if you think about it, we can see this play out in everyday life all the time. For example, at the front of most supermarkets there are typically two great scanners that will sound an alarm if you take a stolen item through them. You and I do not steal goods from the supermarket, partly because we are good citizens, and partly because we know that if we tried to do so the alarm would sound. The truth is that most items in the supermarket would not trigger the alarm. This is just one of many examples where we see Foucault's Panopticism in action.

However, for Foucault *all* power seems to work like it does in the Panopticon; there are no RSAs because they are deemed superfluous. This break with the material base is something for which the structural Marxist Nicos Poulantzas reproached Foucault sharply in 1978:

> Inevitably, Foucault is led to underestimate at the very least the role of law in the exercise of power within modern societies, but he also underestimates the role of the State itself, and fails to understand the function of the repressive apparatuses (army, police, judicial system, etc.) as means of exercising physical violence that are located at the heart of the modern State. They are treated instead as mere parts of the disciplinary machine which patterns the internalization of repression by means of normalization.[110]

One might expect this from Poulantzas, another of Althusser's former students, but more recently Slavoj Žižek has echoed these criticisms:

> . . . the relationship between Althusser and Foucault is of special interest. The Foucauldian counterparts to Ideological State Apparatuses are the disciplinary procedures that operate at the level of 'micro-power' and designate the point at which power inscribes itself into the body directly, bypassing ideology – for that precise reason, Foucault never uses the term 'ideology' apropos of these mechanisms of micro-power. This abandoning of the problematic of ideology entails a fatal weakness of Foucault's theory. Foucault never tires of repeating how power constitutes itself 'from below', how it does not emanate from some unique summit: this very semblance of a Summit (the Monarch or some other embodiment of Sovereignty) emerges as the secondary effect of the plurality of micro-practices, of the complex network of their interrelations. However, when he is compelled to display the concrete mechanism of this emergence, Foucault resorts to the extremely suspect rhetoric of complexity, evoking the intricate network of lateral links, left and right, up and down. . . . a clear case of patching up, since one can never arrive at Power this way – the abyss that separates micro-procedures from the spectre of Power remains unbridgeable. Althusser's advantage over Foucault seems evident: Althusser proceeds in exactly the opposite direction – from the very outset,

he conceives these micro-procedures as parts of the ISA; that is to say, as mechanisms which, in order to be operative, to 'seize' the individual, always-already presuppose the massive presence of the state, the transferential relationship of the individual towards state power, or – in Althusser's terms – towards the ideological big Other in whom the interpellation originates.[111]

Both Poulantzas and Žižek criticize Foucault's theory of power for being too diffuse and lacking materiality. Also, they both seem to imply that the move from Althusser's homogenous state-centric model to Foucault's more heterogeneous and decentralized model – typically seen as a good thing by literary critics – is in fact a mistake, presumably because in the real world there is such a thing as state power and it should not be overlooked. I am inclined to agree that this is a significant blind spot in Foucault's concept of power. In my opinion, the chief cause of this unsatisfactory aspect of Foucault's thought lies in his disregard for the traditional economic base. I agree with Althusser, that any rational theorization of power must maintain the prospect of violence, in the last instance. For example, we have seen in recent years outbreaks of violent rioting and looting across London and the United Kingdom, not to mention the extraordinary events of the Arab Spring; to pretend that there is no need for a 'RSA' or for state law to maintain law, order and power would be, among other things, supremely irresponsible.

However, Foucault's disregard for the material base has seeped into Shakespeare studies. To take just one example, Richard Wilson's cultural materialist appropriation of Foucault in *Will Power* seems, at times, to oscillate between the material and the purely discursive. Here, Wilson is referring to the practice of branding in Elizabethan and Jacobean state punishment and, more specifically, to the letter 'T' branded on Ben Jonson's thumb in 1598: 'The Renaissance text is a vivid material inscription, scoring the flesh to impose subjection, and authorised by its place within a repertoire of penal practices.'[112] Why must the body become a sign in order to be subjected? True, it is a clever example of a moment in which the repressive and ideological state apparatuses converge, but what is important here for Wilson (as it would be for Foucault) is the process of *internalisation*. The body is marked so as to ensure that the individual internalizes his or her subjection to power. In Marxism, both classic and Althusserian, it would be equally important that *physical violence* has occurred here. The immense physical pain that branding causes is surely *as* significant to the person receiving it as the final impression that it leaves on them. It occupies an analogous position to other forms of repressive state action. In as much as they disturb 'the active life process' (the means of production, the material conditions of the individual) these acts of state violence belong to the economic material sphere. The emphasis on the material existence of ideology in Althusser distinguishes his model from Foucault's discursive theory of power in that, ideology rests ultimately upon physical matter in this way. Let us re-examine Althusser's much quoted formulation: 'ideology represents the imaginary relationship of individuals to their real conditions of existence'.[113] What are these 'real conditions'? Partly, Althusser is referring to the Lacanian sense of 'the real' that lies beyond ideology; but I think the stronger sense here is the Marxist notion of economic reality, the material conditions in which an individual finds him or herself. To unpack this further: ideology constitutes the *imaginary* relations between material objects and human beings – it is the force that allows one to have a name, a job and social status, that interpellates arbitrary, non-signifying matter so as to give it connotations that have a wider social significance. It is the difference between a man simply placing a formless piece of metal on his head (the 'real conditions') and a king wearing a crown (the 'imaginary relations'). In Foucault there is no such distinction between 'real' and 'imagined', because power is always-already both discursive and internalized. To bring it back to the Panopticon, if the prisoners tried to stage a mass breakout, in Althusser's prison they would probably be captured and beaten by several dozen wardens and officers; in Foucault's prison there wouldn't be anybody in the tower. Of course, for Foucault, who if you recall speaks unironically about 'the perfection of power', such an attempt would be almost *unthinkable*.

We can summarize Foucault's theory as follows:

1   History is discontinuous and comprises a series of epistemes.

2   These epistemes can be analysed structurally.

3   Each episteme is made up of, and governed by, a mass of 'discursive fields'.

4 There is no discourse without a power relation; where we find 'discursive fields' we also find power – this is the chief object of study when analysing epistemes.

5 Individuals submit to power by internalizing it, as in the example of the prisoners in Bentham's Panopticon, so there is no need for a material RSA.

6 Since it mainly takes place inside people's heads, there is no 'outside' of this power: where there are people there is discourse and knowledge, where there is discourse and knowledge there is power. In effect, the very act of thinking always already entails a power relation.

Of all the theorists we have looked at, Foucault has been undoubtedly the most influential for new historicists and cultural materialists, especially the former group. A crude short-hand version of new historicism would posit that it essentially takes Geertz's methods of 'thick description' and 'local knowledge' and marries them with Foucault's discourse analysis and obsession with power.

Key questions for students

- Do you find Foucault's more disparate and chaotic account of power relations more or less convincing than Althusser's theory of ideology? Why?
- Do you agree with Foucault that there is no discourse or knowledge without power? Why?
- Can you think of five examples of Panopticism in everyday life? List them.
- What do you think about the points made by Poulantzas and Žižek, that Foucault is wrong to ignore the state and the 'RSA'?
- How might Foucault's methods be appropriated for the study of Shakespeare's plays?

Selected further reading

Deluze, Gilles, *Foucault*, trans. Seán Hand (London: Continuum, 1999).

Dreyfus, Herbert L. and Paul Rainbow, *Michel Foucault: Beyond Structuralism and Hermeneutics* (Chicago: University of Chicago Press, 1983).

Foucault, Michel, *Discipline and Punish: The Birth of the Prison*, trans. Alan Sheridan (New York and London: Penguin Books, 1991).

—, *The History of Sexuality, Volume 1: The Will to Knowledge* (New York and London: Penguin, 1998).

—, *Archaeology of Knowledge and The Discourse on Language*, trans. Alan Sheridan (New York and London: Routledge, 2002).

—, *The Order of Things: An Archaeology of the Human Sciences*, trans. Alan Sheridan (New York and London: Routledge, 2002).

Hamilton, Paul, *Historicism* (New York and London: Routledge, 1996).

Harpham, Geoffrey, 'Foucault and the New Historicism', *American Literary History*, 3(2) (Summer 1991), 360–75.

Lentricchia, Frank, 'Foucault's Legacy: A New Historicism?', in *The New Historicism*, ed. H. Aram Veeser (New York and London: Routledge, 1989), pp. 231–42.

Montag, Warren, '"The Soul is the Prison of the Body": Althusser and Foucault 1970–1975', *Yale French Studies*, 88 (1995), 53–77.

Wilson, Richard, *Will Power: Essays on Shakespearean Authority* (Hemel Hempstead: Harvester Wheatsheaf, 1993).

Notes

1 Karl Marx, 'The Eighteenth Brumaire of Louis Bonaparte', in *Karl Marx: Selected Writings*, ed. David McLellan (New York and Oxford: Oxford University Press, 1977), p. 300.

2 Note that this would not be true of the structuralists such as Roman Jakobson or Roland Barthes, or of Jacques Derrida.

3 Clifford Geertz, *The Interpretation of Cultures: Sketched Essays* (New York: Basic Books, 1973), p. 48.

4 Ibid., pp. 48–9.

5 Ibid., p. 89.

6 Ibid., p. 452.

7 Geertz, *The Interpretation of Cultures*, p. 9.

8 Renato I. Rosaldo Jr, 'A Note on Geertz as a Cultural Essayist', *Representations*, 59, Special Issue: The Fate of 'Culture': Geertz and Beyond (1997), p. 30.

9 Ibid., p. 27.

10 Ibid., p. 28.

11 Clifford Geertz, *Local Knowledge: Further Essays in Interpretative Anthropology* (New York: Basic Books, 1983), p. 4.

12 Geertz, *The Interpretation of Cultures*, pp. 448–52.

13 See Donald E. Brown, *Human Universals* (New York: McGraw-Hill, 1991).

14 Vincent P. Pecora, 'The Limits of Local Knowledge', in *The New Historicism*, ed. H. Aram Veeser (New York and London: Routledge, 1989), p. 258.

15 Antonio Gramsci, *Selections from the Prison Notebooks*, ed. and trans. Quintin Hoare and Geoffrey Nowell Smith (London: Lawrence and Wishart, 1973), p. 43.

16 Karl Marx, *Capital*, ed. David McLennan (New York and Oxford: Oxford University Press, 1995), p. 205.

17 Gramsci, *Prison Notebooks*, p. 9.

18 Lisa Athos, *In Carcere con Gramsci* (Milan: Terracini, 1973), p. 84.

19 Karl Marx and Friedrich Engels, *The Communist Manifesto*, ed. Gareth Stedman Jones, trans. Samuel Moore (New York and London: Penguin, 2002), p. 268.

20 Christine Buci-Glucksmann, *Gramsci and the State*, trans. David Fernbach (Southampton: Lawrence and Wishart, 1980), p. 242.

21 Roger Kojeckey, *T.S. Eliot's Social Criticism* (London: Faber and Faber, 1971), p. 13.

22 See Karl Mannheim, *Ideology and Utopia* (London: Kegan Paul & Co., 1936).

23 T. S. Eliot, *Notes Towards a Definition of Culture* (London: Faber and Faber, 1948), p. 28.

24 Kenneth Asher, *T.S. Eliot and Ideology* (Cambridge: Cambridge University Press, 1998), p. 93.

25 Eliot, *Notes Towards a Definition of Culture*, p. 27–8.

26 Asher, *T.S. Eliot and Ideology*, p. 94.

27 Eliot, *Notes Towards a Definition of Culture*, p. 21.

28 Gramsci, *Prison Notebooks*, pp. 8–12.

29 Michael Freedman, *Ideology: A Very Short Introduction* (New York and Oxford: Oxford University Press, 2003), p. 23.

30 Gramsci, *Prison Notebooks*, p. 18.

31 Terry Eagleton, 'Eliot and a Common Culture', in *Eliot in Perspective* (London: Macmillan, 1970), p. 286.

32 Eliot, *Notes Towards a Definition of Culture*, p. 31.

33 Gramsci, *Prison Notebooks*, p. 12.

34 Eliot, *Notes Towards a Definition of Culture*, p. 24.

35 Antonio Gramsci, *Il Risorgimentio* (Turin: Einaudi, 1949), p. 70.

36 David Hawkes, *Ideology* (New York and London: Routledge, 1996), p. 119.

37 Joseph V. Fernia, *Gramsci's Political Thought: Hegemony, Consciousness, and the Revolutionary Process* (Oxford: Clarendon Press, 1987), p. 51.

38 Gramsci, *Prison Notebooks*, p. 120.

39 Ibid., pp. 181–2.

40 Ibid., p. 182.

41 Niccolò Machiavelli, *The Prince*, trans. Geoffrey Bull, 4th edn (New York and London: Penguin, 2003), pp. 58, 59.

42 Pechter, 'The New Historicism and its Discontents', p. 292.

43 Alan Liu, 'The Power of Formalism: The New Historicism', *ELH*, 56(4) (Winter 1989), p. 736.

44 Walter Cohen, 'Political Criticism of Shakespeare', in *Shakespeare Reproduced: The Text in History and Ideology*, ed. Jean E. Howard and Marion F. O'Connor (New York and London: Methuen, 1987), p. 27.

45 Louis Althusser, 'Cremonini, Painter of the Abstract', in *Lenin and Philosophy and Other Essays*, ed. Fredric Jameson (New York: Monthly Review Press, 2001), p. 165.

46 Louis Althusser and Etienne Balibar, *Reading Capital*, trans. Ben Brewster (London: New Left Books, 1986), pp. 119–44.

47 Marx and Engels, *The Communist Manifesto*, p. 233.

48 Louis Althusser, 'Ideology and the Ideological State Apparatus', in *Lenin and Philosophy and Other Essays*, ed. Fredric Jameson, trans. Ben Brewster (1971; rpr. New York: Monthly Review Press, 2001), pp. 109, 116, 117.

49 Ibid., pp. 87, 97, 119, 123.

50 Terry Eagleton, *Literary Theory: An Introduction* (Oxford: Blackwell, 1996), p. 149.

51 See *The Matrix*, dir. Andy Wachowski and Larry Wachowski (Warner Bros. Pictures, 1999).

52 Althusser, 'Ideology and the Ideological State Apparatus', pp. 122–3.

53 See Jacques Lacan, 'The Mirror Stage as Formative of the Function of the I as revealed in Psychoanalytic Experience', in *Écrits: a Selection*, trans. Alan Sheridan (London: Tavistock, 1977), pp. 1–7.

54 Louis Althusser, *For Marx*, trans. Ben Brewster (1969; New York and London: Verso, 2005), p. 103.

55 Althusser, 'Ideology and the Ideological State Apparatus', pp. 89, 110.

56 Ibid., p. 105.

57 See George Orwell, *Nineteen Eighty-Four* (London: Penguin, 2003).

58 Althusser, 'Ideology and the Ideological State Apparatus', p. x.

59 John Fiske, 'British Cultural Studies and Television', in *Channels of Discourse: Television and Contemporary Criticism*, ed. Robert C. Allen (London: Methuen & Co., 1987), pp. 310–11.

60 E. P. Thompson, *The Poverty of Theory* (London: Merlin Press, 1978), p. 197.

61 Althusser, *For Marx*, pp. 99–100.

62 Ibid., p. 100.

63 William S. Lewis, *Louis Althusser and the Traditions of French Marxism* (Oxford: Lexington Books, 2005), p. 174.

64 Althusser and Balibar, p. 96.

65 Lehan, 'The Theoretical Limits of New Historicism', pp. 538, 540, 542–3, 552.

66 John Higgins, 'Raymond Williams and the Problem of Ideology', *boundary*, 2(1) (Autumn 1982), p. 149.

67 Paul Smith, *Discerning the Subject* (Minneapolis, MN: University of Minnesota Press, 1989), p. 18.

68 Stephen Cohen, 'Between Form and Culture', in *Renaissance Literature and Its Formal Engagements*, ed. Mark David Rasmussen (New York and Basingstoke: Palgrave, 2002), p. 20.

69 See Francis Mulhern, 'Althusser in Literary Studies', in *Althusser: A Critical Reader*, ed. Gregory Elliott (Cambridge, MA and Oxford: Blackwell, 1994), pp. 159–76; Warren Montag, '"The Soul is the Prison of the Body": Althusser and Foucault 1970–1975', *Yale French Studies*, 88 (1995), pp. 35–77.

70 Nicos Poulantzas, *State, Power, Socialism* (London: Verso, 1980), p. 31.

71 Niccolò Machiavelli, *The Historical, Political, and Diplomatic Writings of Niccolò Machiavelli, Volume 2*, trans. Christian E. Detmold (Boston: J. R. Osgood and Company, 1882), p. 102.

72 Gramsci, *Prison Notebooks*, p. 247.

73 Louis Althusser, *Machiavelli and Us*, ed. François Matheron, trans. Gregory Elliott (New York and London: Verso, 2000), p. 81.

74 Judith Butler, 'Performativity's Social Magic', in *Bourdieu: A Critical Reader*, ed. Richard Shusterman (Malden, MA and Oxford: Blackwell, 1999), p. 122.

75 Thompson, *The Poverty of Theory*, p. 333; Tony Judt, *Marxism and the French Left: Studies on Labour and Politics in France, 1830–1981* (New York and London: New York University Press, 2011), p. 215. See also Valentino Gerratana, 'Althusser and Stalinism', *New Left Review*, 101–2 (January–April 1977), pp. 110–24.

76 Althusser, 'Letter on Art to André Daspre', in *Lenin and Philosophy*, pp. 149–55, and 'Cremonini Abstract Painter', in ibid., pp. 157–66.

77 Althusser, 'Letter on Art', p. 152.

78 See, for example, Terry Eagleton, *Criticism and Ideology* (London: Verso, 1978) and Fredric Jameson, *The Political Unconscious: Narrative as a Socially Symbolic Act* (Ithaca, NY: Cornell University Press, 1981).

79 Warren Montag, 'Introduction', in Pierre Macherey, *In a Materialist Way: Selected Essays*, ed. Warren Montag, trans. Ted Stolze (London: Verso, 1998), p. 1.

80 See CCCS, *On Ideology* (London: Hutchinson, 1978); for an account of the CCCS see also, Vincent B. Leitch, *Cultural Criticism, Literary Theory, Poststructuralism* (New York: Columbia University Press, 1992), pp. 145–61; Cary Nelson and Lawrence Grossberg (ed.), *Marxism and the Interpretation of Culture* (Urbana and Chicago: University of Illinois Press, 1988); Ernesto Laclau and Chantal Mouffe, *Hegemony and Socialist Strategy: Towards a Radical Democratic Politics*, 2nd edn (New York and London: Verso, 2001); Slavoj Žižek, *The Sublime of Ideology* (New York and London: Verso Books, 1989); Slavoj Žižek, 'Introduction', in *Mapping Ideology*, ed. Slavoj Žižek (New York and London: Verso Book, 1994), pp. 1–33.

81 Pierre Macherey, *A Theory of Literary Production*, trans. Geoffrey Wall (London: Routledge and Kegan Paul, 1978), p. 64.

82 Peter Dews, 'Althusser, Structuralism, and the French Epistemological Tradition', in *Althusser: A Critical Reader*, ed. Gregory Elliott (Cambridge, MA and Oxford: Blackwell, 1994), p. 104.

83 Robert Paul Resch, *Althusser and the Renewal of Marxist Social Theory* (Berkley, CA: University of California Press, 1992), p. 229.

84 Michel Foucault, *Discipline and Punish: The Birth of the Prison*, trans. Alan Sheridan (New York and London: Penguin Books, 1991), p. 27; Michel Foucault, *Archaeology of Knowledge and The Discourse on Language*, trans. Alan Sheridan (New York and London: Routledge, 2002), p. 30.

85 Foucault, *Discipline and Punish*, p. 26.

86 Michel Foucault, *The Order of Things: An Archaeology of the Human Sciences*, trans. Alan Sheridan (New York and London: Routledge, 2002), p. xxii.

87 Foucault, *Discipline and Punish*, pp. 26–7.

88 See Althusser and Balibar, *Reading Capital*, pp. 56–64.

89 Foucault, *Discipline and Punish*, p. 26.

90 Especially good on Foucault's disjunctive vision of history: Paul Hamilton, *Historicism* (New York and London: Routledge, 1996), pp. 133–44.

91 Foucault, *Archaeology of Knowledge*, pp. 23, 25.

92 Ibid., pp. 25–6.

93 Ibid., pp. 30, 54.

94 Foucault, *The Order of Things*, p. xxiv.

95 John Nichols (ed.), *The Progresses and Public Processions of Queen Elizabeth [To which are subjoined some of the Early Progresses of King James I]*, 4 vols (London, 1788–1821), vol. 1, pp. 325–7; Katherine Eisaman Maus, 'Richard II', in *The Norton Shakespeare* eds Stephen Greenblatt, Walter Cohen, Jean E. Howard and Katharine Eisman Maus (New York and London: W.W. Norton and Co., 1997), p. 944.

96 Terry Eagleton, 'Body Work', in *The Eagleton Reader*, ed. Stephen Regan (Oxford: Blackwell, 1998), p. 161.

97 Veeser, 'The New Historicism', in *The New Historicism Reader*, ed. H. Aram Veeser (New York and London: Routledge, 1994), p. 3.

98 Ibid., p. 11.

99 Veeser, 'The New Historicism', in *The New Historicism Reader*, p. 13; he quotes Edward W. Said, *Culture and Imperialism* (New York: Knopf, 1993), p. 278.

100 Edward W. Said, *Power, Politics and Culture* (New York and London: Bloomburg, 2004), p. 138.

101 Althusser, *For Marx*, p. 111.

102 Marx and Engels, *The German Ideology*, pp. 42, 47–8.

103 Marx, *Capital*, p. 31.

104 Marx and Engels, *The German Ideology*, p. 47.

105 Michel Foucault, *The History of Sexuality, Volume 1: The Will to Knowledge* (New York and London: Penguin, 1998), pp. 95, 97.

106 Foucault, *Discipline and Punish*, p. 203.

107 Foucault, *The History of Sexuality, Volume 1*, p. 97.

108 Foucault, *Discipline and Punish*, pp. 201, 202–3.

109 Ibid., p. 201, emphasis mine.

110 Poulantzas, *State, Power, Socialism*, p. 77.

111 Slavoj Žižek, 'Introduction', in *Mapping Ideology*, ed. Slavoj Žižek (New York and London: Verso Book, 1994), p. 13.

112 Richard Wilson, *Will Power: Essays on Shakespearean Authority* (Hemel Hempstead: Harvester Wheatsheaf, 1993), p. 145.

113 Althusser, 'Ideology and the Ideological State Apparatus', p. 109.

CHAPTER FOUR

New historicism

Summary

- The battlefield of Shakespeare studies: 'The Alliance' versus 'The Dissenters'
- Why new historicism is 'new'
- Jonathan Goldberg, Leonard Tennenhouse and early Stephen Greenblatt: 'Shakespeare-as-instrument-of-state-power'
- Catherine Gallagher and later Greenblatt: cultural poetics
- The textualization of culture
- Anecdotes
- Commitment to anti-humanism
- Criticisms of new historicism
- Five-point definition of new historicism

Before continuing, it is important to recognize that new historicism and cultural materialism have been around for almost 30 years,[1] and that their critical reception has a long history. With '"ismic" tagging' still rife in Renaissance studies,[2] one might be forgiven for feeling lost when trying to navigate one's way through the various competing 'isms' on offer. The remainder of this book can be seen as a sort of field map to help you understand the recent criticism you may encounter when studying Shakespeare at university, it is useful to be aware of various allegiances and standpoints. Although they have been dominant in Shakespeare studies over the past three decades, new historicism and cultural materialism have never formed a homogenous movement or had a monopoly in the field, and there are many divergent positions both between and within those groups and among their adversaries. In the rest of this book, I will survey and define the most significant of these positions, so that the aims and allegiances of individual critics are clearly situated and understood. To help you understand the various positions clearly, I am going to use the metaphor of a battlefield. Obviously these various critics are not at war and in many (although not all!) cases two staunchly opposed scholars would probably enjoy an amicable cup of tea or coffee together. In the 1980s, I am led to believe that things were a lot more fierce and heated, 'the battlefield' is generally calmer these days – but that is perhaps because the historicist status quo rules the day. Most of the principal new historicists and cultural materialists are reaching retirement age or have already retired, so it is safe to assume that the older generation of humanists and formalists with whom they sparred in the 1980s are long gone, give or take a Richard Levin or Graham Bradshaw.

A survey of the terrain of Shakespeare studies over the last three decades reveals numerous encampments, each of which contains its own factions. The first battle-line to draw is between the two main antagonists: those who argue from within the new historicist and cultural materialist alliance, and those who dispute its authority. For the purposes of this field map, let us call this second group 'The Dissenters', a heterogeneous diaspora of scholars with alternative views who share a common purpose of challenging 'The Alliance', who now constitute the critical establishment in the academy. New historicists and cultural materialists who once wrote from a marginalized position against the formalist and liberal humanist centre – and were, in turn, attacked from this centre – now find themselves in the seats of power. As a consequence, anyone writing against them today finds himself or herself in the same position that the new historicists and cultural materialists were once in themselves. Geoffrey Galt Harpham's wry observation that the original critical reception of new historicism was akin to 'a professional wrestling match in which a professional "scientific" wrestler, a gentleman of style and class, makes a few remarkable and ingenious gestures, only eventually to be clubbed senseless by an infuriated 450-pound brute',[3] must now give way to Don E. Wayne's farsighted prediction that new historicism would become the 'new orthodoxy in Renaissance studies'.[4] The 'massed forces of principled objections, self-righteous thuggery, scholastic quibbling, and debonair condescension' are still there,[5] but they are now outnumbered and represent the minority view.

Behind the lines of 'The Alliance' are, of course, the two major camps: new historicism and cultural materialism, each of which contains several sub-camps. This chapter will outline new historicism. As Kiernan Ryan notes, 'the phrase "new historicism" adverts . . . to the "new criticism" in which so many of its American luminaries were first schooled, but whose principles and procedures it seeks to demolish'.[6] The phrase 'new historicism' has built into it the very concept of reacting to something else, something 'old' that it uses to define itself against. In order to understand exactly what 'new historicism' is, it is first necessary to know just what these 'old' things are. Ryan suggests that it is the new critics, but let us not forget E. M. W. Tillyard's 'old historicism' either. It is 'new' not only because it is *historicism* and not formalism, but also because it is a very specific type of historicism distinct from the historical Shakespeare critics from the 1940s we looked at in Chapter 2. That said, the immediate climate in which the new historicists found themselves was dominated by formalism, be it the New Critics, the structuralists or the emerging deconstructionists. So much of the early theoretical talk from Stephen Greenblatt and the others focuses on their departure from formalism.

Greenblatt found in New Criticism 'no escape from contingency'.[7] The principal objection was that current literary analysis, as practised by the New Criticis, failed adequately to contextualize the texts that they were reading. At first, they simply produced what might be called 'old historicist' readings in the manner of Tillyard. Witness, for example, Stephen Orgel's *The Illusion of Power* (1975), often seen as a 'definite proto-new historicist work'.[8] However, after reading Geertz and Foucault, Greenblatt could not continue unquestioningly producing what he called 'mainstream literary history', with its received Tillyardian assumptions about 'the collective mind of the people', what the alliance have come to call 'the monological approach of historical scholarship'.[9] Such criticism is 'concerned with discovering a single political vision, usually identical to that said to be held by the entire literate class or indeed the entire population' and therefore prone to making sweeping generalizations and to ignoring large swathes of the general populace in the historical periods they study. Greenblatt would prefer to focus the critic's scrutiny on 'fields of force, places of dissension and shifting interests, occasions for the jostling of orthodox and subversive impulses'. New historicism is thus 'set apart from both the dominant historical scholarship of the past [the monological approach] and the formalist criticism that partially displaced this scholarship in the decades after World War Two [new criticism]'.[10] This bears out what I said above, Greenblatt's new historicism is 'new' on two counts: first, because it is a return to a historically contextualized (and therefore politicized) reading of literature after the dominance of new criticism and its formalist cousins and, second, because it is distinct from the old, monological historicist practices of the 1930s and 1940s.

Let us return to our battlefield. In the new historicist camp, Leonard Tennenhouse, Jonathan Goldberg, and the Stephen Greenblatt of the early-to-mid-1980s occupy what we might call the 'Shakespeare-as-instrument-of-state-power' tent, maintaining that a Shakespearean play is ultimately 'a vehicle for disseminating court ideology'.[11] This position, which is often dismissed as crude or 'primitive'[12] by commentators, has all too frequently been mistaken for the new historicist position as a whole. Nevertheless, not to acknowledge that a fixation with state power has been synonymous with new historicism since its inception would be negligent. In particular, many new historicists have been much taken with the idea that power is able to contain subversion by allowing a moderate degree of agency to (and in some cases actively fostering) dissent. As Greenblatt contends in *Learning to Curse* (1990), just as in the anti-humanist writings of Althusser and Foucault:

> Actions that appear to be single are disclosed as multiple; the apparently isolated power of the individual genius turns out to be bound up with collective, social energy; a gesture of dissent may be an element in a larger legitimation process, while an attempt to stabilize the order of things may turn out to subvert it.[13]

This theme was central not only for Greenblatt in the 1980s but also for other 'first wave' new historicists, such as Jonathan Goldberg and Leonard Tennenhouse, both of whom described fully functioning monarch-centred state ideologies or discourses in early modern England. For example, in an essay on *Measure for Measure*, Leonard Tennenhouse argues that although the ruler is 'bound by the conditions for the social milieu over which he presides',[14] through the trick of substitution he is able to ratify the marriage institution and, through that ratification, create the need for the regulation of sexual behaviour which, as ruler, he will administer: all of which serves to reinforce his own power. Tennenhouse would go on to make similar readings of Shakespeare's plays seemingly making the same argument time and again in his book *Power on Display* (1986), perhaps the best example of this crude early form of new historicism. In another early new historicist study, *James I and the Politics of Literature* (1983), James Goldberg invokes a system of power transmission (from God to monarch to literary discourse) to conclude that 'the ideological function of writing is an instrument of royal power'.[15] In these two examples, the acts of marriage and writing both serve and reinforce the monarch's power. Both are seen as constituting (and it is easy to substitute Althusser's language for theirs here) ideological state apparatuses that serve to reproduce the conditions of the monarch's role as head of state.

It was this fascination with hegemony that made new historicism's emergence in the 1980s a much-debated and controversial event, since its tenets proved naturally contentious with both Marxists and liberal humanists. The Marxist objection, as raised by Jean E. Howard, Walter Cohen and others, was that the new historicists leave no scope for genuine resistance, because 'any apparent site of resistance ultimately serves the interests of power.[16] Greenblatt answered this curtly: 'the Marxist critique . . . rests upon an assertion that new historicism argues that "*any* apparent site of resistance" is ultimately co-opted. Some are, some aren't'.[17] The most vehement attack from the liberal humanists came from Edward Pechter, who lambasted the persistence of a pseudo-Althusserian power model in which 'power is still reified in the monarch, or in a particular set of dominant institutions, and discourse is located in a starkly simple model of domination and subversion'.[18] Greenblatt responded with a similarly blunt rebuke, this time contending that the idea of a 'human essence' to which his humanist critics subscribed 'is precisely what new historicists find vacuous and untenable'.[19] Haunted by his own much-quoted

catchphrase from his reading of *Henry IV Parts 1 and 2*, 'subversion, no end of subversion, only not for us',[20] Greenblatt here
asserts his anti-humanism while pointedly rejecting the claim that
new historicism finds genuine resistance and subversion an impossible feat. He sees enormous, indeed vital, scope for social change:
'structures may be broken in pieces, the pieces altered, inverted,
rearranged'. However, for him, 'the point is that certain aesthetic
and political structures work to contain the subversive percep-
tions they generate'.[21] Greenblatt finds himself in a critical bind
here: on the one hand he is arguing that change through social
dissent *is* possible, though 'it will not do to imagine that it is easy,
automatic, without cost or obligation', and on the other hand he is
restating his claim that in the case of the *Henry IV* plays the scope
for such dissent is precluded. Moreover, he views the suggestion
that a literary work could count as an 'authentic' act of political
subversion or liberation as 'fatuous and presumptuous'. This in a
nutshell is the classic new historicist dilemma: authentic subversion *is* possible, somehow, but it is very difficult to achieve because
the dominant ideology is so effective and successful at reproducing itself and its own modes of discourse. When ideology controls
whole spheres of action and agency, such as marriage, writing,
thought and even the *concepts* of those things – the very conditions of their possibility – its reach becomes almost inescapable.
And this, in my understanding, is one of Greenblatt's key ideas in
both *Shakespearean Negotiations* and *Learning to Curse*: power
can be explicit and oppressive but it can also be, through ideology
and its discourses, insidious, hidden and unseen like the disguised
Duke in Tennenhouse's reading of *Measure for Measure*.

The neighbouring new historicist tent, draped with the banner of 'cultural poetics', is occupied by critics such as Catherine
Gallagher, Stephen Mullaney and the Stephen Greenblatt of the
late 1980s and beyond. Their position is more subtle and flexible than that of Tennenhouse or Goldberg. This position takes its
cue from Greenblatt's *Shakespearean Negotiations* (1988), which
posits the idea that 'works of art . . . are the products of collective negotiation and exchange'.[22] In contrast to the more simplistic
model adopted by Tennenhouse and Goldberg, Greenblatt's idea
of 'negotiation' draws on Foucault's notion of 'discursive formations'. Like Foucault, Greenblatt studies 'the relations between

statements',[23] but what interests him in particular are the moments of overlap, exchange, conflict and negotiation that arise when, to use Stephen Mullaney's phrase, two different 'discursive cultural practices' come into contact.[24] Greenblatt's essay, 'Martial Law in the Land of Cockaigne', for example, is interested in an 'instance of transcoding and naturalization' when Hugh Latimer, the Bishop of Worcester, 'attempts to transfer the practice of purification from the religious to the civil sphere'. In the same essay, Greenblatt finds a similar 'transcoding' move from the civil sphere to the theatrical sphere in Shakespeare's theatrical appropriation of 'salutary anxiety'.[25] In this model, 'social energy' moves swiftly and smoothly from sphere to sphere through silent transactions. In many ways this echoes the economic exchanges, 'the circulatory rhythms of American politics' and of 'production and consumption',[26] that move ceaselessly through US society. H. Aram Veeser was keen to argue in 1989 that this sort of new historicism demonstrates that 'symbolic exchanges have a cash value',[27] but it seems to me that the point is subtler than that. Greenblatt's 'cultural poetics' traces the movement of ideas and practices not only to show their likely origins in hegemony but also to demonstrate how such movement is the stuff of the 'real world',[28] the recovery of which offers us a glimpse of what Gallagher calls the long-lost 'counter-historical life'.[29]

Proponents of cultural poetics would support Catherine Gallagher's claim to be interested in 'the gaps and fissures, the points of stress and incoherence, inside the dominant ideology' and the idea of 'ideological contradiction'.[30] Hence, in theory at least, cultural poetics seeks to recover evidence of political agency in the past by searching those gaps and fissures for echoes of the lost voices of the past. Stephen Greenblatt's 'desire to speak with the dead' is in fact the desire to speak with the forgotten dead, with those who have tended to be ignored by mainstream history. He views his task as trying 'to track what can only be glimpsed, as it were, at the margins of the text . . . the half-hidden cultural transactions through which great works of art are empowered'. [31]

Another significant dimension of cultural poetics is the relative autonomy and creativity it affords the individual critic of literary texts through the difference and distance it insists upon between past and present. For both Gallagher and Greenblatt – following the work of the historian Hayden White,[32] and reflecting the general shift in literary criticism and the humanities to Derridean deconstruction at the time – new historicism hinges on the 'linguistic turn in the social and humanistic disciplines'; by which they mean 'the conceiving of cultures as texts' (with 'text' here occupying a position analogous to that of Foucault's discursive fields). In *Practicing New Historicism* (2000), Gallagher and Greenblatt see this move as 'powerfully attractive for several reasons. It carries the core hermeneutical presumption that one can occupy a position from which one can discover meanings that those who left traces of themselves could not have articulated.'[33] The influence of Clifford Geertz is plain to see. Here, the critic is no mere recipient of an autotelic text (as in formalism), but rather the occupant of an empowered and privileged position of hindsight from which he or she can survey and piece together discursive formations from the past. More importantly, new historicism approaches texts from *outside* the particular discursive formations or ideologies from which they sprang, so it is always privy to structural insights that would be invisible to the authors of texts. Hence, as Howard Felperin argues, new historicism is 'distinctly academic' in this respect. It maintains 'a carefully measured distance between . . . subject matter and its investigator'.[34] As John Brannigan claims, new historicism 'attempts to show the past as alien to us',[35] or, as Catherine Belsey puts it: the new historicist project is one that must 'specify the *difference* between *distinct* historical moments, and in consequence read *differently*'.[36] Cultural poetics can be said to gain much of its interpretative force (and relative autonomy) from this insistence on difference.

This insistence on difference has drawn criticism from some quarters. Felperin, for example, attacks what he perceives as a 'pseudo-scientific, empiricist'[37] academic mindset unveiling the residue of New Criticism. His penetrating analysis finds buried at the heart of new historicism 'the concept of a "deep structure" with which it cannot dispense',[38] which, ironically, positions new historicism as a kind of formalism, something it would profess to be fundamentally opposed to.[39] Louis Montrose, a new historicist himself, has acknowledged that 'certain . . . empiricist tendencies' can partly account for new historicism's 'sudden installation as the new academic orthodoxy',[40] because it is only an appropriation of 'old' historicism and of the dominant ideology rather than a real critique of it. Paul Hamilton articulates the more standard objection that, due to this privileged, distanced position,

> Greenblatt it seems, hasn't the option of seeing things differently. He can't help being right; and [was] Shakespeare's play to see its own ideology . . . it could only concur further with Greenblatt . . . Greenblatt's present seems incapable of self-criticism, past subversions always prefigure his enlightened present . . . the hermeneutical circle is drawn tight.[41]

There is the glimmer of the accusation here that new historicism is a form of what Fredric Jameson would call 'genetic' history, characteristic of the eighteenth-century ideology of Enlightenment, which constructs 'an imaginary past term as the evolutionary precursor of a fuller term, which has historical existence'.[42] It is possible to detect this in the very phrase that Greenblatt helped to popularize: 'early modern'; the implication is that you can draw a straight line from the early modern era to the 'late modern era', our own time. Incidentally, this diachronic and progressive view of history is exactly what Althusser and Foucault are opposing in their synchronic and discontinuous view of history as a series of ruptures. Suffice it to say, that as good readers of Foucault, Greenblatt, Gallagher and new historicists in general *do not* see themselves doing this. Like Althusser and Foucault, they too have a disjunctive notion of history. It is precisely *because* there is a 'rupture' between Shakespeare's time and our own that it appears so remote and alien to Greenblatt and company. It is for this very reason that they start their analysis by focusing on the *difference* between the cultural past and our cultural present. As Jameson elaborates, through this difference:

> The doors of comprehension begin to swing closed and we find ourselves separated by the density of our own culture from objects or cultures thus initially defined as Other from ourselves and they [are] irredeemably inaccessible.[43]

This is the problem the cultural materialist, Catherine Belsey, faces in the manor house of Llancaiach Fawr at the start of her

Shakespeare and the Loss of Eden (1999). Belsey witnesses actors playing seventeenth-century servants in a 'living museum', but when she comes to speak with them she finds herself 'tongue-tied' and unable to enter into dialogue or any meaningful discourse. As she notes, 'when the familiar present ceases to be a secure foothold, the past becomes more remote . . . harder to read because the only frame of interpretations available to the modern reader is relegated to distance, out of reach'.[44] Belsey's dilemma, essentially a repackaging of Foucault's encounter with Borges's Chinese encyclopaedia in *The Order of Things*, frames the basic historicist predicament. New historicists resolve this predicament by highlighting and analysing the constitutive factors of the past culture *as distinct from ours*. As John Brannigan argues, new historicism 'attempts to show the past as alien to us', or as Belsey herself puts it elsewhere: the new historicist project is one that must 'specify the *difference* between *distinct* historical moments, and in consequence read *differently*'.[45] New historicism can be said to gain much of its interpretative force (and relative autonomy) from this insistence on difference.

Gallagher and Greenblatt also move to distance themselves from Marxism:

> As we were from the beginning uncomfortable with such key concepts as superstructure and base or imputed class-consciousness, we have found ourselves . . . slowly forced to transform the notion of ideology critique to discourse analysis.[46]

This, of course, is a clear turn from Althusser to Foucault, although Gallagher and Greenblatt never expand on *why* they are uncomfortable with the concepts of base, superstructure and ideology or on their reasons for making this turn. At its most basic, the turn from ideology to discourse frees the new historicists from merely looking at forms of state control thereby enabling them to explore myriad marginal discourses, and perhaps find genuine subversion (of power) in those places. As we saw in Chapter 3, Althusser's concept of ideology and ISAs is specifically materialist, whereas Foucault's concept of power is purely discursive and dispenses altogether with the material 'base'. In preferring Foucault to Althusser, Gallagher and Greenblatt repeat this move and complete the near-total textualization of culture.

Gallagher and Greenblatt view the idea of culture-as-text as attractive because it broadens the field of analysis to include texts not traditionally included in the literary canon. Authors can be 'newly recovered',[47] which has proven to be the departure point of many feminists working in new historicism, not least Gallagher herself. In this respect, cultural poetics can be seen as a liberating force for literature in that it levels the playing field by attributing equal status to all texts – an idea, of course, totally at odds with notions of aesthetic value such as those found in the work of I. A. Richard or F. R. Leavis. Paradoxically, then, despite draining the traditional, hierarchical canon of aesthetic value, cultural poetics 'aestheticises' *all cultures* by viewing them as texts, turning the entirety of the human social product into an art object. In this essentially formalist insistence on an aestheticized world, a cultural *poetics*, we can trace the institutional residue of New Criticism – more on this later.

Another important dimension of cultural poetics is the production of what Gallagher and Greenblatt call 'counter-histories' that stand as an alternative to mainstream history; apparently, the key to unlocking them is to be found in the anecdote. New historicist criticism, especially Greenblatt's, is teeming with anecdotes, both historical and modern in origin, including anecdotes drawn from the critic's own experience. Accordingly, they take on unusual significance in moments when new historicists attempt to articulate their theoretical enterprise. For Greenblatt, anecdotes offer:

Access to the everyday, the place where things are actually done, the sphere of practice that even in its most awkward and inept articulations makes a claim on the truth that is denied to the most eloquent of literary texts . . . The anecdote was a way into the 'contact zone', the charmed space where the *genius literarius* could be conjured into existence.[48]

Greenblatt's sense of delight in the power of the anecdote is palpable here, bearing out Jeremy Hawthorn's claim that he is 'generally more concerned with experienced realities than with objectified facts'.[49] Indeed, the earlier Greenblatt had been very keen to insist that 'the existence or absence of a *real* world, *real* body, *real* pain, makes a difference'.[50] The anecdote thus serves as a kind of 'living museum' where the modern reader can experience what life must *really* have been like, as opposed to the ideologically framed version we receive in history and literature, or as Greenblatt himself puts it: 'it helps us to conjure up a "*real*" as opposed to an "imaginary" world'.[51] It is important to note Greenblatt's choice of words here. Despite its not being imagined, we still '*conjure up*' this 'real' (in inverted commas): it has no existence *outside* culture; it is still simply an understanding of what is 'real' *as opposed to* the 'not real', that is, 'imaginary' version that the discursive practices of power (traditional history, official tracts, etc.) offer us. It should thus be understood that Greenblatt's 'lived realities', his 'truth that is denied' in literary texts, offer no escape from the discursive web of power-knowledge. Catherine Belsey puts it succinctly when she writes, 'in the work of Stephen Greenblatt reality is understood to be synonymous with the cultural conception of reality, and this in turn is historically relative'.[52]

For Gallagher, whose chapter on anecdotes follows Greenblatt's in *Practicing New Historicism*, anecdotes 'divulge a different reality, which is behind or beside the narrative surface and composed of things that historians cannot assimilate into typicality or coherent significance . . . the undisciplined anecdote appealed to those of us who wanted to interrupt the Big Stories'. New historicists are particularly fond of 'outlandish and irregular ones . . . overlooked anomalies, suppressed anachronisms', because they 'serve to undermine "epochal truths", to puncture on purpose . . . to chip away at the familiar edifices and make plastered-over cracks appear'.[53] Thus, Gallagher holds that the anecdote demystifies discourses and ideologies and exposes them as the illusions they really are. Inevitably, she returns to Foucault's encounter with Borges's Chinese encyclopaedia and his three-tier model of 'the unspoken order of things'.[54] The encounter with the encyclopaedia is characterized as 'a vague and sickening encounter with thought in ruins' as opposed to the 'quotidian experience of order in its "pure primary state"'. For Gallagher, both of these experiences serve to

> estrange us from 'our thought, the thought of our time'. They both bring the mind up against the given empirical codes as . . . initiations, causing them 'to lose their original transparency' and introducing the notion that these orders are perhaps not the only possible ones.[55]

This strongly echoes Althusser's 'Letter on Art', in which, if you recall, he claims that through distantiation, that is, a process that *estranges* the viewer or reader from his or her ideological present by refusing the usual process of interpellation, art can ' "make us see", "make us perceive", "make us feel" something which *alludes* to reality!'.[56] Gallagher would reserve a similar special category for the anecdote. (Note that in Gallagher's model art *itself* does not have this special status.) However, the difference is that Althusser's 'distantation' is internal, so that the ideological subject recognizes his or her *own* ideological construction in the moment of estrangement; whereas Gallagher's is external, so that whilst she recognizes and exposes the lines of construction in the historical subject or culture, her own ideological or discursive construction, her own world-view, is left relatively unscathed.

Gallagher goes on to make further claims for the anecdote. Not only can it be used to reveal discursive formations in cultural artefacts, but it can also serve the altogether more noble purpose of reinvigorating literary texts and criticism:

> [In the anecdote] literature's own dormant counter-historical life might be reanimated: possibilities cut short, imaginings left unrealised, projects half-formulated, ambitions squelched, doubts, dissatisfactions, and longings half felt, might all be detected there. They were buried beneath the surface, no doubt, but would stir one hoped 'at the touch of the real'.[57]

This is Gallagher at both her most vague and her most deterministic: it is difficult to see *who* the subject of these 'possibilities', 'imaginings' or 'ambitions' are: are these 'the dead' Greenblatt spoke of in *Shakespearian Negotiations*? If so, assuming it is possible to recover the unrequited wants of dead people, can they really be found in literary texts? Gallagher's own *Nobody's Story* (1994) does not even try. It explicitly states that it is not interested in *real* dead people (who actually lived) but rather with 'fictional Nobodies',[58] by which she means anyone or anything that was not a real person. So much for 'the touch of the real'. In the passage quoted above, Gallagher ascribes to the anecdote 'extraordinary powers'. She writes as if counter-historical meanings were all interned somewhere 'beneath the surface' of the text, just waiting for the right new historicist to come along with the right anecdote and resurrect them. It remains unclear how these goals can be achieved.

Why should anecdotes have so much power and significance? It comes back to their view of culture as being a giant text which comprises smaller texts, which ironically means that Gallagher and Greenblatt's view of culture has an unmistakably formalist character. The irony of this has not been lost on critics of new historicism, not least myself. In *Shakespeare's History Plays* (2012), I argue that new historicism, far from being an antidote to the three decades of formalism that preceded it, is in fact a type of 'hidden formalism'. Recall in Chapter 3 how Geertz treated culture as a kind of poem. For Geertz, culture seems to be a unified whole, the parts of which can be treated as synecdoches giving the anthropologist a key with which to unlock 'the whole' in microcosm. Because culture is a 'whole' in this way, it follows that any two parts of that culture are connected and share a certain cultural logic. The boys playing on their video game and the reading group in Women's Institute, while seemingly totally random and different parts of the culture, *are* in fact connected and share this 'cultural logic'. So we are likely to see the same sorts of symbols and values in both sets of people, and, ergo, an analysis of the boys playing video games will reveal something about the reading group. Walter Cohen calls this 'arbitrary connectedness'.[59] New historicists repeat all of these Geertzian moves wholesale. This is how they are able to take obscure little anecdotes and use them to 'open up' Shakespeare's plays. Greenblatt's trick, again and again, is to show how the cultural logic of the anecdote is mirrored in Shakespeare. David Scott Kastan puts it a little more scathingly: the typical Greenblatt essay advances by 'offering some bizarre incident as the point of generation of a cultural principle that is then discovered in a canonical text'.[60] Kiernan Ryan makes a similar point:

> . . . in the end the eccentric anecdote repeatedly turns out to be a synecdoche, an exemplary illustration of a pervasive cultural logic, which even the wildest imaginations of the age are powerless to escape.[61]

For Kastan, as for myself, the readings of new historicists are 'not properly historical at all but rather formalist practices, discovering pattern and order, unity and coherence, in the culture . . . exactly as an earlier generation of formalist critics found them in works of literature'.[62] We might even take Kastan's criticisms further: new historicists are meant to be against Tillyard's 'Elizabethan world view' approach, but in treating culture as if it were a poem with a governing logic they replicate it. What's the difference between Tillyard saying that every Elizabethan believed in the Great Chain of Being and then seeing it everywhere in Shakespeare's plays and Greenblatt 'transcoding' ideologies from one 'discursive field' to another, from anecdotes to Shakespeare's play? We started out by saying that new historicism was 'new' because it opposed both formalism and 'old historicism', but upon further analysis it seems to me that it is both formalist and, unwittingly, more Tillyardian than it professes to be. This may seem like a negative account of new historicism, at least as practised by Gallagher and Greenblatt, but I think it is an accurate one. They have been consistently praised for breaking with formalism and their heterogeneous and non-monolithic view of culture, but I think we have seen enough to suggest that the opposite is true in both cases if you really think about what they are doing.

Jean E. Howard, Walter Cohen, Don E. Wayne, Phyllis Rackin, Peter Erikson and Marion F. O'Connor represent another group in the new historicist camp, who rallied round the banner: *Shakespeare Reproduced* (1987).[63] These critics generally support the aims of new historicism but harbour major political and methodological reservations about the work of the other new historicists. As we have seen, it was Cohen who first pointed out 'arbitrary connectedness'. While this group houses divergent approaches, what all of its critics have in common is a sympathy for the commitment of British cultural materialism to the political causes of feminism and the subversion of hegemony. They each aim, in their own individual ways, 'not only to *describe*, but to *take a position on*, the political uses of texts' and, even more importantly, to work towards 'a critical practice in which the critic acknowledges his or her own interested position within a social formation, rather than laying claim to an Olympian disinterestedness'.[64] As shall become evident, this cohort of critics, which has originated many of the classic critiques of new historicism from a forward-looking, constructive position, has been as influential in the development of new historicism as Greenblatt or Goldberg has been.

It is also worth mentioning briefly another member of the new historicist camp, Louis Montrose, though he is something of a renegade among critics of this stamp. Montrose's work has been hailed as 'exemplary New Historicism',[65] and 'the exception that almost proves the rule'.[66] This is perhaps because, in many ways, he has been ahead of his time. In his early essays, Montrose pre-empted many of the criticisms that would be levelled against Tennenhouse, Goldberg and Greenblatt.[67] Later, in 1986, he recognized that it is important to acknowledge that 'the critic exists in history', and argued that 'we should resist the inevitably reductive tendency to think in terms of subject/structure opposition',[68] well before either of these views became standard critiques of new historicism. Later, in *The Purpose of Playing* (1996), he is concerned with the problem of the individual and political agency. His solution to this is what a cultural materialist might do: to turn from Althusser's 'closed and static, monolithic and homogeneous' version of ideology to Raymond Williams and more recent theorists, such as Pierre Bourdieu, who provide more 'heterogeneous and unstable, permeable and processional' structural frameworks that explain more adequately social and political change.[69]

In all its incarnations, new historicism is above all an antihumanist mode of criticism that rejects the notion of a 'human essence' in favour of the idea that the individual is inextricably bound and, indeed, formed by a network of social practices embodied in material institutions and governed by the discourses of the hegemonic ideology or dominant culture. Montrose is quite eloquent on this point:

> Although it continues to thrive in the mass media, in the rhetoric of politicians, and in the hearts and minds of the general population, the freely self-creating and world-creating Individual of so-called bourgeois humanism has, for quite some time, been defunct in the texts of academic theory.[70]

From this standpoint, it is no longer possible to speak of a text as the autonomous creation of a single author. Rather it is a social product that is inextricably bound to the patchwork 'mastertext' of the culture that produced it. Just as in Geertz, by looking at a text it is possible to find aspects of that culture's complex

structural constitution stitched into it and, conversely, it is possible to find in the culture previously unseen aspects of the text's
discourse. By privileging the position of the critic, Gallagher's
and Greenblatt's insistence that culture itself is a text and their
insistence on the difference of the past from our present enable
the new historicist to conduct analyses of, and draw inferences
from, particular literary texts in particular historical moments.
The main purpose of conducting such analyses is to expose and
explore the conditions of the possibility of the text's constitution
and the ideological or discursive rules that helped to create that
possibility. Invariably, this analysis takes the form of a critique
of power and its subjects, and of how power has manifested and
reproduced itself through institutions, symbols and individual
rulers, and above all through ideology and discourses, in various historical moments. New historicism does search for the possibility of resistance to and, ultimately, liberation from power,
but more often than not finds power too adept at maintaining
its hegemony. Let us therefore replace Veeser's five-point definition,[71] which is too centred on notions of capitalism and the economy to serve as a *general* definition, and say that new historicism
assumes the following:

1   That there is no 'human essence' and that every expressive
    act is embedded in a network of material practices in a
    particular time and place.

2   That culture has the structural properties of a text and can
    therefore be analysed in the same way as a text.

3   That literary texts are inextricably bound to this cultural
    text through a network of other texts and discourses, all of
    which are open to the same form of analysis.

4   That power will always seek to contain dissidence and that
    this drive for containment must be overcome if genuine
    subversion is to be achieved.

5   That it is possible to produce 'counter-histories', that is,
    histories that explore what is only glimpsed or ignored in
    dominant historical accounts, through an engagement with
    the 'real' lived experiences of people, as documented by
    anecdotes.

For the remainder of this book, when I speak of 'new historicism', it is on the assumption that it has been broadly defined as displaying these core characteristics. The influence of this approach to Shakespeare since the 1980s has been incalculable; it would be like trying to measure the influence of Bob Dylan or The Beatles on the development of popular music. The question we need to ask ourselves is whether or not that influence is necessarily a good thing, or to follow my music analogy, whether we just need to do something *different* from what has come before us. I will leave that for you to ponder.

Key questions for students

- To what extent do you believe that new historicism is really 'new'?
- Do you think that the early new historicists, such as Jonathan Goldberg and Leonard Tennenhouse, had a valid point in arguing that Shakespeare was essentially a puppet of the Tudor state and his plays simply conduits of the dominant ideologies of his time?
- Are Catherine Gallagher and Stephen Greenblatt right to follow Clifford Geertz in treating culture as a text, essentially as a giant poem? Why?
- Are they right to follow Michel Foucault in dispensing with the materiality of ideology? Why?
- Do you agree with myself, David Scott Kastan and others that new historicism is, despite appearances, in fact a type of 'hidden formalism'? If so, why? And if not, why not?

Selected further reading

Barry, Peter, *Literature in Contexts* (Manchester: Manchester University Press, 2007).

Belsey, Catherine, 'Historicizing New Historicism', in *Presentist Shakespeares*, ed. Hugh Grady and Terence Hawkes (New York and London: Routledge, 2007), pp. 27–45.

Brannigan, John, *New Historicism and Cultural Materialism* (London: Palgrave Macmillan, 1998).

Dutton, Richard and Richard Wilson (eds), *New Historicism and Renaissance Drama* (New York and London: Longman, 1992).

Gallagher, Catherine and Stephen Greenblatt, *Practicing New Historicism* (Chicago, IL and London: University of Chicago Press, 2000).

Goldberg, Jonathan, *James I and the Politics of Literature* (Baltimore, MD and London: Johns Hopkins University Press, 1983).

—, 'Making Sense', *New Literary History*, 21(3) (Spring 1990), 457–62.

—, *Sodometries: Renaissance Texts, Modern Sexualities* (Stanford, CA: Stanford University Press, 1992).

Greenblatt, Stephen, *Renaissance Self-Fashioning: From More to Shakespeare* (Chicago and London: University of Chicago Press, 1980).

—, *Shakespearean Negotiations: The Circulation of Social Energy in Renaissance England* (Oxford: Clarendon Press, 1988).

—, *Learning to Curse: Essays in Early Modern Culture* (New York and London: Routledge, 1990).

Hamilton, Paul, *Historicism* (New York and London: Routledge, 1996).

Hawthorn, Jeremy, *Cunning Passages: New Historicism, Cultural Materialism and Marxism in the Contemporary Literary Debate* (London: Arnold, 1996).

Howard, Jean E., 'Old Wine, New Bottles', *Shakespeare Quarterly*, 35(2) (Summer 1984), 234–7.

—, 'The New Historicism in Renaissance Studies', *English Literary Renaissance*, 16 (Winter 1986), 13–43.

Howard, Jean E. and Marion F. O'Connor (eds), *Shakespeare Reproduced: The Text in History and Ideology* (London: Methuen, 1987).

Howard, Jean E. and Phyllis Rackin, *Engendering a Nation: A Feminist Account of Shakespeare's History Plays* (New York and London: Routledge, 1997).

Montrose, Louis, '"Eliza, Queen of Shepheardes," and the Pastoral of Power', *English Literary Renaissance*, 10 (Spring 1980), 153–82.

—, '"Shaping Fantasies": Figurations of Gender and Power in Elizabethan Culture', *Representations*, 2 (Spring 1983), 61–94.

—, 'Renaissance Literary Studies and the Subject of History', *English Literary Renaissance*, 16 (Winter 1986), 5–12.

—, 'Professing the Renaissance: The Poetics and Politics of Culture', in *The New Historicism*, ed. H. Aram Veeser (New York and London: Routledge, 1989), pp. 15–36.

—, *The Purpose of Playing: Shakespeare and the Cultural Politics of the Elizabethan Theatre* (Chicago, IL and London: University of Chicago Press, 1996).

Mullaney, Steven, 'After the New Historicism', in *Alternative Shakespeares, Volume 2*, ed. Terence Hawkes (New York and London: Routledge, 1996), pp. 17–37.

Pechter, Edward, 'The New Historicism and its Discontents: Politicizing Renaissance Drama', *PMLA*, 102(3) (May 1987), 292–303.

Porter, Carolyn, 'History and Literature: After New Historicism', *New Literary History*, 21(2) (Winter 1990), 252–72.

Ryan, Kiernan (ed.), *New Historicism and Cultural Materialism: A Reader* (London: Arnold, 1996).

Tennenhouse, Leonard, 'Representing Power: *Measure for Measure* in its Time', in *The Power of Forms in the English Renaissance*, ed. Stephen Greenblatt (Norman, OK: Pilgrim Books, 1982), pp. 139–56.

—, *Power on Display: The Politics of Shakespeare's Genres* (New York and London: Methuen, 1986).

Veeser, H. Aram (ed.), *The New Historicism* (New York and London: Routledge, 1989).

— (ed.), *The New Historicism Reader* (New York and London: Routledge, 1994).

Notes

1 Assuming that the publication of Stephen Greenblatt's *Renaissance Self-Fashioning: From More to Shakespeare* (Chicago and London: University of Chicago Press, 1980) marks its birth.

2 Graham Bradshaw, *Misrepresentations: Shakespeare and the Materialists* (Ithaca, NY and London: Cornell University Press, 1993), p. 1.

3 Geoffrey Harpham, 'Foucault and the New Historicism', *American Literary History*, 3(2) (Summer 1991), 368.

4 Don E. Wayne, 'Power, Politics, and the Shakespearean Text: Recent Criticism in England and the United States', in *Shakespeare Reproduced: The Text in History and Ideology*, ed. Jean E. Howard and Marion F. O'Connor (New York and London: Methuen, 1987), p. 48.

5 Harpham, 'Foucault and the New Historicism', p. 363.

6 Kiernan Ryan, 'Introduction', in *New Historicism and Cultural Materialism: A Reader*, ed. Kiernan Ryan (London: Arnold, 1996), p. xiii.

7 Stephen Greenblatt, *Shakespearean Negotiations: The Circulation of Social Energy in Renaissance England* (Oxford: Clarendon Press, 1988) p. 3.

8 Kevin Curran, *Marriage, Performance, and Politics at the Jacobean Court* (Burlington, VT and Farnham: Ashgate, 2009), p. 14n. See Stephen Orgel, *The Illusion of Power: Political Theater in the English Renaissance* (Berkeley, CA: University of California Press, 1975).

9 Stephen Greenblatt, 'Introduction', in *The Power of Forms in the English Renaissance*, ed. Stephen Greenblatt (Norman, OK: Pilgrim Books, 1982), p. 5; E. M. W. Tillyard, *The Elizabethan World Picture* (London: Vintage, 1959), p. 18; Jonathan Dollimore, 'Shakespeare, Cultural Materialism and the New Historicism', in *Political Shakespeare: Essays in Cultural Materialism* ed. Jonathan Dollimore and Alan Sinfield (1985; Manchester: Manchester University Press, 1994) p. 4.

10 Greenblatt, *The Power of Forms*, pp. 5, 6.

11 Leonard Tennenhouse, *Power on Display: The Politics of Shakespeare's Genres* (New York and London: Methuen, 1986), p. 77. It must be noted here that, although Jonathan Goldberg has turned to concentrate more on the issues of gender and sexuality, the complicity of the text with state power is still an assumption underpinning his practice. Consider, for example, Goldberg's conclusion that 'the misogyny of the second tetralogy is complicit with homophobia' (*Sodometries: Renaissance Texts, Modern Sexualities* (Stanford, CA: Stanford University Press, 1992), p. 175), which he regards as yet another example of Shakespeare reflecting and reinforcing court attitudes. Although Goldberg's focus has changed in recent years, the central thesis of *James I and the Politics of Literature* remains implicit in much of his work.

12 Bradshaw, *Misrepresentations*, p. 23.

13 Stephen Greenblatt, *Learning to Curse: Essays in Early Modern Culture* (New York and London: Routledge, 1990), pp. 164–5.

14 Leonard Tennenhouse, 'Representing Power: *Measure for Measure* in its Time', in *The Power of Forms in the English Renaissance*, ed. Stephen Greenblatt (Norman, OK: Pilgrim Books, 1982), p. 147.

15 Jonathan Goldberg, *James I and the Politics of Literature* (Baltimore, MD and London: Johns Hopkins University Press, 1983), p. 55.

16 Walter Cohen, 'Political Criticism of Shakespeare', in *Shakespeare Reproduced: The Text in History and Ideology*, ed. Jean E. Howard

and Marion F. O'Connor (New York and London: Methuen, 1987), p. 33.

17 Greenblatt, *Learning to Curse*, p. 165.

18 Edward Pechter, 'The New Historicism and its Discontents: Politicizing Renaissance Drama', *PMLA*, 102(3) (May 1987), 297.

19 Greenblatt, *Learning to Curse*, p. 165.

20 Greenblatt, *Shakespearean Negotiations*, p. 45.

21 Greenblatt, *Learning to Curse*, p. 166.

22 Greenblatt, *Shakespearean Negotiations*, p. vii.

23 Michel Foucault, *Archaeology of Knowledge and The Discourse on Language*, trans. Alan Sheridan (New York and London: Routledge, 2002), pp. 42, 34.

24 Stephen Mullaney, 'After the New Historicism', in *Alternative Shakespeares, Volume 2*, ed. Terence Hawkes (New York and London: Routledge, 1996), p. 19.

25 Stephen Greenblatt, *Shakespearean Negotiations*, p. 136.

26 Greenblatt, *Learning to Curse*, p. 154.

27 H. Aram Veeser, 'Introduction', in *The New Historicism*, ed. H. Aram Veeser (New York and London: Routledge, 1989), p. xv.

28 Greenblatt, *Learning to Curse*, p. 15.

29 Catherine Gallagher, 'Counterhistory and The Anecdote', in *Practicing New Historicism* (Chicago, IL and London: University of Chicago Press, 2000), p. 74.

30 Catherine Gallagher, 'Marxism and the New Historicism', in *The New Historicism*, ed. H. Aram Veeser (New York and London: Routledge, 1989), pp. 51, 43.

31 Greenblatt, *Shakespearean Negotiations*, pp. 1, 4.

32 See Hayden White, *Metahistory: The Historical Imagination in Nineteenth-Century Europe* (Baltimore, MD and London: Johns Hopkins University Press, 1973).

33 Catherine Gallagher and Stephen Greenblatt, *Practicing New Historicism* (Chicago, IL and London: University of Chicago Press, 2000), p. 8.

34 Felperin, *The Uses of the Canon: Elizabethan Literature and Contemporary Theory* (Oxford: Clarendon Press, 1990), pp. 146–7.

35 John Brannigan, *New Historicism and Cultural Materialism* (London: Palgrave Macmillan, 1998), p. 123.

36 Catherine Belsey, 'Richard Levin and Indifferent Reading', *New Literary History*, 21(3) (Spring 1990), 452, emphasis mine.

37 Felperin, *The Uses of the Canon*, p. 152.

38 Ibid., p. 152.

39 This and the problems inherent in it will be expanded upon later. For now, it is worth keeping in mind the residue of Althusser and Foucault's structuralism. It might be helpful to think of Roland Barthes's account of literature as 'a construction of layers . . .' etc. (quoted earlier) as being roughly analogous to the new historicist view of culture and of history.

40 Louis Montrose, 'Professing the Renaissance: The Poetics and Politics of Culture', in *The New Historicism*, ed. H. Aram Veeser (New York and London: Routledge, 1989), p. 18.

41 Paul Hamilton, *Historicism* (New York and London: Routledge, 1996), p. 155.

42 Fredric Jameson, 'Marxism and Historicism', *New Literary History*, 11(1) (1979), p. 42.

43 Ibid., pp. 43–4.

44 Catherine Belsey, *Shakespeare and the Loss of Eden* (London: Macmillan, 1999), p. 3.

45 Brannigan, *New Historicism and Cultural Materialism*, p. 123; Belsey, 'Richard Levin and Indifferent Reading', p. 452, emphasis mine.

46 Ibid., p. 9.

47 Gallagher and Greenblatt, *Practicing New Historicism*, p. 10.

48 Stephen Greenblatt, 'The Touch of the Real', in *Practicing New Historicism* (Chicago, IL and London: University of Chicago Press, 2000), p. 48.

49 Jeremy Hawthorn, *Cunning Passages: New Historicism, Cultural Materialism and Marxism in the Contemporary Literary Debate* (London: Arnold, 1996), p. 147.

50 Greenblatt, *Learning to Curse*, p. 15, emphasis mine.

51 Greenblatt, 'The Touch of the Real', p. 30, emphasis mine.

52 Catherine Belsey, *Culture and the Real* (New York and Oxford: Routledge, 2005), p. 4.

53 Gallagher, 'Counterhistory and the Anecdote', pp. 51–2.

54 Note that Gallagher defines this three-tier model as the following: 1. reflexive knowledge: the mental grid or code according to which

people process information and live their lives; 2. 'wild space': the fact that order exists; 3. the fully articulated justification for that order (ibid., pp. 72–3).

55 Ibid., pp. 73, 74.

56 Louis Althusser, 'A Letter on Art in Reply to André Daspre', in *Lenin and Philosophy and Other Essays*, ed. Fredric Jameson, trans. Ben Brewster (1971; rpr. New York: Monthly Review Press, 2001), p. 152.

57 Gallagher, 'Counterhistory and the Anecdote', p. 74.

58 Catherine Gallagher, *Nobody's Story: The Vanishing Acts of Women Writers in the Marketplace 1670–1820* (Oxford: Clarendon Press, 1994), p. xix.

59 Cohen, 'Political Criticism of Shakespeare', p. 30.

60 Kastan, *Shakespeare After Theory*, p. 29.

61 Ryan, 'Introduction', p. xvii.

62 Ibid., p. 30.

63 Jean E. Howard and Marion F. O'Connor (eds), *Shakespeare Reproduced: The Text in History and Ideology* (London: Methuen, 1987).

64 Jean E. Howard and Marion F. O'Connor, 'Introduction', in *Shakespeare Reproduced*, p. 4.

65 Veeser, 'Introduction, in *The New Historicism*', p. xv.

66 Cohen, 'Political Criticism of Shakespeare', p. 37.

67 See, for example, Louis Montrose, '"Eliza, Queen of Shepheardes," and the Pastoral of Power', *English Literary Renaissance*, 10 (Spring 1980), 153–82, and '"Shaping Fantasies": Figurations of Gender and Power in Elizabethan Culture', Representations, 2 (Spring 1983), 61–94.

68 Louis Montrose, 'Renaissance Literary Studies and the Subject of History', *English Literary Renaissance*, 16 (Winter 1986), 8–9. Both of these arguments picked up steam after the publications of *Shakespeare Reproduced* and Veeser's *The New Historicism*.

69 Louis Montrose, *The Purpose of Playing: Shakespeare and the Cultural Politics of the Elizabethan Theatre* (Chicago, IL and London: The University of Chicago Press, 1996), p. 12.

70 Ibid., p. 13.

71 In which new historicism assumes, '1) that every expressive act is embedded in a network of material practices; 2) that every act of unmasking, critique, and opposition uses the tools it condemns and

risks falling prey to the practice it exposes; 3) that literary and non-literary "texts" circulate inseparably; 4) that no discourse, imaginative or archival, gives access to unchanging truths or expresses unalterable human nature; and 5) that a critical method and a language adequate to describe culture under capitalism participate in the economy they describe' (Veeser, 'The New Historicism', in *The New Historicism Reader*, p. 2).

CHAPTER FIVE

Cultural materialism

Summary

- Subversion and dissidence
- Raymond Williams
- Reading Shakespeare in our own time as opposed to from the remote past
- Writing from marginalized perspectives
- Cultural materialism and subjectivity
- Criticisms of cultural materialism
- Three-point definition of cultural materialism
- Opponents of new historicism and cultural materialism

Over in the cultural materialists' camp, Jonathan Dollimore and Alan Sinfield appear to have centralized power much more effectively than their new historicist counterparts. Graham Holderness, Catherine Belsey, Richard Wilson, Michael Bristol and Annabel Patterson might all be said to belong to this camp. Although they might not all display the political fervour of Sinfield, their work shares a concern for the possibility of genuine political agency and subversion in the teaching of Shakespeare today. The classic Marxist narrative of the class struggle still informs much of their analyses, which tend to take the form of ideology critique rather than 'cultural poetics'. Instead of tracing the effects of quasi-essentialist notions such as 'social energy', these critics focus on the function of social practices, because, as Richard Wilson contends, 'texts [are] inextricably social in their logic, and imbricated in specific material contexts, such as buildings, regions, customs, professions, and laws'.[1] This is quite different from Greenblatt's more elastic interpretation of Foucault; the emphasis on the material, ritualistic nature of ideology as working through 'raw material, fixed installations (buildings), instruments of production (machines), etc.' in 'Churches, Parties, Trade Unions, families, some schools, most newspapers, cultural ventures, etc., etc.'[2] is more Althusserian, and perhaps more importantly, more openly Marxist in emphasis. So the materialist methodology of this critical school inevitably exhibits a more radical character, orientated towards social change, 'resistance and renewal'.[3] Although there are a few sub-camps, the cultural materialists maintain, on the whole, a fairly unified position. One possible reason for this is that, while it has grown powerful, it has maintained something of its original marginality.[4]

The American new historicists have always been reluctant to produce explicit theoretical tracts. Greenblatt himself has obstinately refused to speak for anyone *but himself* at several points in his career, stating in 1990 that he was not 'overly sympathetic to calls for [new historicism's] systemization',[5] and then ten years later, still insistent that he and Gallagher 'remain deeply sceptical of the notion that we [new historicists] should formulate an abstract system and then apply it to literary works'.[6] Whereas it is clear that Greenblatt is reticent about speaking for anyone but himself, the practitioners of cultural materialism have always been more than happy to define themselves explicitly both historically and politically. Jonathan Dollimore's introduction to cultural materialism's flagship study, *Political Shakespeare* (1985), reads like a manifesto announcing the arrival of a pioneering new way of reading. 'Materialist criticism', Dollimore proclaims, 'refuses to privilege "literature" in the way that literary criticism has done hitherto'; it 'eliminates the old divisions between text and context'. Dollimore is keen to point out where cultural materialism differs from new historicism: 'The most significant divergence within cultural analysis is that between those who concentrate on culture as . . . [instrumental in the] making of history, and those who concentrate on the unchosen conditions which constrain and inform that making process.' Here, of course, cultural materialism is aligned with the former position. Whereas new historicism is 'explicitly concerned with the operations of power',[7] cultural materialism is far more interested in what Alan Sinfield calls in a later study 'the scope of feasible political change'.[8]

The key issue for cultural materialists, as for new historicists, is the issue of subversion and dissidence. But where new historicism searches for subversion and finds only the illusions and strategies of containment employed by the dominant ideology, cultural materialists find genuine subversion. Sinfield complains that 'Greenblatt looks for "subversion", but finds, often brilliantly, that it is constructed within the discourse of power . . . an unbearable circle of power'. The new historicist vision of power is too simple and 'idealised' for Sinfield who seeks 'a more complex model, one that envisages the operations of power and ideology as more disjunctive'. For Sinfield, 'the insistence in representations upon unity in a simple hierarchy does not mean that is how the state *actually worked*, only that this is the way major parts of the ruling fraction represented it as working'.[9] New historicists are thus accused of overestimating the pervasiveness and efficiency of power in the historical moments they treat, because they oversimplify the relationship between power and ideology and mistakenly suppose, for example, that Elizabethan England was an absolutist state.[10]

In contrast to this unified model, cultural materialists lay claim to a more heterogeneous view of ideology, which affords individuals scope for disengaging from and even challenging power. In *Faultlines* (1992), Sinfield argued that contradictions or 'faultlines' in ideology generate dissidence in individuals, which the state has to strive to restrain:

> The contradictions inscribed in ideology produce very many confused or dissident subjects, and control of them depends upon convincing enough of the rest that such control is desirable and proper. Soldiers have to believe that they are different from terrorists, prison officers that they are different from kidnappers, judges that they are different from muggers; and most of us have to be persuaded to agree.[11]

Sinfield rewrites Althusser by making the effects of ideology far more explicit and conscious. The implication here is that Althusser himself was writing of the machinations of a *totally successful* ideology or the 'ideal form' of ideology, and that, in actuality, in the *real world*, things are more complicated. Ideology is not always totally successful in interpellating its subjects. As Sinfield says elsewhere in *Faultlines*, though State 'institutions' work 'to achieve ideological unity' they are 'not always successful'.[12] Seven years earlier, following the reception of his book *Radical Tragedy* (1984), Dollimore had outlined three possibilities in historical and cultural processes: (a) consolidation (which is essentially Althusser's ideology working to perfection); (b) containment (the phenomenon new historicists are habitually disposed to discern) and 3. *genuine* subversion. Dollimore deals with the new historicist subversion/containment model by redefining ideology:

> To some extent the paradox [of authority *producing* subversion for its own ends] disappears when we speak not of a monolithic power structure producing its effects but of one made up of different, often competing elements . . . If we talk only of power producing the discourse of subversion we not only hypostatise power but also efface the cultural differences – and context – which the very process of containment presupposes.[13]

Here Dollimore finds scope for a genuine resistance to authority distinct from that of Sinfield's *Faultlines*. In Dollimore's view subversion is produced from a multitude of sources that vie with the dominant ideology for hegemony: subversion can thus arise from the cumulative impact of specific differences within a culture. This accounts for historical paradigm shifts that have come from 'the people', such as the February Revolution and the overthrow of the Russian Tsar in 1917 or the Islamic revolution and the overthrow of the Shah of Iran in 1979. Dollimore also suggests that subversion can take place at the level of the dominant ideology itself in the form of a 'counter-faction',[14] which directly opposes the ruling authority but subsequently maintains that authority's current structure and form. This accounts for historical changes initiated by discontent and internal divisions at the level of government, such as Henry Bolingbrook's usurpation of Richard II or Henry Tudor's usurpation of Richard III. Thus, for cultural materialism, culture is seen not 'as a static totality . . . but as diverse and changing, the site of profound contradictions';[15] and accordingly, as Dollimore writes elsewhere: 'subversive knowledge emerges under pressure of contradictions in the dominant ideology which also fissure subjectivity'.[16] In such a model, dissent and change are seen as an *inevitability* built into the structure of authority. As Catherine

Belsey writes: 'the condition of subjectivity' itself 'is a location of change'.[17]

Much of this thought, in particular the rejection of a singular model of domination in favour of 'something more substantial and more flexible than any abstract imposed ideology' and the idea of a mass of competing forces under a dominant hegemony, reflects the influence of Raymond Williams, who coined the term 'cultural materialism' in the first place.[18] This is why I have saved discussion of Williams until now, because in many ways he was the first cultural materialist – certainly, without Williams it is unlikely that the thought of Dollimore or Sinfield or others of their generation, such as Graham Holderness and Terry Eagleton, would have taken the direction it did. His key theory in the pioneering *Marxism and Literature* (1977) is that culture is irreducibly complex and made up at any given time by numerous cultures which are dynamically linked to each other. At any given time, there is not just one 'culture' but lots of different cultures with their own geneses in different epochal moments. Williams gives the examples of 'feudal culture', 'bourgeois culture' and 'socialist culture' which are all part of a cultural *process*. Culture is not static but processional and its different subcultures are in competition for hegemony. The status of a single subculture is liable to change over time. Williams identifies three different statuses: 'residual', 'emergent' and 'dominant'. These are fairly self-explanatory. To use his examples: bourgeois culture is 'dominant' because it has hegemony; socialist culture is 'emergent', because it is still being created and perhaps may one day become dominant; and feudal culture is 'residual' because it is the remnant of a by-gone era, essentially an anachronism, but crucially it is still 'active in the cultural process . . . as an effective element of the present'.[19] A very good example of this might be the role that the Catholic Church – an ancient institution – still plays in many people's lives and in global politics. Clearly, Catholicism is something 'from the past', but it would be churlish to suggest that it is not an 'effective element' of the present. Williams talks about the 'residual' as a 'reaching back to those meanings and values which were created in actual societies and actual situations of the past, and which still seem to have significance because they represent areas of human experience, aspiration, and achievement which the dominant culture neglects, undervalues, opposes, represses, or even cannot recognize.' Since Williams is a Marxist thinker, however, unsurprisingly he is more interested in the 'emergent': 'the formation of a new class, the coming to consciousness of a new class, in actual process, the (often uneven) emergence of elements of a new cultural formation'.[20] Williams gives the example of the emergent working class in the industrialized nineteenth century. Another example would be the middle classes – 'bourgeois culture' if you will – in Tudor England. It is not difficult to spot that one of the key differences between Williams and Althusser and Foucault, is that Williams remained committed to the idea of diachronic history. History is not a series of ruptures but a process: any given culture will contain both the traces of its own past and the seeds of its own future, as well as its own defining features. If you recall the account I gave in Chapter 3, it is not difficult to see either, how Williams was profoundly influenced by Antonio Gramsci. In fact, Williams often reads as an erudite and sophisticated rewrite of Gramsci: essentially he adds an interesting twist on Gramsci's theory of hegemony and class struggle.

The influence of Williams and Gramsci, to whom Dollimore and Sinfield acknowledge their debt, demonstrates a further difference between cultural materialism and new historicism. Whereas new historicists like Greenblatt are 'uncomfortable' talking about ideology and seek to distance themselves from it at every turn, cultural materialists are left-wing critics working in the Marxist *materialist* tradition (remember the discussion of base and superstructure in Chapter 3). This Marxist genealogy, as Howard Felperin says, has given it 'an enormous headstart in becoming a genuinely historical and political criticism'.[21] Kiernan Ryan articulates the key difference between cultural materialism and new historicism: that the former's Marxism had produced:

The summons to pursue a *materialist* critique of culture, as opposed to establishing a cultural *poetics*, speaks volumes about the differences between these two styles of radical criticism . . . Cultural materialism seeks actively and explicitly to use the literature of yesterday to change the world today. It is a brazenly engaged political stance, committed to activating the dissident potential of past texts in order to challenge the present conservative consensus inside the educational institutions where it is forged.[22]

Felperin makes a similar point: 'these critics read and write to change the world, or at least the structure of British society, through the state ideological apparatus of higher education'.[23] This is in sharp contrast to Greenblatt's dismissal of such possibilities as 'fatuous and presumptuous' in *Learning to Curse*. What is of particular note here is the cultural materialist awareness of the context in which he or she is writing. Both Sinfield and Dollimore are acutely aware of their status as academics working in universities and, more broadly, in the British system of higher education. This can be demonstrated by a consideration of the titles of some of their contributions to *Political Shakespeare*: Dollimore's 'Shakespeare Understudies: The Sodomite, the Prostitute, the Transvestite and their Critics' or Sinfield's tongue-in-cheek, 'Give an account of Shakespeare and Education, showing why you think they are effective and what you have appreciated about them. Support your comments with precise references'.[24] In these titles it is clear to see something of cultural materialism's antagonistic, radical character. Cultural materialism would support the new historicist, Louis Montrose's, assertion that

> The politics of the academy extend beyond what we casually refer to as 'academic politics' . . . There are those of us . . . who believe our most important work as teachers and scholars is to interrogate the legacy that we are charged (and paid) to transmit . . . If, by the ways in which we choose to read Renaissance texts, we bring to our students and to ourselves a sense of our own historicity, then we are at the same time demonstrating the limited but nevertheless tangible possibility of contesting the regime of power and knowledge that at once sustains and constrains us.[25]

Thus by planting the seed of ideological self-doubt into their students, individuals who, in most cases, go on to leave university and get jobs in other fields, occupying social functions in other discourses, the cultural historicist sows the possibility of future social dissonance or – if one stretches the argument to its logical extreme – revolution.

One interesting symptom of this is the collapse of the model of reading 'differently' advocated by new historicism. This is the key insight of Felperin in his essay '"Cultural Poetics" Versus "Cultural

Materialism"': rather than construing history 'as a remote subject' as new historicists do, cultural materialists write very much 'in the moment', by which I mean they replace new historicism's model of difference with one of partial identification and dialogue.[26] This is a distinctly Marxist vision of history, one which Fredric Jameson put forward in 1979:

> We must try to accustom ourselves to a perspective in which every act of reading, every local interpretative practice, is grasped as the privileged vehicle through which two distinctive modes of production confront and interrogate each other . . . [the past] radically calls into question the commodified daily life, the reified spectacles, and the simulated experience of our own plastic-and-cellophane society . . . the privatised and instrumentalized speech, the commodity reification, of our own way of life . . . it is the past that sees us, and judges us remorselessly, without any sympathy or complicity with the scraps of subjectivity we try to think as our own fragmentary and authentic life experience.[27]

Unlike Greenblatt, writing under the shelter of academic distance and cultural difference, cultural materialists are faced head-on with the problems history might throw up in our own culture. In fact, this judgement on us from the past is the *aim* of cultural materialism. Thus when Catherine Belsey talks about finding a place for women in Renaissance drama it is with a view to 'changing the present' concluding that 'the pressure to do so is increasingly urgent'. Belsey's critique of the seventeenth century's 'discourse of patriarchalism' and how 'women disrupt the discourses designed to contain them . . . find unauthorized forms of speech . . . exceed the space allotted to them' is equally relevant to the here and now because 'we . . . have no choice to but read [a text] from the present, to produce for it a meaning intelligible from *our own* place in history'.[28]

   In this movement from past issues projected onto the present to produce a *new* future, Felperin has found what he calls a 'nostalgia for the future . . . for an England that in certain respects was and might be again'. This can certainly be glimpsed in Fredric Jameson's dissatisfaction with our 'plastic-and-cellophane society'. It is enough for now to say that cultural materialism derives much if its forward impetus from such a dissatisfaction, not necessarily the same dissatisfaction as Jameson's, but one that recognizes that 'the principal strategy of ideology is to legitimate inequality and exploitation by representing the social order that perpetuates these things as immutable and unalterable' and this, in prejudices, stereotypes, received views and attitudes, *persists today* as much, if not more than it did in Shakespeare's day.[29]

This last concern is perhaps the most crucial for understanding what cultural materialism is doing. Cultural materialists tend to be concerned with the subjects that have been marginalized by the dominant culture – Sinfield talks of the 'subcultures of class, ethnicity, gender, and sexuality' and how the individual academic must 'break out of the professional subculture and work (not just live personally) in dissident subcultures'.[30] The vast majority of cultural materialist studies are, almost overwhelmingly, concerned with the issues of these 'dissident subcultures': in particular, if the critic is gay, that of homosexuality, and if the critic is female, the role of women, construction of female identity and so on. At least one of these tendencies is easily demonstrated by drawing a list of just some of the cultural materialist studies that have been published in the past two decades: *Homosexuality in Renaissance England* (1988), *Sexual Dissidence* (1991), *Sodometries* (1992), *Passions Between Women* (1993), *Queering the Renaissance* (1994), *Men in Women's Clothing* (1996), *The Homoeroticism of Early Modern Drama* (1997), *Homosexualities in the English Theatre* (1997), *Queer Virgins and Virgin Queans on the Early Modern Stage* (2000), *Figuring Sex Between Men from Shakespeare to Rochester* (2002), *The Renaissance of Lesbianism in Early Modern England* (2002), *On Sexuality and Power* (2004), *Shakespeare, Authority, Sexuality* (2006).[31] The sheer volume of feminist studies that cultural materialism has produced is too vast to list here, but the point is made: as well as being politically committed to the present, cultural materialists characteristically write from the margins, from 'dissident subcultures' and their work always therefore, implicitly, attacks the dominant centre. But it is possible to see how these critics' personal interests set the agenda of their studies. They will read texts 'against the grain' if necessary to get the study they want from it. Sinfield himself calls this the 'affirmative habit . . . [in which] the critic will indulge in whatever strenuous reading is necessary to get the Shakespearean text onto his or her side'. But he argues that cultural materialism is above such readings: 'the self conscious stratagems of cultural materialism blow the whistle on the affirmative habit'. In fact he sees this as a key achievement of cultural historicism in general: 'it allows to be seen that critics have *always* done that'; Greenblatt was attacked for his denying subversion because he 'was drawing attention to the affirmative habit'.[32] It is difficult to accept this from Sinfield *and* account for the amount of books that give special attention to sodomy in Renaissance texts which, after all, is not implied more than a handful of times in the entire Shakespeare canon.

Dollimore commented on this problem back in 1994, defending himself and others against similar criticisms from Hugh Grady:

> If the gay-identified critics who have written on same-sex desire in this period were as institutionally or contemporary-bound as Grady implies we all are, or should be, the temptation would presumably have been to find in Shakespeare reflections of themselves. The paradoxical reality is that, following the argument of Michel Foucault, these critics mostly insist that there are no homosexuals in Shakespeare. In doing that they are embroiled in an important current debate about the historical 'nature' of homosexuality.[33]

But this does not really answer the question of *why* we should look for the answers of this current debate in Shakespeare, especially if there are no homosexuals in Shakespeare. One probable answer is that, in asking these questions, they can 'denaturalise' the present and thereby shed light on their own, present-day concerns; Sinfield admits 'I focus on [these issues of] dissident sexuality – because they are a site of ongoing political agitation, and because *they concern me* as a gay man'.[34] In fairness, this is a problem of which cultural materialism is acutely aware. Cultural materialists explicitly do not want to make affirmative readings, they want texts to speak for themselves, rather than to ventriloquize. They will search for dissidence and lost voices but will not conjure them if they do not exist, as Dollimore promised in 1985: 'we will listen in vain for voices from the past or search for their traces in a "history" they never officially entered.'[35]

Nonetheless, it seems paradoxical to me to insist, on the one hand on anti-humanism at all costs, and on the other to encourage students, in Scott Wilson's words, 'to read with their genitals, argue with their background, or theorize with their skin colour'.[36] How can cultural materialism be po-facedly and militantly against essentialist humanism and committed to theorists, such as Althusser and Foucault, who as we have seen have no place for the autonomous free-thinking individual in their systems of control, *and* argue for a critical practice of *subjectivity*? Where is this magical subjectivity coming from? Is it not just the 'culture' or 'ideology' that made you and to which you are entirely subjected, reflected back on that same culture or ideology? Are 'gay-identified critics' *really* nothing but a set of ideological effects? Is homosexuality an ideological effect? These sorts of questions appear to have no answer and the tension between anti-humanism and 'subjective' criticism strikes me as being hopelessly contradictory.

Furthermore, cultural materialism itself comes from a position of embattled marginality and it seeks marginality and 'the scope for dissidence' in texts. One question to ask here is whether it is possible for someone like me, neither a woman nor a homosexual, to *be* a cultural materialist (if I so wished) or do I need to belong to a marginalized 'subculture'? The questions of female identity or of dissident sexuality do not necessarily *concern* me in any direct way. Does this mean I am excluded from cultural materialism and condemned to write from the centre or, heavens forbid, the right? This question is not intended as a criticism *per se*, rather I put it forward to highlight the highly personal and *necessarily marginal* nature of much cultural materialist criticism as compared with new historicism. Power, replication, allegory, the state machinations of Renaissance England and so on – the concerns of new historicism – can be seen as universal concerns because the subject is objectified; the personal politics and concerns of the individual critic seldom come into focus other than in one of Greenblatt's supposedly entertaining anecdotes. In complete contrast, cultural materialist studies are often littered with the personal politics and concerns of their authors, the cultural or textual subject often serves as the setting in which these concerns play out, but the agenda is set by the critic and not the text. So a cultural materialist reading by me, Neema Parvini, will be set by essentially my own concerns whatever they may be. If I was to think like a cultural materialist, then I would have to take into account that my father is from an upper middle-class family in Iran and my mother from a working-class mining

town in the Welsh valleys. I would have to think about what it is
to be of mixed race in this way, and what it is like to have parents
from two different cultures – a picture complicated by the fact that
I have essentially replicated their choice of 'interracial' marriage,
because my wife is the child of an Indian couple, who like my father
are first-generation migrants to the United Kingdom. Presumably
then, when I come to read Shakespeare I should be interested in
how he treats mixed-race relationships and how he deals with the
meeting of cultures: think of Jessica and Lorenzo in *The Merchant
of Venice*, or Desdemona and Othello in *Othello*. For a cultural
materialist, this would not only be a perfectly legitimate way to
proceed, but also more than likely an exciting prospect. For me,
I am afraid it seems intellectually suspect. If I were really to have
a deep-rooted interest in mixed-race marriages in twentieth- and
twenty-first century Britain to the extent where I would research
and write about it, then I suspect that Shakespeare's plays would
not be my starting point and would be surprised to see them figure
at all in any substantial way.

My point is that coming *to Shakespeare* with these sorts of questions already in mind seems a little arbitrary: it puts the cart before
the horse. It seems to me to make much more sense to pick up a text
and see where it takes you than to come at it with a pre-planned
agenda. Richard Levin argues along similar though far from identical lines: 'the materialism of [the cultural materialist] doctrine
is highly selective and that selectivity is determined . . . by politics'.[37] He is implying that cultural materialists bend history and
Shakespeare's plays to confirm their own view of the world:

> A common tactic is to assert that some aspect (always a bad one)
> of Shakespeare's world or the world of his play is basically the
> same in our world, often translating it into an abstract problem
> (like class-division) that floats free of history and the many
> material differences between our society and his. That does not
> 'matter' so long as their equation of the two worlds enables them
> to derive from the play a Marxist lesson for today.[38]

I do not necessarily agree with this. While it is true that cultural
materialists, as I said, put the 'cart before the horse', it is not clear
to me why the differences between Shakespeare's time and our own
should prohibit readings of the kind Levin describes. I also think

that he has rather missed the point: cultural materialists are more concerned with how Shakespeare has been appropriated by our own culture than how he might have been understood in his own time. They care about now, not then. The typical cultural materialist essay will take a reading of a Shakespeare play made by one of the old essential humanists – anyone from A. C. Bradley to Moody E. Prior (see Chapter 2), but most often Tillyard – and show how they have been responsible for mystifying or supporting or suppressing the exposure of the 'bad' aspect of Shakespeare's world, which has consequences for how those things are thought about in our own time, and then they attempt to set the record straight. I have no problem with this endeavour and view it as something that needed to happen in Shakespeare studies – it is undoubtedly a positive development. My objection is only to the practice of letting one's 'subjectivity' dictate the agenda prior to making the reading of the text. There is a difference between the two statements below:

1   'Tillyard suppressed the radical ideas of Shakespeare's history plays to further his own conservative ends, which in turn gave a generation of students a conservative Shakespeare, and now I want to show that these history plays are not so conservative after all'

2   'I am interested in mixed-race marriage because they concern me as a child of mixed-race who happens also to be in a mixed-race marriage. I believe X, Y and Z about mixed-race marriage. With this in mind, I am going to look for X, Y and Z in the depictions of mixed-race marriage in Shakespeare's plays.'

In my view, the first of these statements represents a worthy cultural materialist endeavour; the second is almost intellectually fraudulent *especially* if the speaker claims to be an anti-humanist.

Even allowing for its complete contradiction with anti-humanism, the avowed subjectivity of cultural materialism would be a sweeter pill to take if it were not so forthright and polarizing. Graham Bradshaw has been one of the most vocal critics of the cultural materialist tendency to moralize. He says that for cultural materialists there is *always* a 'humanist Enemy', who harbours 'an "essentialist", quasi-theological concern with "man", but that to identify the target in this way is itself a theological move, which creates and demonizes the "humanist" Other'.[39] Marcus Nordlund concurs: 'once they have been defined as essentialist . . . alternative views have typically been associated with a reactionary outlook . . . and then been assigned to the critical dustbin'.[40] As does Bradshaw's spiritual ally, Richard Levin, as we have seen, another very vocal 'Dissenter': cultural materialists 'posit a fundamental conflict between right and wrong' and artificially 'conflate this conflict with the opposition . . . associating formalism (and so humanism) with the upper class or patriarchy and their own approach with the victims'.[41] Bradshaw's attack continues by accusing cultural materialists of reducing the complexity of Shakespeare down to the binary terms of good and evil:

> [The cultural materialist] substitutes an evil, reactionary, and repressively authoritarian Shakespeare for the good crypto-materialist Shakespeare whose true content and intentions were allegedly misrepresented and suppressed by the essentialist-idealist-liberal-humanist Enemy. As ever, the contradiction doesn't matter as long as the critically contradictory readings advance the ideological objective . . .
>
> . . . Primitive neo-Tillyardian materialists like Dollimore and Sinfield assume, like Tillyard, that *the* Shakespearian Meaning exists, but also assume, since Tillyard is the ideological Enemy, that the Meaning must be somewhere else, or something else. So this approach delivers either the good, subversive crypto-materialist Shakespeare, whom the 'essentialist humanists' appropriate, misrepresent and suppress because They Are Evil; or the evil, authoritarian Bard whom 'essentialist humanists' take to be Good, again because They Are Evil.[42]

Bradshaw accuses cultural materialism of 'group think',[43] or to put it in less kind terms, of a kind of mob mentality. He claims that cultural materialists will make an issue political so as to avoid really discussing it. 'Politicized issues deflect or divert us from discussing Shakespeare plays'.[44] Bradshaw describes a nightmare vision of censorship with cultural materialists as a kind of '"thought police": any "dissident perspective" is presented as not only superior but transhistorically, transculturally true', and those who oppose such a perspective are necessarily conservative, inferior and mistaken.[45]

Before closing, it is worth noting in passing that a relatively new strain of materialist, often feminist, criticism – sometimes called 'new materialism' – has recently emerged. Following Foucault's *The History of Sexuality*, these materialists have become increasingly focused on the human body as 'the site of identity formation' or of cultural resistance. As Ewan Fernie and Clare McManus observe, this type of materialism displays a 'critical obsession with human materiality'.[46] Dympna Callaghan might be said to represent a sophisticated version of this approach, one that argues that 'the material should not be confined to the binarism brute-material/ discursive . . . [because] the social and cultural always *exceed* the discursive'. In other words, physical matter such as the female body is not simply 'material' but socially and culturally inscribed. For Callaghan this move has important political consequences that are 'pertinent to feminist struggle because the politics of the body are exacerbated and more urgent there: as the object of patriarchal subjugation, which has been simultaneously and problematically marked as the ground of feminist resistance'. Opposed to both humanism and deconstruction, Callaghan wishes to reclaim women's bodies 'without regressing into biological essentialism (the very rationale for women's subordination), the phenomenology of lived experience, or the political evasions of poststructuralism'.[47]

To summarize: cultural materialism, like new historicism, maintains the anti-humanist conception of the individual as formed and constrained by social forces such as ideology. However, following Gramsci and Williams, in the cultural materialist model the dominant ideology's sphere of influence is less impregnable, because it is subject to a myriad contradictions and competing discourses that serve to undermine it; and herein lies the scope for genuine dissidence. Springing as it avowedly does from a Marxist tradition, cultural materialism never ceases to be politically engaged. Its aim is to change the present and it will do this by searching for dissidence in the past. Thus, rather than writing from a privileged position of academic and temporal detachment, the cultural materialist faces the past with the present very much in mind: the fate of the present is as much at stake as the meaning of the text from the past. Cultural materialist criticism is therefore inherently polemical. Part of its manifesto is to speak for those whose voices have generally been silenced by the dominant ideology, such as women or gay men. In contrast to new historicism, which endeavours to maintain a degree of objectivity, cultural materialism is therefore a frankly *subjective* form of criticism in that the concerns of its practitioners invariably become the concerns of its studies. The present is the chief concern, so the present sets the agenda. It is thus possible to characterize cultural materialism as proceeding on the following general assumptions:

1 That social dissidence is not only possible but *inevitable* as a result of the competing discourses that foster contradictions in any dominant ideology.

2 That the present is in need of radical change and the process of change can be advanced in the sphere of education by searching for moments of contradiction and dissidence in the culture of the past.

3 That genuine dissidence comes from 'dissident subcultures' and hence the search for dissidence itself must first come from a 'dissident subculture', an attack on hegemony from the margins of discourse where the hegemonic ideology has the weakest hold over its subjects.

When I speak of 'cultural materialism' it is with the assumption that it has been broadly defined as having these core characteristics. It should be noted here that four of the five assumptions attributed to new historicism in Chapter 4 *also* hold for cultural materialism.[48] We could argue, then, that cultural materialism subsumes and moves beyond the new historicist model. It makes at least three assumptions that new historicism does not make and yet shares *all but one* of new historicism's assumptions. The cultural materialist project is one of political activism, which rejects new historicism's 'subversion / containment' model as too totalizing and its consistent focus on state power as too conservative. Most new historicists, on the other hand, would baulk at what they would perceive as the cultural materialists' idealism and naivety in thinking that they might actually be able to change something by reading and writing about books. Hence, Felperin's statement that while new historicism and cultural materialism 'have much in common, they are in crucial respects not only "different" . . . but actually *opposed*',[49] is a fair and valid conclusion.

Behind enemy lines, in territory occupied by 'The Dissenters', we have several small, but no less vocal, camps. In the 'liberal humanist' camp, we have the motley trio of Edward Pechter, Richard Levin and Graham Bradshaw. I have grouped them in this way, not because they are explicitly allied or because they agree on all issues, but because they have all been constant thorns in the side of new historicism and cultural materialism and refuse (with varying degrees of pragmatism and sophistication) to abandon their humanism. These critics have fundamental ideological and political objections to new historicism and cultural materialism and reject their anti-humanism. This camp has been at the forefront of the battle since new historicism's inception. It has led the charge relentlessly, in what Richard Dutton calls a 'long-running crusade',[50] from the mid-1980s right up until the twenty-first century, when Alan Sinfield and Richard Levin brought their disputes onto the internet in a heated and quite personal exchange.[51] In a series of polemical attacks, these critics have each subjected new historicism and cultural materialism to thorough scrutiny.[52] Their chief allegation is that, while proposing to do something radically new, new historicism and cultural materialism simply repeat the mistakes and traps of Tillyard's 'old' historicism. They produce, as Bradshaw describes, 'a thoroughly Tillyardian inversion of Tillyard'.[53] It is clear that these critics come from a lineage of thought quite distinct from that of the cultural historicists. This is even reflected in their prose, which is markedly more acidic in tone than the sort of prose one finds in most essays by new historicists or cultural materialists; they employ rhetorical devices such as sarcasm, mock-bombast and, at times, outright ridicule to formulate their attacks. Their language is much less laden with terms borrowed from postmodern French theory, though they demonstrate with great lucidity that they have read and understood it. Given that 'The Alliance' has set itself up as an attack on humanism, the rebukes it has received from Pechter, Levin, Bradshaw and other humanist critics were always inevitable.

No less inevitable, perhaps, has been the emergence of a movement known as 'presentism' in Renaissance studies. Hugh Grady and Terence Hawkes had long had strong affinities with the cultural materialists but broke with that camp, and cultural historicism in general, to satisfy their desire to 'talk to the living' as well as, or instead of, the dead. Attempting to redeem the term 'presentism' from its pejorative associations, Grady and Hawkes recognize that 'we can never, finally, evade the present', arguing that criticism must finally come clean and admit that 'it speaks always and only to – and about – ourselves'.[54] The 'carefully measured distance between . . . subject matter and its investigator' that Howard Felperin discerned in new historicism is eradicated.[55] One obvious reaction to this is to ask how 'presentism' differs from cultural materialism, which, as we have seen, also has a strong commitment to the present. Ewan Fernie, another critic associated with the movement, argues that 'presentism' marks 'a major methodological departure' from both new historicism and cultural materialism in that it recognizes that Shakespeare is 'more embedded in our modern world than he ever was in the Renaissance'.[56] The suggestion is that, unlike cultural materialism, presentism is no longer concerned with Shakespeare's contemporary audience or his reception in Renaissance England or, indeed, with the machinations of the Elizabethan or Jacobean court to maintain hegemony, or with contemporary efforts to subvert it. 'Presentism' posits a completely different orientation, which exists 'to challenge the dominant fashion of reading Shakespeare historically'.[57]

Other 'Dissenter' camps include: historians such as Hayden White, who find some aspects of new historicist and cultural materialist methodology objectionable;[58] new aestheticism;[59] 'historical formalism';[60] Marxists who do not subscribe to the cultural materialists' assumptions;[61] and 'post-theory' literary historians, such as David Scott Kastan, for whom 'new historicism is neither new enough nor historical enough to serve'.[62] Finally, we have the imperious 'big names' of the 1980s – Terry Eagleton, Stanley Fish, Fredric Jameson, J. Hillis Miller, Jonathan Culler and even the godfather of cultural materialism, Raymond Williams – who each cast a glance at, and passed judgement on, the new historicist and cultural materialist project at various moments. These are the major areas of opposition to the current hegemony of 'The Alliance'.[63] H. Aram Veeser's boast that 'meta-critical essays build up like Chinese lacquer around every new historicist twist and angle' would still appear to carry weight.[64]

Key questions for students

- Do you think that the cultural materialists are correct to follow Louis Althusser in insisting on a *material* analysis of ideology and culture?
- Do you think Raymond Williams's ideas about 'emergent', 'residual' and 'dominant' cultures improve on the more static model of ideology that Althusser gives us? Why?
- Do you prefer the notion of subversion and dissidence that cultural materialists such as Jonathan Dollimore and Alan Sinfield offer to Stephen Greenblatt's ideas about power and containment? Why?
- What do you think of the more radically political character of cultural materialism? Are they right to appropriate their readings of Shakespeare's plays for their own political ends?
- Scott Wilson has said that cultural materialism encourages students 'to read with their genitals, argue with their background, or theorize with their skin colour'. Is that a good thing or a bad thing in your opinion? Why?

Selected further reading

Belsey, Catherine, *Critical Practice* (New York and London: Methuen, 1980).

—, *The Subject of Tragedy: Identity and Difference in Renaissance Drama* (London: Methuen, 1985).

—, 'Richard Levin and Indifferent Reading', *New Literary History*, 21(3) (Spring 1990), 449–56.

—, *Desire: Love Stories in Western Culture* (Oxford: Blackwell, 1994).

—, *Shakespeare and the Loss of Eden* (London: Macmillan, 1999).

Bradshaw, Graham, *Misrepresentations: Shakespeare and the Materialists* (Ithaca, NY and London: Cornell University Press, 1993).

Callaghan, Dympna, *Shakespeare without Women: Representing Gender and Race in the Renaissance* (New York and London: Routledge, 2000).

Dollimore, Jonathan, 'Shakespeare, Cultural Materialism and the New Historicism', in *Political Shakespeare: Essays in Cultural Materialism*, ed. Jonathan Dollimore and Alan Sinfield, 2nd edn (1985; Manchester: Manchester University Press, 1994), pp. 2–17.

—, *Radical Tragedy: Religion, Ideology and Power in the Drama of Shakespeare and His Contemporaries*, 3rd edn (Basingstoke: Palgrave Macmillan, 2004).

Dollimore, Jonathan and Alan Sinfield, 'Culture and Textuality: Debating Cultural Historicism', *Textual Practice*, 4(1) (1990), 91–100.

—, 'History and Ideology, Masculinity and Miscegenation: The Instance of *Henry V*', in *Faultlines: Cultural Materialism and the Politics of Dissident Reading* (Oxford: Clarendon Press, 1992), pp. 109–42.

— (eds), *Political Shakespeare: Essays in Cultural Materialism*, 2nd edn (Manchester: Manchester University Press, 1994).

Holderness, Graham, *Shakespeare's History* (New York: St Martin's Press, 1985).

—, *Shakespeare Recycled: The Making of Historical Drama* (Hemel Hempstead: Harvester Wheatsheaf, 1992).

—, *Shakespeare: The Histories* (London: Macmillan, 2000).

Levin, Richard, 'The Cultural Materialist Attack on Artistic Unity, and the Problem of Ideological Criticism', in *Ideological Approaches to Shakespeare*, ed. R. P. Merrix and N. Ranson (Lewiston, NY: Edwin Mellen Press, 1992), pp. 39–56.

—, 'The Old and the New Materialising of Shakespeare', in *The Shakespearean International Yearbook, Vol. 1: Where Are We Now in Shakespearean Studies?*, ed. W. R. Elton and John M. Mucciolo (Brookfield, VT and Aldershot: Ashgate, 1999), pp. 87–107.

Sinfield, Alan, 'Power and Ideology: An Outline Theory and Sidney's *Arcadia*', *ELH*, 52(2) (Summer, 1985), 259–77.

—, *Faultlines: Cultural Materialism and the Politics of Dissident Reading* (Oxford: Clarendon Press, 1992).

—, *Shakespeare, Authority, Sexuality: Unfinished Business in Cultural Materialism* (New York and London: Routledge, 2006).

Williams, Raymond, *Marxism and Literature* (Oxford: Oxford University Press, 1977).

—, *Problems in Materialism and Culture* (London: Verso, 1980).

Wilson, Richard, *Will Power: Essays on Shakespearean Authority* (Hemel Hempstead: Harvester Wheatsheaf, 1993).

Wilson, Scott, *Cultural Materialism: Theory and Practice* (Oxford: Blackwell, 1995).

Notes

1 Richard Wilson, *Will Power: Essays on Shakespearean Authority* (Hemel Hempstead: Harvester Wheatsheaf, 1993), p. 15.

2 Louis Althusser, 'Ideology and the Ideological State Apparatus', in *Lenin and Philosophy and Other Essays*, ed. Fredric Jameson, trans. Ben Brewster (1971; rpr. New York: Monthly Review Press, 2001), pp. 86, 97. This point is made more explicitly in Richard Wilson, 'Introduction: Historicising New Historicism', in *New Historicism and Renaissance Drama*, ed. Richard Wilson and Richard Dutton (New York and London: Longman, 1992), pp. 1–18, where Wilson argues that cultural materialism is 'above all inflected by Althusser's theory that though ideology is produced "in words", it has a material existence' (p. 15).

3 Graham Holderness, *Shakespeare Recycled: The Making of Historical Drama* (Hemel Hempstead: Harvester Wheatsheaf, 1992), p. 42.

4 New historicism, on the other hand, originating at Berkeley, never boasted an especially rebellious character in its politics or methods of persuasion. Its battles with deconstruction in the 1980s and 1990s have tended to be characterised as 'an 80s West Coast, politically savvy and even earnest rival to what many saw as the apolitical, ahistorical, basically East Coast school of deconstruction that flourished in the 70s' (Geoffrey Harpham, 'Foucault and the New Historicism', *American Literary History*, 3(2) (Summer 1991), 360) rather than as an assault on the establishment. Greenblatt's move from Berkeley to Harvard in 1997, though doubtless a purely professional one, might be taken as marking the symbolic defeat of deconstruction by new historicism in the American academy.

5 Stephen Greenblatt, *Learning to Curse: Essays in Early Modern Culture* (New York and London: Routledge, 1990), p. 3.

6 Catherine Gallagher and Stephen Greenblatt, *Practicing New Historicism* (Chicago, IL and London: University of Chicago Press, 2000), p. 2.

7 Jonathan Dollimore, 'Shakespeare, Cultural Materialism and the New Historicism', in *Political Shakespeare: Essays in Cultural Materialism*, ed. Jonathan Dollimore and Alan Sinfield (1985; Manchester: Manchester University Press, 1994), pp. 4, 3.

8 Alan Sinfield, *Faultlines: Cultural Materialism and the Politics of Dissident Reading* (Oxford: Clarendon Press, 1992), p. 32.

9 Alan Sinfield, 'Power and Ideology: An Outline Theory and Sidney's *Arcadia*', *ELH*, 52(2) (Summer 1985), 259–60, 261, emphasis mine.

10 When Sinfield is discussing new historicism, he has in mind the 'first wave' new historicists. The account of Catherine Gallagher's position described in the previous section, which prizes Foucauldian heterogeneity and marginality, might be said to represent a second

wave, which occupies a position closer to that of Sinfield and Dollimore. While the areas of overlap are, generally, much larger now than in the mid-1980s, a distinction between American new historicism and British cultural materialism remains in the former's insistence on the textuality of culture and the latter's insistence on a more properly materialist criticism.

11 Sinfield, *Faultlines*, pp. 244–5.

12 Ibid., p. 113.

13 Dollimore, 'Shakespeare, Cultural Materialism and the New Historicism', p. 12.

14 Ibid.

15 Sinfield, 'Power and Ideology', p. 265.

16 Dollimore, 'Shakespeare, Cultural Materialism and the New Historicism', p. 482.

17 Catherine Belsey, *The Subject of Tragedy: Identity and Difference in Renaissance Drama* (London: Methuen, 1985), p. 224.

18 Raymond Williams, *Problems in Materialism and Culture* (London: Verso, 1980), p. 38.

19 Raymond Williams, *Marxism and Literature* (Oxford: Oxford University Press, 1977), pp. 121–2.

20 Ibid., pp. 123–4.

21 Felperin, *The Uses of the Canon*, p. 157.

22 Ryan, 'Introduction', in *New Historicism and Cultural Materialism*, p. xv.

23 Felperin, *The Uses of the Canon*, p. 157.

24 In *Political Shakespeare*, pp. 129–53 and pp. 158–81.

25 Montrose, 'Professing the Renaissance', *The New Historicism* ed. Veeser, pp. 30–1.

26 Felperin, *The Uses of the Canon*, p. 155.

27 Jameson, 'Marxism and Historicism', pp. 70–1.

28 Belsey, *The Subject of Tragedy*, pp. 1–2, 158, 222, 224, 223–4, emphasis mine.

29 Felperin, *The Uses of the Canon*, pp. 114, 161–2.

30 Sinfield, *Faultlines*, p. 294.

31 Some of these books, do, of course, come from the new historicist lineage, for example Goldberg's *Sodometries* and *Queering the Renaissance*. Again, it is possible to see a convergence of interests

between new historicism and cultural materialism as their focuses become less State-centric and more marginal – they do, after all, form an 'Alliance'.

32 Jonathan Dollimore and Alan Sinfield, 'History and Ideology, Masculinity and Miscegenation: The Instance of *Henry V*', in *Faultlines: Cultural Materialism and the Politics of Dissident Reading* (Oxford: Clarendon Press, 1992), p. 114; Alan Sinfield, *Shakespeare, Authority, Sexuality: Unfinished Business in Cultural Materialism* (New York and London: Routledge, 2006), pp. 198, 199.

33 Jonathan Dollimore, 'Shakespeare Understudies: the Sodomite, the Prostitute, the Transvestite and their Critics', p. 131.

34 Sinfield, *Shakespeare, Authority, Sexuality*, p. 22, emphasis mine.

35 Dollimore, 'Shakespeare, Cultural Materialism and the New Historicism', p. 15.

36 Scott Wilson, *Cultural Materialism: Theory and Practice* (Oxford: Blackwell, 1995), p. 21.

37 Richard Levin, 'The Old and the New Materialising of Shakespeare', in *The Shakespearean International Yearbook, Vol. 1: Where Are We Now in Shakespearean Studies?*, ed. W. R. Elton and John M. Mucciolo (Brookfield, VT and Aldershot: Ashgate, 1999), p. 88.

38 Ibid., p. 91.

39 Graham Bradshaw, *Misrepresentations: Shakespeare and the Materialists* (Ithaca, NY and London: Cornell University Press, 1993), pp. 7, 9.

40 Marcus Nordlund, *Shakespeare and the Nature of Love: Literature, Culture, Evolution* (Evanston, IL: Northwestern University Press, 2007), p. 17.

41 Richard Levin, 'The Poetics and Politics of Bardicide', *PMLA*, 150(3) (May, 1990), 492.

42 Bradshaw, *Misrepresentations*, pp. 16, 23.

43 Graham Bradshaw, 'State of Play', in *The Shakespearean International Yearbook, Vol. 1: Where Are We Now in Shakespearean Studies?*, ed. W. R. Elton and John M. Mucciolo (Brookfield, VT and Aldershot: Ashgate, 1999), p. 4.

44 Ibid., p. 5.

45 Bradshaw, 'State of Play', p. 7.

46 Ewan Fernie and Clare McManus, 'Materiality', in *Reconceiving the Renaissance: A Critical Reader* (New York and Oxford: Oxford University Press, 2005), pp. 278, 280.

47 Dympna Callaghan, *Shakespeare Without Women: Representing Gender and Race in the Renaissance* (New York and London: Routledge, 2000), pp. 29, 30, 280.

48 The new historicist assumption that cultural materialism rejects is '2) That culture has the structural properties of a text and can therefore be analysed in the same way as a text'. It must reject this or it would cease to be materialist; cultural materialist analysis always starts from the material base and this is crucial to its methodology.

49 Felperin, *The Uses of the Canon*, p. 144.

50 Richard Dutton, 'Postscript', in *New Historicism and Renaissance Drama*, ed. Richard Wilson and Richard Dutton (New York and London: Longman, 1992), p. 224.

51 See: Alan Sinfield, 'Selective Quotation', *Early Modern Culture, issue 2* (updated 2001) <http://emc.eserver.org/1-2/sinfield.html>, accessed 18 March 2007; Richard Levin, 'Selective Quotations and Selective Marxisms: A Response to Alan Sinfield and David Siar', *Early Modern Culture, issue 2* (updated 2001) <http://emc.eserver.org/1-2/levin.html>, accessed 18 March 2007; Alan Sinfield, 'Counter-response to Richard Levin', *Early Modern Culture, issue 2* (updated 2001) <http://emc.eserver.org/1-2/sinfield2.html>, accessed 18 March 2007. This type of vitriolic exchange has become something of a habit in Levin's career. He had previously clashed with Catherine Belsey and Jonathan Goldberg in *New Literary History*, 21(3) (Spring, 1990) and, notoriously, a year earlier, with over 20 furious left-wing feminists (Janet Adelman, Margaret J. Arnold, Linda Bamber and Catherine Belsey, 'Feminist Criticism', *PMLA*, 104(1) (January 1989), 77–80), the fallout from which was reproduced in Ivo Kamps (ed.), *Shakespeare Left and Right* (New York and London: Routledge, 1991). More recently, Edward Pechter kept the tradition of quoting Bob Dylan in anger alive in a spat with Peter Hulme. See Edward Pechter, 'Misrepresentation, Ego, Nostalgia: Misreading "Misreading the Postcolonial Tempest"', *Early Modern Culture, issue 3* (updated 2003) <http://emc.eserver.org/1-3/pechter_response.html>, accessed 27 March 2007.

52 See bibliography for a complete list, but, apart from Bradshaw's *Misrepresentations*, which I draw on in Chapter 5, the major attacks were (in chronological order): Edward Pechter, 'The New Historicism and its Discontents: Politicizing Renaissance Drama', *PMLA*, 102(3) (May 1987), 292–303; Richard Levin, 'Unthinkable Thoughts in the New Historicizing of English Renaissance Drama', *New Literary History*, 21(3) (Spring 1990), 433–47; Edward Pechter, 'Against "Ideology"', in *Shakespeare Left and Right*, ed. Ivo Kamps

(New York and London: Routledge, 1991), pp. 79–98; Richard Levin, 'The Cultural Materialist Attack on Artistic Unity, and the Problem of Ideological Criticism', in *Ideological Approaches to Shakespeare*, ed. R. P. Merrix and N. Ranson (Lewiston, NY: Edwin Mellen Press, 1992), pp. 39–56; Edward Pechter, *What Was Shakespeare? Renaissance Plays and Changing Critical Practice* (Ithaca, NY and London: Cornell University Press, 1995); Richard Levin, 'The Old and the New Materialising of Shakespeare', in *The Shakespearean International Yearbook, Vol. 1: Where Are We Now in Shakespearean Studies?*, ed. W. R. Elton and John M. Mucciolo (Brookfield, VT and Aldershot: Ashgate, 1999), pp. 87–107; Graham Bradshaw, 'State of Play', in *The Shakespearean International Yearbook, Vol. 1: Where Are We Now in Shakespearean Studies?*, ed. W. R. Elton and John M. Mucciolo (Brookfield, VT and Aldershot: Ashgate, 1999), pp. 3–25.

53 Bradshaw, *Misrepresentations*, p. 9.

54 Grady and Hawkes, 'Introduction: Presenting Presentism', pp. 4, 5.

55 Howard Felperin, *The Uses of the Canon: Elizabethan Literature and Contemporary Theory* (Oxford: Clarendon Press, 1990), p. 147.

56 Ewan Fernie, 'Shakespeare and the Prospect of Presentism', in *Shakespeare Survey 58: Writing About Shakespeare*, ed. Peter Holland (New York and Cambridge: Cambridge University Press, 2005), pp. 174–5.

57 Ewan Fernie, 'The Last Act: Presentism, Spirituality and the Politics of *Hamlet*', in *Spiritual Shakespeares*, ed. Ewan Fernie (New York and London: Routledge, 2005), p. 106.

58 See Hayden White, 'New Historicism: A Comment', in *The New Historicism*, ed. H. Aram Veeser (New York and London: Routledge, 1989), pp. 293–303.

59 See Isobel Armstrong, *The Radical Aesthetic* (Oxford: Blackwell, 2000), and John J. Joughin and Simon Malpas (eds), *The New Aestheticism* (New York and Manchester: Manchester University Press, 2003).

60 See Patricia Parker, *Shakespeare from The Margins: Language, Culture, Context* (Chicago and London: University of Chicago Press, 1996); *Modern Language Quarterly*, 61(1) (March 2000), a special edition with a polemical introduction by Susan J. Wolfson; David Rasmussen (ed.), *Renaissance Literature and Its Formal Engagements* (New York and Basingstoke: Palgrave, 2002); and Stephen A. Cohen (ed.), *Shakespeare and Historical Formalism* (Aldershot: Ashgate, 2007). Patricia Parker's *Shakespeare from the Margins* is listed as

a precursor of historical formalism, because she shares many of its objections to the cultural historicist method.

61 See, for example, Gabriel Egan, *Shakespeare and Marx* (New York and Oxford: Oxford University Press, 2004).

62 David Scott Kastan, *Shakespeare After Theory* (New York and London: Routledge, 1999), p. 29.

63 There are, of course, a plethora of other commentators – John Brannigan, Ivo Kamps, Claire Colebrook, Howard Felperin, Jeremy Hawthorn, Richard Lehan, Jürgen Pieters, Carolyn Porter, Kiernan Ryan and H. Aram Veeser to name but ten prominent ones – who each have their own allegiances. Five of them consider new historicism and cultural materialism in book-length treatments, Lehan and Porter offer lengthy essays, and the remaining four have all edited collections of cultural historicist work. Their positions are so nuanced that it would be impossible to map and place all of them. It is worth noting that, Felperin, Lehan and perhaps Ryan aside, all these commentators are generally sympathetic to the cultural historicist cause and might expect to be included in their number. Veeser and Kamps in particular adopt a rather celebratory tone when discussing new historicism and cultural materialism in the introductions to their respective volumes. In short, the pro-cultural historicists outnumber those opposed to them.

64 H. Aram Veeser, 'The New Historicism', in *The New Historicism Reader*, ed. H. Aram Veeser (New York and London: Routledge, 1994), p. 7.

CHAPTER SIX

Alternative views in new historicism and cultural materialism

Summary

- Broadening the parameters of new historicist and cultural materialist work
- Lee Patterson
- Alan Liu
- Postcolonial scholarship
- Patricia Parker
- The recent work of Catherine Belsey
- Jerome McGann

As we run the gamut of new historicist and cultural materialist positions, the need for an umbrella term like 'The Alliance' becomes ever clearer. The return to historicism is no longer confined to studies of the Renaissance or, indeed, to models of power containment or power subversion. The body of historical and materialist work since the early 1980s has been so vast, and the range of positions so great, that any claim to be comprehensive when summarizing it would constitute an act of some fraudulence. What follows is a brief field survey of the major *strands* of historicist work in literary criticism to date that do not fall neatly into the definition I provided of new historicism in Chapter 4, or of cultural material-ism in Chapter 5. The works and writers that I have chosen to com-ment on here can be seen as representative of positions that might have a wider purchase in particular quarters. It is useful to think of new historicism and cultural materialism as polar extremes in the broader church of recent contextual scholarship. Lee Patterson takes exactly this view and offers a set of three axes with which to plot the various positions within this broader realm:

1 'A truly materialist analysis' versus 'A symbolic approach that seeks to maintain the unity of the social whole by applying an anthropological conception of culture as driven by semiotic rather than material needs'.

2 'Those who insist on the priority of agency over impersonal processes in the making of history, who maintain the efficacy of subjective meanings, intentions, and beliefs, and who see the literary work as bespeaking but also simultaneously criticising the ideology of the time' versus 'those who hold a darker, Foucauldian conception of an inescapable metaphysics of power, for whom, social life as lived is different from but ultimately controlled by the social as hegemonically thought, and for whom the unities of culture finally override its differences'.

3 'Literary historians who believe in the power of the exemplary instance' versus 'those for whom historical understanding requires empirical completeness . . . for whom the illustrative instance can never do more than illustrate the presence of forces whose efficacy requires other forms of demonstration'.[1]

Crudely speaking, in each case the first axis represents cultural materialism and the second represents new historicism. These axes offer a good starting point but are in need of updating to reflect the concerns that have developed in the time since Patterson was writing. Therefore, my aim in this chapter is to add to this list new axes by looking to further developments.

The logical place to start is with Patterson's own work, which has set itself in dialogue with, if not in opposition to, new his-toricism. Patterson is an American medievalist and his work has contested two major issues. The first of these issues is the matter of methodology. In *Negotiating the Past* (1987), Patterson rejects the Geertzian new historicist model of 'absorbing the historical into the textual'. He finds in this textual method a deconstructionist tendency to endow the text with what he calls 'irresolution' and warns: 'to adopt an interpretative method that history is not merely known through but constituted by language is to act as if there are no acts other than speech acts.'[2] As an alternative to this, Patterson puts forward a materialist argument:

> History is impelled by consequential and determinative acts of material production: building cities, making wars, collecting wealth, imposing discipline, seizing and denying freedom – these are material processes that . . . possess a palpable force and an intentional purposiveness . . . that stand against the irresolutions and undecidabilities valued by contemporary techniques of interpretation.
>
> . . .
>
> The sceptical self-cancellations of contemporary textuality should not subvert the category of the historical real.[3]

Deep in this textualized vision of the world, Patterson finds the root cause of new historicism's problems: Foucault and his 'totalising vision of an entrapping world organized by structures of domination and submission'. Patterson argues that all Foucauldian analysis is ultimately doomed to reconfirm its own hypothesis by denying any agency to the individual and ascribing all action and motive to a 'monolithic culture' because that is the only conclusion available to it: 'there is no space outside of power because power is the only term in the analyst's arsenal.' Patterson argues that these problems are compounded because new historicism's method, following Clifford Geertz, is 'relentlessly synchronic'. Patterson claims that 'the current distrust of diachronic historicism' has been 'impelled by the discrediting of the concept of origin, the collapse of the classic model of cause-and-effect causality'. Thus freed from the traditional laws of logic, new historicists are 'released from the narrow criterion of relevance that constrained older literary historians'. Implicit in this statement is the accusation, *a la* Walter Cohen (see Chapter 4), that new historicists forge their argument through 'arbitrary connectedness' justified by the claim that because culture is a text any one part of culture must therefore be relevant and have a structural relationship with any other part of culture.[4] Instead of this, rather than simply resurrecting diachronic history and the logic of cause and effect as one might expect his argument to be heading, Patterson turns to a difficult passage in Theodor Adorno's 'Subject and Object':

> The preponderant exertion of knowledge is destruction of its usual exertion, that of using violence against the object. Approaching knowledge of the object is the act in which the subject rends the veil it is weaving around the object. It can do this only where, fearlessly passive, it entrusts itself to its own experience. In places where subjective reason scents subjective contingency, the primacy of the object shimmering through – whatever in the object is not a subjective admixture.[5]

From this Patterson infers that 'historical understanding is by definition a vacillation between contradictions that must not yield to closure'.[6] What Patterson is moving towards, like Fredric Jameson and the cultural materialists, is roughly a situation of equivalence between past and present in which 'negotiation' can take place. He sees this as being both a viable and preferable alternative to the new historicist privileging of the critic, which devalues and denies the historical subject's own historical and critical faculties and invokes an 'absolute historicism' (Antonio Gramsci's phrase) from which there is no escape and in which real action is impossible.[7]

This leads to Patterson's second major issue: the relationship between the individual and what he calls 'social totality'. His major concern is that in modern America 'Foucault's dystopic vision of the carceral society is on the way to fulfilment' through fundamentalist conservativism, the growth of state power, corporate and military hegemony and the ever more naked and exploitative goals of ribald capitalism. But, if this is indeed the case, 'then surely our scholarly task should be to stand against it'.[8] Hence Patterson sees the new historicist infatuation with Foucauldian power structures as *itself* a form of collusion with American state power. He argues instead for a renewed commitment to humanist individualism and this is where Patterson is crucially different from the British cultural materialists in that the latter remain stoically and stubbornly within the theoretical framework of anti-humanism though they have a similar political investment in their negotiations with the past. This is an argument Patterson takes further in *Chaucer and the Subject of History* (1991), which begins with a desperate portrait of an America in the throes of an identity crisis. In this portrait, the United States of America is itself in the grip of the ideology of individualism where 'human life is conceived in terms of a basic unit, the autonomous, free, self-determining individual' and 'the behaviour of these individuals is in turn typically understood as freely chosen rather than socially or historically determined' and 'modern individuals tend to see themselves as self-made'.[9] Patterson understands this as the disavowal of (diachronic) history and notions of society that take on a truly political dimension when they are set against the political backdrop of Ronald Reagan's America and Margaret Thatcher's Britain. He even quotes Thatcher's 'there is no such thing as society; only individuals exist' and traces similar sentiments being expressed by, of all people, Miss World 1985, to underline just how pervasive the individualist ideology had become in the mid-1980s. He goes on to argue that the prevalence of social determinism (Althusser, Foucault, etc.) in the modern academy is largely because of a reaction against this culture of rabid individualism running rampant in the hegemonic mainstream. Patterson foregrounds what he sees as the chief problem of the modern Western world:

> The 'improvisional self' of the modern American is revealed as 'radically empty', an emptiness that allows for its appropriation by a range of powerful determinants. Individuals isolated from the social whole replicate within the enclave of their personal experience the bureaucratic practices that dominate modern capitalism.
>
> . . .
>
> The very freedom that individualism takes as its central premise, the ability of individuals to separate themselves from the social totality in order to choose to change their lives, is being subverted by the ideology of individualism itself.[10]

Though this is a fairly standard Althusserian critique of capitalist culture, it frames Patterson's project politically, gives it a sense of purpose and, most importantly, gives him *a reason* to return to 'Chaucer's explorations of the dialectic between an inward sense of selfhood – subjectivity – and the claims of the historical world to perhaps find a different understanding of individuality.[11]

Patterson's criticism is thus built on an understanding of his own historical moment and the assumptions and ideals that underpin it – something he finds lacking in new historicism. He builds a bridge to the past by recognizing that 'the dilemmas we now face [in our present historical situation] are not a function of a wholly new phenomena'.[12] Patterson rejects the assumption that the struggle between subjectivity and deterministic social forces is something peculiar to capitalism or even, to the condition of modernity, rather, 'subjectivity is a human characteristic that has *always* been part of history'.[13] This, in part, summarizes the chief drive of Patterson's whole career: to demonstrate how this issue of subjectivity, the relationship between individual and social totality, was not 'invented' by the Renaissance but exists in Chaucer and before. Thus in *Chaucer and the Subject of History* his aims are twofold: first, to return to Chaucer to tackle the issue of individualism relevant to the present cultural problem; and second, to challenge the misconception of the medieval period – and of history in general – as being the archetypal 'Other' 'esoteric and obscure . . . alien . . . feudal, knightly, courtly, antiquated, old-fashioned, out-dated, quaint'[14] and to dismiss as arrogant the assumption that because we are concerned with subjectivity now that it did not exist before.

With all this theoretical work done, both Patterson and his fellow American medievalist Paul Strohm embark on their studies of Chaucer in a pragmatic, scholarly manner by maintaining the logic of cause and effect, moving in a straightforwardly diachronic history, clearly defining the terms of their present day dilemmas before locating Chaucer precisely in his cultural moment through meticulous archival work, looking at his tax records, his social rank, the circles he moved in, the jobs he held and how each of those things relates to the broader picture of medieval life.[15] Although this approach is undoubtedly materialist, with his commitment to humanism and his insistence on the practical consequences of real actions, Patterson's method might be described as a modern variant of American pragmatism in the tradition of William James, John Dewey, Richard Rorty, etc., but one that rejects old-fashioned positivist objectivism in favour of a model based on negotiation and dialogue (between past and present) achieved through the recognition of similarity where it exits and of difference, 'a kind of historicism that can range freely across the discursive field as a whole and is no longer blind to its own historicity'. The most important factor for Patterson is for the critic to remain politically engaged and this, he argues, in typically pragmatist fashion, 'can never be achieved by appeals to theory . . . but to *political* efficacy', which is achieved through critical practice 'since all forms of . . . criticism are evidently and by definition political, which form we choose to practice is an act with consequences'.[16] In many ways Patterson's work is remarkable and can be considered at least twenty years ahead of its time. He shows us a very useful and interesting way of utilizing concepts taken from new historicism and cultural materialism without inheriting many of their problems. Perhaps because he is a Chaucerian scholar and not a Shakespearean, there have been few to follow Patterson. I think there are a great many PhD theses that could be pursued along the lines that he draws.

Another major evaluation and appropriation of new historicism has come from a scholar of the Romantic period, Alan Liu. Liu remains committed to the idea of a properly historicist criticism but is frustrated by its current manifestation in new historicism, a manifestation he finds one-dimensional, rigidly formalist and yet undisciplined and under-theorized. In 'The Power of Formalism: The New Historicism' (1989), he argues that the centrality of the monarch in new historicist Renaissance studies is invariably replaced by the centrality of the bourgeoisie in studies of the eighteenth century, a change precipitated by the conception of 'a shift in power from aristocratic and monarchical rule to the middle classes and the rule of the individualistic self'.[17] But this replacement of one mode of power by another enacts no change at all; rather it replicates the structural relationship between individuals and the hegemonic power that consumes and subordinates them and, at the level of critical practice, merely replicates the new historicist fascination with nodes of power. To combat this, Liu turns to Mikhail Bakhtin's notion of the carnivalesque, which he understands as:

> a universe of authority exactly congruent with that of theatricality – but with the opposite emphasis. Rather than stress

the dominance of a ruling or central perspective, it watches as perspective itself dips and waves, gets drunk, gets lost in a plural recession of funhouse mirrors.[18]

Bakhtin's carnival inverses the totalizing power modality of Foucault through the momentum of and impetus to the disruptive rather than the unified. Liu revels in the Gramscian conflict over hegemony, the discontinuities and discontents bubbling under the surface that come to the fore in this carnival play. He sets up a dialectic between what he calls 'the Disturbed Army', described in his characteristically flamboyant manner as 'the grid that dissolves into the moiré pattern, the asylum that erupts in Bedlam, the Mardi-gras parade that jazzes up the pedestrian rhythm of everyday life' and 'the Governing Line', which is defined as 'the self-centred axial gaze of Foucault's Benthamite Inspector'.[19] This grandiose formulation amounts to an essentially dualistic vision of possibilities within historicism, but Liu argues that new historicism is too focused on the 'Governing Line' and ignores the 'Disturbed Army'. Similar to Patterson's earlier critique, Liu says that this intense focus on power is the symptom of a self-confirming hypothesis:

> The new historicist interpreter is . . . a subject looking into the past for some other subject able to define what he himself, or she herself, is; but all the search shows in its uncanny historical mirror is the same subject he/she already knows: a simulacrum of the poststructuralist self insecure in its identity . . . This is why new historicist books and essays, despite their splendid diversity of material, 'feel' so much the same.[20]

For Liu then, new historicism is itself invested with ideological presuppositions, and thus fails to achieve Foucault's 'archaeological' objectivity and, ironically, to account for the differences that might exist between cultural moments.

This is where Liu's essay comes into its own. Like Patterson's earlier critique, Liu spots the synchronic tendency in new historicist work in which all of culture is a text, frozen in a static moment, begging the question of whether 'any *action* is conceivable at all?'. Liu posits a relocation of emphasis from 'expressive action to action *qua* action – as action' by which he means, *real* 'lived' action such as kicking a football or punching somebody in the face. For Liu this is 'an alternate ground of explanation definitive of what we mean by identities and their coercive representations'. Liu's world, like Patterson's, is one of action – we are judged in history by what we do and the consequences those actions have. Liu takes a critical practice that is 'under the sway of Althusser' and, rather than seeking to remove its structuralist presuppositions, he calls for a renewed definition of new historicism and for a refinement of its theory and method. He criticizes new historicism for being unsystematic and messy, a 'wonder-cabinet of ill-sorted methods . . . the most seriously underthought critical, pedagogical, and institutional concept in the modern academy'.[21] Liu approaches the crux of his critique:

> At best, the new historicism is either pseudo-Foucauldian in 'feel' or, when it alludes to its methodological base at all, merely points without reflection or overall perspective to select extrapolations of the structural development of formalism – e.g. anthropology or Althusser.[22]

This is a key insight by Liu. He is perhaps the first to recognize the artificial commingling of contradictory ideas: the unhappy union of the Hegelian dialectic and Althusser (whose project as we saw in Chapter 3 was anti-Hegelian); the insistence on deconstructionist indeterminacy married to an entirely synchronic methodology; and, finally, the contradiction of drawing on Bakhtin's carnivalesque (e.g. in the work of John Bender[23]) while maintaining the principles of Foucauldian Panopticism. But this is not the argument Liu makes here, it is only implied in what he says. What Liu places emphasis on instead is the idea that new historicism has failed to move beyond its formalist roots:

> The *exact* forms of formalism the new historicism claims to have left behind ('ambiguity', 'paradox', 'contradiction', 'irony' and so forth) drift from their organisation in literary study to figure the operations of history.[24]

In other words, new historicists take a Derridean *post*-structuralist stance with regard to linguistics and the indeterminacy of meaning in language, yet fail to recognize that their concept of history is itself rooted, indeed, founded upon structuralist notions and the problems that such notions surely encounter. Much as in the analysis I put forward in Chapter 4, new historicism is itself then a type of formalism, but one that lacks an adequately analytical rhetoric or a 'full-scale theory'.[25]

Liu blames the lack of these things on what he describes as an 'embarrassment of the post-modern intellect' caught up in endless Derridean relativism.[26] He characterizes the relationship between past and present in current new historicist theory as symptomatic of this 'post-modern intellect' and its tendency to see itself manifested in all places:

> The subversion of the present, after all, can only truly be mapped over that of the past if the *relation* between subversive and dominant elements in the present is like that of the past.[27]

These fretful postmodern critics search for an answer to their present crisis and find hope (or rather the illusion of hope) in the Renaissance period. Hence, for Liu, new historicism is one of a long series of instances where intellectuals have sought to ratify an active role for themselves in society by making the Renaissance a simulacrum of contemporary society – 'it is our latest Romanticization of the Renaissance'. The only answer for Liu is a full-scale reworking of new historicist theory that must start with 'a new historicist study of new historicism', in which there is greater introspection and an acknowledgement of the movement's own place in its historical moment. New historicism needs to 'overcome the embarrassment of its own implication in history . . . [it needs] to build the awareness of post-modernity into our criticism as *method* rather than as . . . narcissistic, in disciplinary nostalgia for subversion'. Liu calls for a 'renewed rhetoric . . . a philosophy of allegory' with which to tackle literary texts from this moment on.[28] Liu's take on new historicism, with its insistence on a systematized 'full-scale theory', a unified critical method and its distrust of purely synchronic analysis is hence diametrically opposed to that of Stephen Greenblatt who, as noted in Chapter 4, has argued many times against any type of unification or systemization in new historicist theory and who remains committed to a 'cultural poetics'.

Liu's call has, to my knowledge, never been answered. In fact, since his essay, written in 1989, the tendency has been the opposite: for new historicism and cultural materialism to become *more* disparate in the range of the topics and texts they appropriate. One interesting development has been the emergence of a more globalized view of Shakespeare and the Renaissance, especially in a new recognition of the extent of cultural exchanges between the West and the East in the Renaissance. The work of Lisa Jardine and of Nabil Matar has done much to overturn the perception of the Renaissance as a phenomenon specific to developments in the West.[29] It has demonstrated, as Gerald MacLean describes, 'just how many of the artistic, social, religious, philosophical, scientific, technical and cultural developments that distinguished the period depended upon the movement and exchange of ideas, skills and goods between East and West.' The dominant method at work in most of this work is that of cultural materialism, following the 'gold, silver, silk, porcelain, sugar, tea, coffee, currants, oil, wine, honey, pepper, leather, carpets, horses, opium' and textile trades up the Silk Road from Asia.[30] In one study in *Global Interests* (2000), for example, Lisa Jardine and Jerry Brotton trace the movement and exchange of art objects between the powers of Renaissance Europe and the Ottoman and Persian empires. This study leads to surprising moments of cultural overlap, including the changing representations and conceptions of St George 'negotiated between Byzantium and Italy' that remained largely unrecognized in studies of Spenser's *Fairie Queene* until now, and some fascinating insights into the cross-breeding of horses between Western and Eastern powers and the undeniable impact such knowledge must have had on subsequent understandings of what the horse symbolizes.[31] Daniel Vitkus has turned postcolonial theory on its head by recognizing in 'Turning the Turk in *Othello*' (1997) that 'what has often been forgotten is that while Spanish, Portuguese, English, and Dutch ships sailed to the New World and beyond . . . the Turks were rapidly colonizing European territory'.[32] This recognition leads to Vitkus' central argument that:

> Shakespeare's *Othello* draws on early modern anxieties about Ottoman aggression and links them to a larger network of moral, sexual and religious uncertainty which touched English Protestants directly. In part, the idea of conversion that terrified and titillated Shakespeare's audience was a fear of the loss of both essence and identity in a world of ontological, ecclesiastical, and political instability.[33]

When read on this level of political understanding, the text of *Othello* is transformed. In this reading it is Islamic and Ottoman imperialism that is feared rather than *Othello's* racial 'Otherness' as a black man. *Othello's* suicide thus comes to represent the metaphorical killing of 'the Turk he has become', an ugly stereotype of Christian Europe's fear of Islam.[34] Ania Loomba has built on this idea in 'Delicious Traffick' (2000), charting the development of the 'biological understanding of race . . . the concept of purity of blood' that prefigures much of modern racism and Fascism as ideas that did not exist in Medieval Europe.[35] She argues that they were born when the Spanish expelled the Jews and the Moors in 1492, and so, for Loomba, *Othello* becomes an English portrait of Spanish racism suggesting 'an affinity between Othello the Moor and the English, an affinity that was evoked by several writers as Elizabethan England tried to establish trade with Barbary'. Loomba argues that the complicity of race and culture has been historically 'produced by colonial relations'. Furthermore, she contends that the *conflation* of race and religion (i.e. the idea that someone is innately Jewish, Christian or Islamic so that true conversion is impossible) came from Christian Protestant anxieties about the authentication of identity because, for perhaps the first time, faith and nationhood had become destabilized due to the dawning age of individualism, self-fashioning and 'the fluidity of the self'.[36]

The majority of this work also has a political dimension, especially in the climate of growing Islamophobia in the post-9/11 global climate and the subsequent 'War on Terror' in which they produced most of this work. It might be characterized as an European and Eastern effort to counteract what Jerry Brotton has described as 'an ever-more narrow parochialism', in Shakespeare studies, especially that of Greenblatt and the new historicists, that 'offer us a fascinating but ultimately provincial Shakespeare with little acknowledgement of the wider world around him'. If you cast your mind back to Chapter 3, this is, in effect, another version of Vincent P. Pecora's criticism of Geertz's of 'local knowledge'. Brotton argues that most of the work produced by American new historicism and postcolonialism has tended to orientate Renaissance Europe towards the emergent American New World and that our understanding of Renaissance texts must be complicated by an increased awareness of 'North African, eastern Mediterranean, Persian and Islamic contexts' which have 'a complex and ambivalent effect upon Shakespeare's plays'.[37] So while the Bush administration insisted on an 'axis of evil' and Mahmoud Ahmadinejad renewed Islamic fervour in the Gulf about 'the Great Satan' of the United States of America, a cultural divide most people have felt in some form living in the twenty-first century, these critics feel the urgent need to bridge that cultural divide by emphasizing our shared past and the fact that the histories of Eastern and Western powers are inextricably linked.

Running parallel to these developments, the work of Patricia Parker has gone in a different direction, positing that recent new historicist and cultural materialist studies have tended to ignore the lively wordplay in Shakespeare's texts. For Parker, 'wordplay [can] make possible glimpses into the relation between the plays and their contemporary culture'. Parker advocates a return to 'a more historically grounded study of language and culture, one that takes seriously the "matter" of language as part of the "material Shakespeare"'.[38] Parker's focus, amazingly, unlike any of the critics we have encountered thus far, is very much on language. However, this is not a return to an older type of formalism but a materialist approach to language centred on the individual *signifier* and its epistemological development. Rather than describing the interrelations of words in poetic devices, its status *as poetry* in a synchronic structure, Parker's investigation is diachronic in the fashion of pre-Saussurean linguistics. Her focus is, almost exclusively, on the word's capacity to *connote* rather than its poetic function or its potential aesthetical effects.

Following many other members of 'The Alliance', Parker's other major concern is with the issues of feminism and of homoeroticism and her turn from the synchronic mode can be attributed to her warning about the dangers of importing 'binaries and boundaries that do not fit the complexities of early modern gendering or erotic wordplay'. The Saussurean linguist's preoccupation with binaries hence imports artificial categories into texts – texts that Parker would argue necessarily resist such glib polarization. Parker's political aim is to move criticism 'away . . . from assumptions about the erotic that reflect modern preoccupations rather than early modern ones'. She contends that the 'reduction' of wordplay 'to the ornamental was itself a historical process' connected with and allied to 'the relegation of women and other marginal subjects to the status of secondary or accessory'. She then makes a Foucauldian move by arguing that words, in their very usage, 'function in relation to a larger field of discourse – in this period, in ways that involve not only language but institutions, practices, and laws. . . . Discourse is inseparable from the social and political'. So, for Parker, the *word* becomes a discursive unit with which to unlock a wider discursive field; and this is the dominant technique of *Shakespeare from the Margins* (1996). Parker takes specific 'terms or networks of terms' as lenses through which to examine the larger cultural issues at stake in Shakespeare's plays and, of course, to understand the culture that produced those plays. It is interesting to note here, that while Parker abandons synchrony in her analysis of the linguistic in literary texts, her approach to *culture* is itself, ironically, entirely synchronic, because it presupposes the inextricable relatedness of all discourses within the structural whole of culture – cultural poetics in its fully realized state.[39]

This intertextualized view of the cultural landscape would appear to plot her position as being close to that of the new historicists. But Parker herself speaks of her work as being 'closer to the assumptions of cultural materialism . . . than the subversion-containment model of a now largely abandoned form of new historicism'. In light of this self-identification, it is not surprising that Parker finds scope for subversion in wordplay: 'Subversion in the period of the plays could operate at the verbal as well as the visual level, transmitted sotto voce in a wordplay that could be taken several ways at once.' So in the hermeneutic indeterminacy of the signifier in which wordplay must anchor itself Parker finds an ideological or discursive 'faultline'. Every utterance is linked to a network of cultural assumptions, every word has an ideological charge. Parker's task is to expose 'the mechanics of its joints and seams' by taking 'key words' and reconstructing the invisible bridges that connect these various discursive networks, in short, to reconstitute 'the lateral working of verbal networks'. And this is the formula she reproduces time and time again in her book. She approaches the Shakespeare canon through 'preposterous', 'rude mechanicals', 'construe', 'increase' and 'dilation', each time masterfully recovering the hidden meanings of each term and outlining their various (potentially subversive) usages in Renaissance culture through careful diachronic investigations into language allied to synchronic linkages between the discursive fields of Shakespeare's texts and their contexts. Parker's is a strange mix of critical techniques – one part diachronic epistemology, one part 'cultural poetics', and one part feminist – but, though formulaic, it is effective in its avoidance of what she identifies as the tendency of some recent critics to 'repeat the gestures of an older historicism' (that of Tillyard) in their seeming inability to account for hermeneutic indeterminacy. Parker recognizes the problem of historicism anchoring texts to specific readings, enacting a form of hermeneutic tyranny, and her close attention to the signifying possibilities of specific words provides one way to historicize without surrendering the polysemy of literary texts.[40]

The penultimate position that I am going to consider here is that of Catherine Belsey, who has spent much of her career as a cultural materialist. However, her *Culture and the Real* (2005) signals a theoretical departure from mainstream cultural materialism that warrants further investigation. As we have seen, 'the real' constitutes an important category for Greenblatt and the new historicism. It is the place that anecdotes can allude to; for Patterson and Liu 'the real' is important too, because it is the place in which genuine action takes place; and for cultural materialists *en masse*, 'the real' represents the 'real them' living in the world working at universities, teaching 'real' students and so on. Belsey's central problem is that in these current conceptions of reality, 'epistemology subsumes or occludes ontology'. Nothing is really 'real' until it is articulated as such. Belsey returns to the psychoanalyst Jacques Lacan who is probably the foremost influence on Althusser after Marx and Lenin, and a thinker whose work anticipates Judith Butler, Julia Kristeva and new historicism's 'cultural poetics'. Belsey ratifies the Lacanian distinction between 'reality', that is, *what is known by culture*, and 'the real' which simply exists 'undefined, unaccountable', inaccessible to the human subject who is caught in the web of language, a web that blankets all things and from which there is no escape.[41] Belsey rejects Slavoj Žižek's postmodern adaptation of Lacan's 'real' as an absence, on the grounds that it is a reaffirmation of the very constructivist idealism from which she is trying to disengage:

> By identifying the real with the void [Žižek] reaffirms, contrary to Lacan, the idealist view that determination is exercised not by a world but only by our idea of it, conscious or unconscious.[42]

There would appear to be little difference between Žižek's position and Greenblatt's in that both insist, in the final analysis, on
the supremacy of the subject's reconstruction of 'the real' in language and/or culture-as-text. The trauma of Žižek's absent real is
transformed by the articulation of that trauma, just as Greenblatt's
Renaissance is transformed by his descriptions of its 'real world,
real body, real pain'.

Instead, Belsey turns, time and time again, to Lacan's own
definition: 'the real is what does not depend on my idea of it'.[43]
It is inaccessible to the human subject yet it still *exists*, unlike
Žižek's 'real' which does not. Against this idea she posits, 'culture'
which 'consists of a society's entire range of signifying practices'.[44]
Belsey's concern is essentially a humanist one, though she would
not admit it:

> If subjectivity is an effect of culture, of the inscription of culture
> in signifying practice, there is no place for human beings outside
> culture. Culture, therefore, *is* all we know, in that sense we are
> always in culture – always in the game.
>
> . . .
>
> Knowledge exists at the level of the symbol, and there is no
> way of knowing that any specific set of symbols map the world
> accurately.[45]

This is Belsey struggling with what she perceives as culturalism's
'thorough-going constructionism' that is 'ultimately reductionist'
in its failure to account for a genuine 'real', but unable to abandon her own anti-humanism and apparently unable or unwill-
ing to see that it is a theoretical straitjacket. This echoes Liu's
complaint about a whole generation of critics writing with postmodern embarrassment about the very fact of their own existence. Belsey finds a solution in applying Lacan's principles of 'the
real' and his idea of sublimation, that 'promises pleasure on the
level of the signifier', to Jean-Francois Lyotard's aesthetic model
of the postmodern. Here the sublime offers an avenue through
which to approach 'the real' as an allusion 'at the level of the symbolic to the inaccessible Thing', which in turn offers the viewer
pleasure from the signifier itself. What Belsey argues is that this
moment where culture apprehends the unknowable 'real' in the

form of sublimation offers a way in which we can understand culture 'without reducing it to something else: ethical instruction, ideological control, or scripted determinism'.[46] Belsey offers a highly theorized and still anti-humanist answer to Althusserian or Foucauldian determinism by putting human pleasure and/ or desire, rather than models of domination, at the centre of culture.

It is important to pause at this juncture to define the new historicist and cultural materialist concept of 'the real'. Let us first consider the cultural materialist position on reality, because it is not enough to say that they would be content with only 'the real them' working in universities. Their position is slightly more complicated than that, insomuch as, implicitly, they hold to the Althusserian–Marxist distinction between the materialist 'real' or 'real conditions' and the ideological 'illusion' or 'allusion'. Physical matter (e.g. a building, a person's body) exists *as matter* independent of its existence in ideology, but its relations are *always-already* represented by that ideology so that while there is no *outside* of ideology for the individual subject (given that any material relation he or she can have will already be represented in this way), such a space must exist as it is central to what the ideology is representing. This is in fact another form of the Lacanian 'real', which is residual in Althusser's theory and more or less gone by the time we get to Foucault's model of power-knowledge. As I said in Chapter 3, this argument depends on the famous Althusserian proviso in that the material existence of ideology is 'rooted in the last instance in "physical" matter'.[47] New historicists, on the other hand, maintain the more post-structuralist Foucauldian view of culture as one inescapable text in which the infinite chain of differences by which all things are defined ensures that there is no position independent of that chain. What is important to note here is that an Althusserian criticism allows for the category of a genuine 'real' *outside* ideology, whereas Foucauldian criticism does not allow a real outside of power-knowledge. I must underline this: for Althusser there is an outside of the structural system, for Foucault there is not. In Althusser, however, this 'outside' is an unknowable X to which the individual, being always already interpellated by ideology, can never gain access – what Fredric Jameson calls 'a replay of the Kantian unknowability of the thing itself'.[48] This indefinable, unknowable X, the 'real' of Belsey's study, is a central tenet of structuralist thought, as Jameson goes on to explain:

> Althusser with his sense of history . . . [and others Jameson lists including Claude Levi-Strauss and Roland Barthes] *do* tend to presuppose, beyond the sign-system itself [beyond language, beyond ideology], some kind of ultimate reality which, unknowable or not, serves as its most distant object of reference.[49]

It is only with Derrida's so-called post-structuralist move – a move Foucault takes but Althusser does not – that *all of Being*, metaphysical, ontological, inexplicable and imagined, is assimilated into the structure of differences, a structure which posits no limits and which has *no outside* (even 'Nothingness' itself is defined against 'Being' as being 'not-Being', etc.; see Chapter 2). For Greenblatt and the other new historicists who insist on a 'cultural poetics' that presupposes that there is no end of possible contexts for a particular text, there can be said to be no reality *outside* of culture, even if these critics *themselves* speak unproblematically of 'the real'.

Before drawing this chapter to a close, it is worth considering briefly the work of Jerome J. McGann, a contemporary of Alan Liu's in editing and in criticism of the Romantic and Modernist periods whose name is associated with a movement called 'the new bibliography', a style of editing texts in a way that attempts to recreate their original context. Whereas new historicism took its point of departure broadly from Foucault and where cultural materialism took its departure from Raymond Williams, McGann's work followed that of Althusser's student Pierre Macherey. Macherey saw the importance of defining a 'text' which:

> is not a tissue of illusions which has to be merely unravelled if we wish to understand its power. An illusion that has been *set to work* becomes more than just an illusion, more than mere deception. It is an illusion *interrupted*, *realized*, completely transformed.[50]

Here we find Macherey writing wholly within the framework of Althusserian materialism. The text is 'transformed' into something more than 'illusion' and by doing so becomes part of the discourse of material 'reality', for, in Marxist terms, what is not illusion is necessarily real. To phrase this less abstractly: the 'illusions' of a text, in that they *allude* to reality', exist in the same way that an individual might 'exist' in a school as a teacher; nobody would argue that a schoolteacher's status in ideology *as* a-teacher-in-a-school is illusory because the illusion is 'set to work', it functions in and affects ideology. In much the same way, a text functions in and affects ideology and therefore its illusions can lay claim to an ideological existence. Furthermore, because (in Althusser) 'ideology has a material existence',[51] this ideological existence constitutes a material reality. However, despite their material existence, as Macherey goes on to say, 'the components fused in the literary text can have no independent reality'[52] from their social contexts. So what we have in effect is a material reality that *only exists* within a particular framework, a reality that is dependent on another reality. From this idea, Macherey develops a complex form of ideology critique. It is also from this idea that McGann begins to develop an idea of the literary text *as social production*.

For McGann, like Macherey, 'literary works are produced *with reference to* the mediational structures [e.g. commercial publishing houses, the "academy", the church, law courts], [which] are in fact embodied in such structures'. Where McGann departs from Macherey is in his claim that 'criticism is obliged to explain and reconstitute such structures in relation to the literary work'.[53] For McGann, 'poetry is best understood within the nexus of its many interesting histories . . . within . . . [which] we may glimpse, if we try, an indeterminate flux of conflicted and competing possibilities'[54]. In order to get to this 'glimpse' 'we' must consider 'the price of a book, its place of publication, even its physical form and the institutional structures by which it is distributed and received' because these 'all bear upon the production of literary meaning, and hence all must be crucially analysed and explained'.[55] Upon such an analysis 'we shall find that poetry possesses ideological investments, and that within its fictional space it . . . delivers – sometimes forthrightly, sometimes in ciphered terms – opinions, ideas, even *propositions*'.[56] The historical contexts of texts, bursting as they are with ideology, contain many 'unexamined tensions and conflicts'.[57] It is up to 'those guardians of our dry bones, the editors, bibliographers, and philologists'[58] to uncover these contexts and bring those dry bones of old texts 'to life'. McGann's statements needed to be put forcefully as he saw himself, with Greenblatt, leading the attack against institutionalized formalism, in a climate where 'the idea that poems operate as autonomous and inter-textual systems [remained] generally in force'.[59]

However, what truly distinguishes McGann from many of the other members of 'The Alliance' is his close attention to the early bibliographical development of any text. He makes this case in *The Beauty of Inflections* (1988):

> The more we pursue the poem's early bibliographical history, the more sharply do we experience the fragility of such a work, and the special human character of the circumstances it defines and perpetuates.[60]

McGann is very much concerned with the specific set of circumstances that lead to a specific text being produced. For example, a particular poem might be circulated among the poet's friends before the poet commits himself to a final draft and sends that draft to the printer who makes amendments to the spelling, punctuation and grammar and perhaps adds a front cover and contents page before the work goes to press. The text can no longer be seen as the product of a single author but must now be seen as a social product. Shakespeare, for example, often worked in collaboration. In fact, since he wrote for the theatre his plays were constantly passing between actors. Can we say for sure if the words on the page were not affected by the original actors who played them? For example, we can see in a turn in Shakespeare's treatment of clowns when the star clown, Will Kempe, left the Lord Chamberlain's Men and Robert Amin took his place. All of a sudden, the country bumpkin clowns we get during Kempe's time (e.g. Bottom in *A Midsummer Night's Dream*, Dogberry in *Much Ado About Nothing*) are replaced by sardonic professional court jesters (e.g. Feste in *Twelfth Night*, Lear's clown in *King Lear*). For McGann, this realization that texts are social has profound implications on the interpretation of any text. So while Lisa Jardine and Jerry Brotton, for example, consider the contexts of global relations that might surround a text, McGann's focus is on the much narrower and more immediate context of a text's genesis bound to a specific time in a specific space.

It is also worth noting that this is not an apolitical theory but one that has a sound political investment in changing the future through the present's reconstruction of the past:

> All poems and cultural products are included in history – *including* the producers and the reproducers of such works, the poet and their readers and interpreters . . . To the historicist imagination, history is the past, or perhaps the past as seen in and through the present; and the historical task is to attempt a reconstruction of the past, including, perhaps, the present of that past. But the *Cantos* reminds us that history includes the future, and that the historical task involves as well the construction of what shall be possible.[61]

This model is distinct from that of the cultural materialists, who tend to posit a specific problem in the present with which they find an affinity in the past (to work towards a future solution). McGann finds his solution, not through history, but in the text. This solution comes from realizing the full potential of something like Pound's *Cantos*, which is a poem that 'does not permit a distanced reading'. The heterological nature of poetry – the fact that it is at once, paradoxically, finite yet infinite, complete yet incomplete, fixed in form but flexible in connotation, reflecting the known and imagining the unknown – is thus able to anticipate the future in a way that history (not having these properties) cannot. This crucially distinguishes McGann from many of the critics we have looked at because, though it maintains the pivotal importance of historical context to any reading, his practice would also insist on the importance of *the text* itself and this goes some way into bringing the text back to the centre of his criticism: 'when we read [poetry] we construct our histories, including our futures'.[62]

It is now time to return to the original list of axes that Lee Patterson outlined in 1990 and add to them some further axes based on some of the positions that have come out of the field survey. To Patterson's original three we can add the following:

4   Those critics who incorporate a diachronic understanding of aspects of culture (e.g. language or race) (Patterson, Parker, Loomba) versus those who rely on a purely synchronic

approach to history and culture (most new historicists and cultural materialists).

5 Those who insist on a reality outside culture, whether it exists in the sphere of 'action' or is unknowable (Patterson, Liu, Belsey, McGann, most cultural materialists) versus those for whom culture subsumes reality (new historicists).

6 Those who consider wider, global contexts, beyond national borders (Matar, Jardine, Brotton, Loomba, postcolonial theory in general) versus those who focus on more localized contexts, with the State representing the limit of their scope (almost all other cultural historicists, especially McGann whose theory of social production insists on specific local contexts).

7 Those who advocate a systematic, fully theorized historicism (Liu, Montrose, cultural materialists) versus those who seek to maintain the loose heterogeneity of historicist practice (Patterson, Greenblatt, Gallagher).

These four axes added to Patterson's three can thus be said to represent the entire spectrum of new historicist and cultural materialist thought to date. However, it should be noted that each axis does not represent only a binary choice between two extreme positions (which it does account for) but a *gradient* line which affords more moderate positions. For example, if we take axis (6) it is clear that Jardine and Brotton are at one extreme and McGann and, let us say, the proto-new historicist Stephen Orgel (who has rarely left Renaissance England, even in recent publications[63]) are at the other. But someone like Catherine Gallagher,[64] partly through virtue of her subject matter, does encompass a fairly wide geographic context, wider than Orgel's, but not as globe-spanning as Brotton's. So it is clear that the range of variable positions available in new historicism and cultural materialism is vast, though certain formations tend to be more popular than others and certain combinations of positions on the various axes fit together more easily than others.

Key questions for students

- Do you think that Lee Patterson is right to insist on a diachronic understanding of history?
- Alan Liu thinks that new historicism is too messy and needs something approaching a list of rules that state its methods clearly. Do you agree?
- What is your assessment of the work being done by Daniel Vitkus, Ania Loomba, Jerry Brotton and others that attempts to trace the undeniable influence of Eastern thought on early modern England and, by extension, Shakespeare's plays?
- Do you think Patricia Parker's fusion of the formalist concern for language with historicist methods is viable?
- What do you think of Catherine Belsey's attempt to find an antidote to Althusser and Foucault by turning to the psychoanalysis of Jacques Lacan?
- Jerome McGann insists on the social production of a given text, citing even the process by which a book comes to press, do you agree with him that texts are inextricably social in this way rather than the work of an individual author? Is the book you are reading right now the work of just one person – that is me – or is it in fact the product of a *social* process?

Selected further reading

Belsey, Catherine, *Culture and the Real* (New York and Oxford: Routledge, 2005).

Jardine, Lisa, *Worldly Goods: A New History of the Renaissance* (London: Macmillan, 1996).

Jardine, Lisa and Jerry Brotton, *Global Interests: Renaissance Art between East and West* (London: Reaktion Books, 2000).

Lacan, Jacques, 'The Mirror Stage as Formative of the Function of the I as revealed in Psychoanalytic Experience', in *Écrits: A Selection*, trans. Alan Sheridan (London: Tavistock, 1977), pp. 1–7.

Liu, Alan, 'The Power of Formalism: The New Historicism', *ELH*, 56(4) (Winter 1989), 721–71.

Loomba, Ania, '"Delicious Traffick": Racial and Religious Difference on Early Modern Stages', in *Shakespeare and Race*, ed. Catherine Alexander and Stanley Wells (Cambridge: Cambridge University Press, 2000), pp. 203–24.

Macherey, Pierre, *A Theory of Literary Production*, trans. Geoffrey Wall (London: Routledge and Kegan Paul, 1978).

MacLean, Gerald, 'Introduction: Re-Orienting the Renaissance', in *Re-Orienting the Renaissance: Cultural Exchanges with the East*, ed. Gerald MacLean (Basingstoke: Palgrave Macmillan, 2005), pp. 1–28.

Matar, Nabil, *Turks, Moors, and Englishmen in the Age of Discovery* (New York: Columbia University Press, 1999).

McGann, Jerome J., 'Introduction: A Reference Point', in *Historical Studies and Literary Criticism* ed. Jerome J. McGann (Madison, WI and London: University of Wisconsin Press, 1985), pp. 3–19.

—, *The Beauty of Inflections: Literary Investigations in Historical Method and Theory*, rev. edn (Oxford: Clarendon Press, 1988).

—, *Social Values and Poetic Arts* (Cambridge, MA: Harvard University Press, 1988).

—, *Towards a Literature of Knowledge* (Oxford: Oxford University Press, 1989).

Parker, Patricia, *Shakespeare from the Margins: Language, Culture, Context* (Chicago, IL and London: University of Chicago Press, 1996).

Patterson, Lee, *Negotiating the Past: The Historical Understanding of Medieval Literature* (Madison, WI: University of Wisconsin Press, 1987).

—, 'Introduction: Critical Historicism and Medieval Studies', in *Literary Practice and Social Change in Britain, 1380–1530*, ed. Lee Patterson (Berkeley and Los Angeles: University of California Press, 1990), pp. 1–14.

—, *Chaucer and the Subject of History* (Madison, WI: University of Wisconsin Press, 1991).

Vitkus, Daniel, 'Turning Turk in *Othello*: the Conversion and Damnation of the Moor', *Shakespeare Quarterly*, 48 (1997), 145–76.

Notes

1 Lee Patterson, 'Introduction: Critical Historicism and Medieval Studies', in *Literary Practice and Social Change in Britain, 1380–1530*, ed. Lee Patterson (Berkeley and Los Angeles: University of California Press, 1990), p. 9.

2 Lee Patterson, *Negotiating the Past: The Historical Understanding of Medieval Literature* (Madison, WI: University of Wisconsin Press, 1987), p. 62.

3 Ibid., pp. 62, 64, 66.

4 Ibid., p. 64.

5 Theodor Adorno, 'Subject and Object', in *The Essential Frankfurt School Reader*, ed. Andrew Arato and Eike Gebhardt (New York: Urizen Books, 1978), p. 506.

6 Patterson, *Negotiating the Past*, p. 71.

7 Antonio Gramsci, *Selections from the Prison Notebooks*, ed. Quintin Hoare and Geoffrey Nowell Smith, trans. Quintin Hoare and Geoffrey Nowell Smith (London: Lawrence and Wishart, 1973), p. 401.

8 Patterson, *Negotiating the Past*, pp. 69, 71.

9 Lee Patterson, *Chaucer and the Subject of History* (Madison, WI: University of Wisconsin Press, 1991), pp. 1, 4.

10 Ibid., pp. 5–6.

11 Ibid., p. 11.

12 Ibid., p. 12.

13 Ibid., emphasis mine.

14 Patterson, 'Introduction: Critical Historicism and Medieval Studies', p. 2.

15 See Paul Strohm, *Social Chaucer* (London and Cambridge, MA: Harvard University Press, 1989).

16 Patterson, 'Introduction: Critical Historicism and Medieval Studies', pp. 8, 10, 14.

17 Alan Liu, 'The Power of Formalism: The New Historicism', *ELH*, 56(4) (Winter 1989), 727.

18 Ibid., p. 729.

19 Ibid., p. 730.

20 Ibid., p. 733.

21 Ibid., pp. 734, 735, 736.

22 Ibid., p. 743.

23 John Bender, *Imagining the Penitentiary: Fiction and the Architecture of Mind in Eighteenth-Century England* (Chicago and London: University of Chicago Press, 1987).

24 Liu, 'The Power of Formalism', p. 743.

25 Ibid., p. 754.

26 Ibid., p. 747.

27 Ibid., p. 750.

28 Ibid., pp. 253–4, 752, 755.

29 See, for example, Lisa Jardine, *Worldly Goods: A New History of the Renaissance* (London: Macmillan, 1996) and Nabil Matar,

Turks, Moors, and Englishmen in the Age of Discovery (New York: Columbia University Press, 1999).

30 Gerald MacLean, 'Introduction: Re-Orienting the Renaissance', in *Re-Orienting the Renaissance: Cultural Exchanges with the East*, ed. Gerald Maclean (Basingstoke: Palgrave Macmillan, 2005), pp. 1, 12.

31 Lisa Jardine and Jerry Brotton, *Global Interests: Renaissance Art between East and West* (London: Reaktion Books, 2000), pp. 22, 132–85.

32 Daniel Vitkus, 'Turning Turk in *Othello*: the Conversion and Damnation of the Moor', *Shakespeare Quarterly*, 48 (1997), 146.

33 Ibid.

34 Ibid., p. 176.

35 Ania Loomba, ' "Delicious Traffick": Racial and Religious Difference on Early Modern Stages', in *Shakespeare and Race*, ed. Catherine Alexander and Stanley Wells (Cambridge: Cambridge University Press, 2000), p. 207.

36 Ibid., pp. 209, 206, 212.

37 Jerry Brotton, 'Shakespeare and Islam', paper presented at Global Perspectives on Shakespeare, British Council Video-conference, London, Cairo, Karachi, Tunis, 4 December 2006.

38 Patricia Parker, *Shakespeare from The Margins: Language, Culture, Context* (Chicago and London: University of Chicago Press, 1996), p. 1.

39 Ibid., pp. 2, 3, 9.

40 Ibid., pp. 11, 13, 17–18, 20, 55, 83, 119, 185, 229.

41 Catherine Belsey, *Culture and the Real* (New York and Oxford: Routledge, 2005), pp. 4, 5.

42 Ibid., p. 56.

43 Originally quoted in Bruce Fink, *The Lacanian Subject: Between Language and Jouissance* (Princeton, NJ: Princeton University Press, 1995), p. 142; quoted in Catherine Belsey, *Culture and the Real* (New York and Oxford: Routledge, 2005), pp. 4, 49, 56.

44 Catherine Belsey, *Culture and the Real* (New York and Oxford: Routledge, 2005), p. 9.

45 Ibid., pp. 9–10.

46 Ibid., pp. 9–10, 146, 155.

47 Althusser, *Lenin and Philosophy*, p. 113. For Althusser's fuller explanation of the relationship between ideology and 'reality' see pp. 109–15.

48 Fredric Jameson, *The Prison-house of Language* (Princeton, NJ and Chichester: Princeton University Press, 1972), p. 109.

49 Ibid., pp. 109–10.

50 Pierre Macherey, *A Theory of Literary Production*, trans. Geoffrey Wall (London: Routledge and Kegan Paul, 1978), p. 62.

51 Althusser, 'Ideology and the Ideological State Apparatus', p. 112.

52 Macherey, *A Theory of Literary Production*, p. 56.

53 Jerome J. McGann, 'Introduction: A Reference Point', in *Historical Studies and Literary Criticism*, ed. Jerome J. McGann (Madison, WI and London: University of Wisconsin Press, 1985), p. 5.

54 Jerome J. McGann, *Social Values and Poetic Arts* (Cambridge, MA: Harvard University Press, 1988), p. 246.

55 McGann, 'Introduction: A Reference Point', p. 4.

56 Jerome J. McGann, *Towards a Literature of Knowledge* (Oxford: Oxford University Press, 1989), p. 8.

57 Jerome J. McGann, *The Beauty of Inflections: Literary Investigations in Historical Method and Theory*, rev. edn (Oxford: Clarendon Press, 1988), p. 17.

58 Ibid., p. 91.

59 McGann, *Towards a Literature of Knowledge*, p. 51.

60 McGann, *The Beauty of Inflections*, p. 101.

61 Jerome J. McGann, 'The Third World of Criticism', in *Rethinking Historicism*, ed. Marjorie Levinson, Marilyn Butler, Jerome J. McGann and Paul Hamilton (New York and Oxford: Basil Blackwell, 1989), p. 105.

62 Ibid., pp. 105, 106.

63 Stephen Orgel, *The Authentic Shakespeare and Other Problems of the Early Modern Stage* (New York and London: Routledge, 2002), which, other than some brief comments on Italian theatre (pp. 53–6), locates Shakespeare and many other Renaissance playwrights squarely as dramatists living in London, subject to state censorship and a multitude of other concerns during the late sixteenth and early seventeenth centuries.

64 See for example her discussion of Aphra Behn's *Oroonoko* in Catherine Gallagher, *Nobody's Story: The Vanishing Acts of Women Writers in the Marketplace 1670–1820* (Oxford: Clarendon Press, 1994), pp. 47–87.

CHAPTER SEVEN

Conclusion

Despite all of the divergent positions we have seen from new historicists and cultural materialists in the last three chapters, they all have one thing in common: a firm commitment to anti-humanism, the belief that there is no such thing as human nature and that individuals are wholly the product of their time and place. This is the orthodox position in most if not all literature departments, and – as I mentioned in Chapter 1 – to challenge it is still considered to be highly controversial, both philosophically and politically. To some feminists, the notion that certain behaviours may be innate either to men or women is offensive. To others, arguments that take 'human nature' as their basis wander into the dangerous territory of eugenics that has been long-tainted by their association with Adolf Hitler and fascism in 1930s. To assert that there is an essential human nature common to all cultures is tantamount to heresy: it is considered deeply conservative, patriarchal, imperialist – a return to the bad old days of E. M. W. Tillyard and company.

In a way, it is easy to see why this might be the case. When we historicize the original new historicists and cultural materialists and consider the worlds in which they lived in the late 1970s and early 1980s, society in Britain and America was very different from the one we know today. Sexism, racism and homophobia went to the very heart and the very top of the social hierarchy, and elitism in the academy was rife. Something needed to change. And the anti-humanist way of seeing individuals as products of their time and place gave academics – and women, and black people, and homosexuals – a powerful weapon with which to expose and attack the status quo. Let there be no doubt that in the 1980s new historicism and cultural materialism *needed* to happen. The period was marked by the ribald individualism and free-market economics of Margaret Thatcher in the United Kingdom and Ronald Reagan in the United States of America. There was a strong ideology of the individual, in the triumph of self-belief and self-interest over society, which as Thatcher once said famously, does not even exist. These governments on the one hand preached self-interest, liberty and hard work, and on the other rapidly closed down mines and factories while privatizing national institutions and putting thousands of people in the public sector out of work. It is not difficult to see how the likes of Jonathan Dollimore and Alan Sinfield would have recognized and been seduced by much of what Louis Althusser and Michel Foucault were talking about.

The problem we face today, over a decade into the twenty-first century, is – if I may be frank – that Althusser and Foucault and the anti-humanists who followed them were wrong to suggest that there is no such thing as human nature, or at any rate that human beings are *wholly* the products of their time and place. In *The Blank Slate* (2002), the cognitive scientist Steven Pinker presents compelling evidence that it is difficult to ignore. He argues that although human beings are conditioned by their cultural surroundings, they are also the products of what they inherit biologically and genetically.[1] Among many other studies, including most significantly Richard Dawkins's *The Selfish Gene*, Pinker draws on the work of the anthropologist Donald E. Brown, who claims to have found hundreds of human universals observable in all known cultures.[2] Things like the idea of conflict and narrative, the classification of colours, body parts, making a distinction between the sexes, emotions such as envy and fear, the division of labour, proper names, language, logic and planning. If you cast your mind back to Chapter 3, recall when Clifford Geertz abstracted the concept of emotion from victory or defeat from the Balinese cockfight and then I did almost exactly the same thing with my imaginary English town. For both Brown and Pinker, the fact that both cultures have the same concept is evidence that it is in some way innate to what makes us human. I will leave you to read Pinker for yourself, but for me it is almost impossible to look at the evidence he presents and then continue acting as if anti-humanist theory were Gospel. At the *very* least, the anti-humanist has to accept that genetics and hormones play a part in what makes us who we are – even if this part is ultimately subordinate to culture.

One cultural materialist, Catherine Belsey, has even made a step towards doing so.[3]

One of the key differences between Pinker and almost all anti-humanist thinkers is in the fact that he is a scientist who is concerned only with studying the evidence. In philosophical terms, we can say he advances his argument *a posteriori*. He observes what there is and then draws conclusions based on what we can see to confirm or deny his hypothesis – the basis of the scientific method. In contrast, most of the thinkers we looked at in Chapter 3 – Althusser and Foucault in particular – advance their theories *a priori*. That is, they come up with their theory – to use the common stereotype, sitting in an armchair in their office – and then apply that theory to the world. There is no need for empirical evidence because we are dealing with a field of pure reason, pure theory. In my view, the question 'is there such a thing as an essential human nature?' is a scientific one with a definite answer. And it is not a question like 'is there a God' that can be answered by nothing short of a miracle, it is a question that *can* be answered. Why? Because there are over six billion people in the world all of whom can be observed, all of whom might provide empirical evidence. Therefore, if plenty of intelligent biologists, psychologists and evolutionary theorists have made such observations and drawn the conclusion that, yes, in fact we are not blank slates but have some aspects to our nature that appear to be intrinsic, then how can I *de facto* reject that claim? To me it seems unreasonably arrogant to reject the ideas that Pinker puts forward in favour of whatever Althusser or Foucault or perhaps Judith Butler happened to come up with in their armchairs in the 1970s, just because it may be inconvenient to one's political beliefs. In fact, it seems absurd and yet something approaching this remains the orthodox position in so many faculties.

In recent years, however, certain critics have ventured to challenge this orthodoxy. Some of these such as Joseph Carroll, Brian Boyd, Marcus Nordlund, William Flesch and Jonathan Gottschall draw directly from the work on evolution I describe and make similar (and much more detailed) versions of the argument I make above.[4] They also go a step further in seeking to understand the evolutionary roots of literature and in this arguably veer from criticism into the territory of anthropology and / or behavioural psychology. Others, such as Andy Mousley, Robin Headlam-Wells and A. D. Nuttall, are tapping into an older humanist perspective.[5] This work signals a renewed focus on individuals: both on Shakespeare as an author with creative intelligence and on the individuals in his plays. You might say that that we are seeing 'the return of the author', and something approaching a return to A. C. Bradley's interest in character. The key insight of this work – captured beautifully and poetically in an image by Nuttall – is that 'the root is not the flower', a twenty-first century re-articulation of Wilbur Sanders' view of Shakespeare's as 'a mind which could read Holinshed and think otherwise'.[6] My own book, *Shakespeare's History Plays* (2012), is also a step in this direction.

My feeling is that this is a step we need to take in Shakespeare studies if we are to continue producing interesting work. What was new and exciting about new historicism and cultural materialism in the 1980s was that critics were suddenly free to talk about politics and cultural issues, things that really matter to themselves and to their students. However, their enthrallment to anti-humanist theory has had some unfortunate consequences: their Shakespeare, much like Tillyard's, is a rather dull individual (if one can call him an individual at all) whose plays are mundane reiterations of the prevailing ideologies of early modern England. At best, almost despite themselves, they expose contradictions between those ideologies; at worst, they are conservative and insidious attempts to reinforce the status quo. The characters who populate these plays are not 'people', but literary constructs whose entire purpose is to expose or confirm and reinforce these ideologies. If nothing else, this strikes me as a particularly boring way to read the plays. Shakespeare gives us wonderful and complex characters and puts them in interesting and complicated situations in which they must make decisions and act. To ignore all of that because of some abstract notion that individuals are cultural products seems to me to ignore the very reason that Shakespeare continues to be read, performed and studied today.

Some of the lessons that new historicism and cultural materialism have taught us cannot be unlearned: of course, historical context is important and we should be aware of dominant ideologies and the official Tudor doctrines; of course, we should consider exactly what sorts of political positions to which Shakespeare was likely to have been exposed; of course, we should think twice about anachronistically importing modern concepts into plays written in the 1590s and early 1600s; and so on. But at the same time, I think there are other lessons with which we can dispense or at least modify: namely the insistence on anti-humanism. I see this as a kind of theoretical straitjacket that, as Annabel Patterson said as far back as 1989, 'seriously inhibit[s] our capacity to talk sensibly about literature'.[7] To an extent Althusser and Foucault were right – yes, we are conditioned by ideology, yes we are constantly caught up in matrices of power relations – but we are also more than just ideology and power. Shakespeare and his plays were and are more than just ideology and power and he had some interesting things to say about those things himself. In fact, he and his characters have interesting things to say about a great many things. What a shame then to reduce them to a set of readymade positions known to any writer who lived in England under Elizabeth I and James I. Is this how we treat the writers of our own time? How would a new historicist or cultural materialist go about interviewing Salman Rushdie or Paul Auster? They both wrote novels in the 'episteme' known as the 1980s, so can we assume that they were writing with a set of readymade positions available to any writer who lived under Ronald Reagan and Margaret Thatcher? Can we assume that ideas found in Rushdie would be commonplace ideas with which Auster would be *au fait*? Or do the 1980s work under a different set of rules from the 1590s? If so, why? How? It seems to me that new historicists and cultural materialists do not afford Shakespeare – one of the greatest writers ever to have lived – the same sort of respect as an individual that writers who are still living enjoy. Maybe now is the right time to start affording him that respect.

Notes

1 Steven Pinker, *The Blank Slate: The Modern Denial of Human Behaviour* (New York and London: Penguin, 2002).

2 Richard Dawkins, *The Selfish Gene*, 2nd edn (Oxford: Oxford University Press, 1989); Donald E. Brown, *Human Universals* (New York: McGraw-Hill, 1991).

3 See Catherine Belsey, 'The Role of Culture', in *Human Nature: Fact and Fiction*, ed. Robin Headlam Wells and Johnjoe Mcfadden (London: Continuum, 2006), pp. 111–27.

4 See Joseph Carroll, *Evolution and Literary Theory* (Columbia, MO: University of Missouri Press, 1995); Joseph Carroll, *Literary Darwinism: Evolution, Human Nature, and Literature* (New York and London: Routledge, 2004); Marcus Nordlund, *Shakespeare and the Nature of Love: Literature, Culture, Evolution* (Evanston, IL: Northwestern University Press, 2007); William Flesch, *Comeuppance: Costly Signalling, Altruistic Punishment, and Other Biological Components of Fiction* (Cambridge, MA and London: Harvard University Press, 2007); Jonathan Gottschall and David Sloan Wilson (eds), *The Literary Animal: Evolution and the Nature of Narrative* (Evanston, IL: Northwestern University Press, 2005); Brian Boyd, *On the Origin of Stories: Evolution, Cognition, and Fiction* (Cambridge, MA and London: Harvard University Press, 2009); Brian Boyd, Joseph Carroll and Jonathan Gottschall (eds), *Evolution, Literature, and Film: A Reader* (New York: Columbia University Press, 2010); Joseph Carroll, *Reading Human Nature: Literary Darwinism in Theory and Practice* (Albany, NY: State University Press of New York, 2011).

5 Robin Headlam-Wells, *Shakespeare's Humanism* (Cambridge: Cambridge University Press, 2005); Andy Mousley, *Re-Humanising Shakespeare: Literary Humanism, Wisdom and Modernity* (Edinburgh: Edinburgh University Press, 2007); A. D. Nuttall, *Shakespeare the Thinker* (New Haven, CT: Yale University Press, 2007).

6 Nuttall, *Shakespeare the Thinker*, p. 11; Wilbur Sanders, *The Dramatist and the Received Idea: Studies in the Plays of Marlowe and Shakespeare* (Cambridge: Cambridge University Press, 1968), p. 74.

7 Annabel Patterson, *Shakespeare and the Popular Voice* (Oxford: Basil Blackwell, 1989), p. 5.

GLOSSARY OF CRITICAL TERMS

Anti-humanism the belief that human beings have no essential nature or innate characteristics and that individuals are little more than cultural products of their time and place.

Base in Marxist theory, the base or 'economic base' (also sometimes called 'infrastructure') is the material basis on which society is built. This is made up of what Karl Marx calls the 'forces of production' – physical tools and machinery used to make things, and the human labour that operates them – and 'relations of production' by which he means the way society is structured by socioeconomic relations, for example, property rights, or the relationship between a factory owner and its workers. The base determines the *conditions* under which the superstructure (see below), which is all the other parts of society (culture, politics, institutions, religion and so on) operates. For Louis Althusser, even though the superstructure appears to be the key determinant in governing human behaviour, he maintains that the economic base is the ultimate cause 'in the last instance'.

Containment an important concept for Stephen Greenblatt and other new historicists. Those with power in a given culture are able to contain subversive or dissident sentiments by briefly giving them voice – allowing a rebellion, for example – only ultimately to maintain order. For example, in a Shakespeare play, we may glimpse moments of genuine subversion, but by the end of the play it has been silenced and its possibility foreclosed by the restoration of order. Although this is a common argument when discussing Shakespeare's comedies, its most famous application is found in Greenblatt's essay on *The Henriad*, 'Invisible Bullets', found in *Shakespearean Negotiations* (1988).

Culture by some critics used interchangeably with 'ideology', by others instead of it, this refers to a society's whole way of life at a particular place and time that governs and determines the behaviour of the individuals who are a part of it.

Diachronic the progressive view of history across time. A diachronic understanding, for example, of a motor car would start by looking at horse-drawn carriages and the first steam-powered engines of the 1670s and move forwards until the modern automobile.

Discourse Michel Foucault's preferred unit of analysis when looking at a given cultural moment (or 'episteme'). Sometimes described as 'language in action', it is any written or verbal statement that pertains to what he calls 'the order of things' (see below). New historicists borrow this term in their analyses of Shakespeare's plays.

Discursive fields for both Michel Foucault and the new historicists, all of the discourse surrounding a given institution. For example, Shakespeare's plays are part of the discursive field of the theatre scene in London during the 1590s and early 1600s.

Dissidence any sentiment that challenges the status quo of the dominant ideology or culture. For cultural materialists this is often a desirable outcome, whether within the confines of Shakespeare's plays or in our own time.

Dominant culture Raymond Williams' phrase for the codes, ideas and values of the ruling class at any given moment. For example, in a capitalist society, the dominant culture is that of the bourgeoisie. Many critics use the phrase 'dominant ideology' or even 'dominant group' instead (see also hegemony). Cultural materialists, especially Alan Sinfield, make extensive use of this concept.

Emergent culture Raymond Williams' phrase for a set of dissident ideas that are in the process of developing with the ultimate aim of supplanting and replacing the dominant culture. For example, in a capitalist society the idea of a socialist society would be 'emergent'. Cultural materialists, especially Alan Sinfield, make extensive use of this concept.

Episteme Michel Foucault's phrase for a particular time and place in history with a particular way of seeing the world, and a set of discourses and practices. For example, we might say that Shakespeare belonged to the episteme of the Renaissance which had very different ideas from both our own time and those found medieval period. In a sense, each episteme has its own 'order of things' (see below).

Epistemelogical break for both Louis Althusser and his followers and Michel Foucault, this refers to a sudden shift from one episteme to another. In Althusser's terms it is the move from one set of ideologies to another – for example, when a country undergoes a revolution. For Foucault, similarly, it is the moment when one 'order of things' is supplanted by another. This view of history is disjunctive and explicitly against any bourgeois theory of 'progress': it is a series of sudden shifts between moments that are largely unconnected. Both new historicists and cultural materialists tend to view history in this way.

Formalism the name given to any approach to literature that focuses primarily on its formal, structural and linguistic features. In the United States of America, New Criticism was the dominant formalist approach from the 1930s to the 1960s, and during the same timeframe in the United Kingdom, formalism manifested itself in the 'practical criticism' of the Cambridge school. Structuralism and post-structuralism are both also considered to be formalist approaches.

Hegemony Antonio Gramsci's term for the predominance of one social class over another by means of subtle coercion. The 'dominant culture' is said to have hegemony over all of the other groups in society. However, it only maintains this position through struggle with the groups it subordinated and must work constantly to keep them subordinated.

Ideological state apparatuses (ISAs) for Louis Althusser, any institution, including schools, families, churches, government buildings and so on that disseminates ideology. These are the primary instruments of ideology through which individuals are 'interpellated' (see below).

Ideology for both Louis Althusser and the cultural materialists, this is the representation of the imagined relations between people and their material surroundings. It is the method through which the ruling class is able to reproduce the 'means of production', or in plainer terms, why people choose to perform their social roles in life without rebelling. Ideology works insidiously by making choices that legitimate the status quo appear to the individual as being the natural order of things, 'common sense'. It also functions by making individuals 'work by themselves' by presenting circumstances that are in fact wholly determined appear as desirable and freely chosen.

Intellectuals Antonio Gramsci's phrase for the key decision-makers in any society or organization. For example, in a factory, the 'intellectuals' would be the board of directors faced with making the key strategic decisions at the highest level. Note, his use of this word is entirely *functional*; he does not mean 'intellectual' in the sense of a clever person or philosopher.

Interpellation Louis Althusser's term for the process by which individuals submit themselves willingly and unquestioningly to the dominant ideology. After this process has taken place an individual becomes an 'ideological subject'.

Langue Ferdinand de Saussure's term for the entirely self-referential system of a given language. The nature of its entirety is necessary for its functioning and governs any single instance of it (see 'parole' below).

Local knowledge Clifford Geertz's method of understanding cultures exclusively in the context of their own particular time and place. For example, truly 'local knowledge' of Shakespeare plays would focus only understanding them in the context of the London theatre of the 1590s and early 1600s.

Narratology the formalist study of narrative and plot.

The 'order of things' this is Michel Foucault's phrase for the prevailing logic of a given cultural moment (or 'episteme'). It is made up of many discursive fields.

Overdetermination Louis Althusser's appropriation of Sigmund Freud's phrase, which refers to the concentration of all of the ideological contradictions in a given society, which can either, in exceptional circumstances, be 'fused' together into a juggernaut in which case a possible revolution (or 'epistemic break') may occur, or more usually, be displaced and neutralized into inertia by the dominant ideology. In both cases the contradictions are said to be 'overdetermined'.

Panopticism derived from Jeremy Bentham's panopticon prison design, this is Michel Foucault's term for the idea of total visibility and constant surveillance which leads individuals to regulate their own behaviour. In Bentham's prison, the prisoners must assume they are being watched at any given time and conform to the rules of the prison. But for Foucault, this phenomenon is present everywhere in modern life.

Parole Ferdinand de Saussure's term for any single instance of *la langue* – any given utterance. An instance of parole can only be understood in relation to *la langue*.

Post-structuralism a difficult and diffuse term to define in a single paragraph, in this book I have generally understood it specifically as the destabilization of binaries to which structuralist thinkers remained in thrall. In structuralism a text has definite limits – an 'inside' and 'outside'; in post-structuralism there is no 'outside' of the text insomuch as there is no 'outside' of culture and both the text and the culture to which it belongs are said to be endlessly intertextual. One example is to contrast the relatively straightforward relationship between a word and the concept (signifier and signified meaning) in Ferdinand de Saussure's structuralist system of language and Jacques Derrida's more complicated view of that relationship as being fundamentally unstable and endlessly deferred. Another example is to contrast Louis Althusser's structuralist insistence of maintaining the binary terms of base and superstructure with Michel Foucault's post-structuralist move of collapsing them onto a single plane. Be aware that other sources may define this term differently, but my understanding is that post-structuralism is almost always in the business of destabilizing binaries that are assumed by structuralists to be fundamental.

Power relations for Michel Foucault all individuals are held in a complex set of power relations with various other individuals and groups. There is no escape from these relations just as there is no 'outside' of power.

Power-knowledge Michel Foucault's idea that there is no knowledge without power and no power without knowledge. Since discourse is also essentially 'made' of knowledge, there is no discourse without power.

Repressive state apparatus (RSAs) for Louis Althusser, when the state is forced into action physically to apprehend or subdue its subjects; for example, if there is civil disorder and the local authorities have to call in the riot police to subdue protesters through the use of violence.

Residual culture Raymond Williams's phrase for a set of ideas that come from the past that still play a role in the current makeup of society. For example, in a capitalist society the role played by organized religion might be said to be 'residual'. Cultural materialists, especially Alan Sinfield, make extensive use of this concept.

Sign/signifier for Ferdinand de Saussure and the many structuralists who developed his ideas, the sign or signifier is a code that has an implied meaning in a symbolic system, in Saussure's case, a word in a language. For Saussure, the signifier is arbitrary and can only be understood in terms of its difference from all of the other signifiers in the system: we only recognize and understand the word 'dog' because it is not 'cat', 'book', 'glass' or any other word.

Structuralism a type of formalism that concerns itself with uncovering the rules of how particular systems function synchronically.

Subversion whereas dissidence is any instance of basic disobedience, this is when the dominant ideology is actively and successfully undermined. This is the ultimate goal of cultural materialist activity.

Superstructure all of the parts of society that do not form part of the economic base: culture, politics, ideology and so on. Although according to orthodox Marxism the base is supposed to be the primary social determinant, in Louis Althusser's work, the superstructure – in particular ideology – is actually doing much of the work.

Synchronic the functioning view of history across space. A synchronic understanding, for example, of a motor car would explain how all the parts of its engine work.

Thick description Clifford Geertz's method of attempting to understand a different culture, as much as possible, from its own point of view. Imagine an alien trying to recognize and understand an impish schoolboy's wink as a signal that he may be about to play a prank on someone rather than as a twitch of the eye. It is easy to see how new historicists borrowed this idea and applied it to the study of Shakespeare's plays: it is the attempt to understand them as his contemporary audiences would have.

BIBLIOGRAPHY

Adelman, Janet, Margaret J. Arnold, Linda Bamber and Catherine Belsey, 'Feminist Criticism', *PMLA*, 104(1) (January 1989), 77–9.

Adorno, Theodor, 'Subject and Object' (1969), in *The Essential Frankfurt School Reader*, ed. Andrew Arato and Eike Gebhardt (New York: Urizen Books, 1978), pp. 497–511.

Althusser, Louis, *Machiavelli and Us*, ed. François Matheron, trans. Gregory Elliott (New York and London: Verso, 2000).

—, 'A Letter on Art in Reply to André Daspre' (1966), in *Lenin and Philosophy and Other Essays*, ed. Fredric Jameson, trans. Ben Brewster (1971; rpr. New York: Monthly Review Press, 2001), pp. 151–5.

—, 'Cremonini, Painter of the Abstract', in *Lenin and Philosophy and Other Essays*, ed. Fredric Jameson (New York: Monthly Review Press, 2001), pp. 85–126.

—, 'Ideology and the Ideological State Apparatus' (1969), in *Lenin and Philosophy and Other Essays*, ed. Fredric Jameson, trans. Ben Brewster (1971; rpr. New York: Monthly Review Press, 2001), pp. 85–126.

—, *For Marx*, trans. Ben Brewster (1969; New York and London: Verso, 2005).

Althusser, Louis and Etienne Balibar, *Reading Capital*, trans. Ben Brewster (London: New Left Books, 1986).

Armstrong, Isobel, *The Radical Aesthetic* (Oxford: Blackwell, 2000).

Asher, Kenneth, *T.S. Eliot and Ideology* (Cambridge: Cambridge University Press, 1998).

Assiter, Alison, *Althusser and Feminism* (London: Pluto Press, 1990).

Athos, Lisa, *In Carcere con Gramsci* (Milan: Terracini, 1973).

Atkins, G. D. and D. M. Bergeron (eds), *Shakespeare and Deconstruction* (New York: Peter Lang, 1988).

Barber, C. L., *Shakespeare's Festive Comedy: A Study of Dramatic Form and Its Relation to Social Custom* (Princeton, NJ: Princeton University Press, 2012).

Barthes, Roland, 'Style and Its Image', in *Literary Style: A Symposium*, ed. Seymour Chatman and Samuel R. Levin (Oxford: Oxford University Press, 1971), pp. 3–15.

—, *Mythologies*, trans. Annette Lavers (London: Paladin, 1973).

—, *S/Z*, trans. Richard Miller (London: Jonathan Cape, 1975).

—, *Essais Critique* (Paris: Seuil, 1977).

—, *Image-Music-Text*, trans. Stephen Heath (New York: Hill and Wang, 1978).

Belsey, Catherine, *Critical Practice* (New York and London: Methuen, 1980).

—, *The Subject of Tragedy: Identity and Difference in Renaissance Drama* (London: Methuen, 1985).

—, 'Richard Levin and Indifferent Reading', *New Literary History*, 21(3) (Spring 1990), 449–56.

—, *Desire: Love Stories in Western Culture* (Oxford: Blackwell, 1994).

—, *Shakespeare and the Loss of Eden* (London: Macmillan, 1999).

—, *Culture and the Real* (New York and Oxford: Routledge, 2005).

—, 'The Role of Culture', in *Human Nature: Fact and Fiction*, ed. Robin Headlam Wells and Johnjoe McFadden (London: Continuum, 2006), pp. 111–27.

Bender, John, *Imagining the Penitentiary: Fiction and the Architecture of Mind in Eighteenth-Century England* (Chicago and London: University of Chicago Press, 1987).

Bonheim, Helmut, 'Shakespeare's Narremes', in *Shakespeare Survey 53: Shakespeare and Narrative*, ed. Peter Holland (Cambridge: Cambridge University Press, 2000), pp. 1–38.

Boyd, Brian, *On the Origin of Stories: Evolution, Cognition, and Fiction* (Cambridge, MA and London: Harvard University Press, 2009).

Boyd, Brian, Joseph Carroll and Jonathan Gottschall (eds), *Evolution, Literature, and Film: A Reader* (New York: Columbia University Press, 2010).

Bradbury, Anne, 'Introduction', in *Shakespeare Criticism 1919–35*, ed. Anne Bradbury (London: Oxford University Press, 1936), pp. v–xi.

Bradley, A. C., *Shakespearean Tragedy: Lectures on Hamlet, Othello, King Lear, Macbeth*, 2nd edn (London: Macmillan, 1905).

Bradshaw, Graham, *Misrepresentations: Shakespeare and the Materialists* (Ithaca, NY and London: Cornell University Press, 1993).

—, 'State of Play', in *The Shakespearean International Yearbook, Vol. 1: Where Are We Now in Shakespearean Studies?* ed. W. R. Elton and John M. Mucciolo (Brookfield, VT and Aldershot: Ashgate, 1999), pp. 3–25.

Brannigan, John, *New Historicism and Cultural Materialism* (London: Palgrave Macmillan, 1998).

Brooks, Cleanth, 'The Formalist Critics' (1951), in *Literary Theory: An Anthology*, ed. Julie Rivkin and Michael Ryan (Oxford: Blackwell, 1998), pp. 52–7.

Brotton, Jerry, 'Shakespeare and Islam', paper given at Global Perspectives on Shakespeare, British Council Video-conference, London, Cairo, Karachi, Tunis, 4 December 2006.

Brown, Donald E., *Human Universals* (New York: McGraw-Hill, 1991).

Buci-Glucksmann, Christine, *Gramsci and the State*, trans. David Fernbach (Southampton: Lawrence and Wishart, 1980).

Butler, Judith, 'Performativity's Social Magic', in *Bourdieu: A Critical Reader*, ed. Richard Shusterman (Malden, MA and Oxford: Blackwell, 1999), pp. 113–28.

Callaghan, Dympna, *Shakespeare Without Women: Representing Gender and Race in the Renaissance* (New York and London: Routledge, 2000).

Camden, William, *Annales: the true and royall history of the famous empresse Elizabeth Queene of England France and Ireland &c. True faith's defendresse of diuine renowne and happy memory. Wherein all such memorable things as happened during hir blessed raigne . . . are exactly described* (London: Printed [by George Purslowe, Humphrey Lownes, and Miles Flesher] for Beniamin Fisher and are to be sould at the Talbott in Pater Noster Rowe, 1625).

Carroll, Joseph, *Evolution and Literary Theory* (Columbia, MO: University of Missouri Press, 1995).

—, *Literary Darwinism: Evolution, Human Nature, and Literature* (New York and London: Routledge, 2004).

—, *Reading Human Nature: Literary Darwinism in Theory and Practice* (Albany, NY: State University Press of New York, 2011).

CCCS, *On Ideology* (London: Hutchinson, 1978).

Clarke, Simon, Terry Lovell, Kevin McDonnel, Kevin Robins and Victor Jeleniewski Seidler, *One-Dimensional Marxism: Althusser and the Politics of Culture* (New York and London: Allison & Busby, 1980).

Clemen, Wolfgang, *The Development of Shakespeare's Imagery*, 2nd edn (Cambridge: Cambridge University Press, 1977).

Cohen, Stephen, 'Between Form and Culture', in *Renaissance Literature and Its Formal Engagements*, ed. Mark David Rasmussen (New York and Basingstoke: Palgrave, 2002), pp. 17–41.

Cohen, Stephen A. (ed.), *Shakespeare and Historical Formalism* (Aldershot: Ashgate, 2007).

Cohen, Walter, 'Political Criticism of Shakespeare', in *Shakespeare Reproduced: The Text in History and Ideology*, ed. Jean E. Howard and Marion F. O'Connor (New York and London: Methuen, 1987), pp. 18–46.

Cooke, Katherine, *A.C. Bradley and his Influence in Twentieth-Century Shakespeare Criticism* (Oxford: Clarendon Press, 1972).

Culler, Jonathan, *Structuralist Poetics* (Ithaca, NY: Cornell University Press, 1975).

—, *Barthes* (London: Fontana Press, 1983).

Cunningham, Valentine, *Reading After Theory* (Malden, MA and Oxford: Blackwell, 2002).

Curran, Kevin, *Marriage, Performance, and Politics at the Jacobean Court* (Burlington, VT and Farnham: Ashgate, 2009).

Dawkins, Richard, *The Selfish Gene*, 2nd edn (Oxford: Oxford University Press, 1989).

Deluze, Gilles, *Foucault*, trans. Seán Hand (London: Continuum, 1999).

Derrida, Jacques, *Of Grammatology*, trans. Gayatri Chakravorty Spivak (Baltimore, MD: John Hopkins University Press, 1976).

—, *Writing and Difference*, trans. Alan Bass (London: Routledge and Kegan Paul, 1978).

—, *Margins of Philosophy*, trans. Alan Bass (Hertfordshire: Harvester, 1982).

Dews, Peter, 'Althusser, Structuralism, and the French Epistemological Tradition', in *Althusser: A Critical Reader*, ed. Gregory Elliott (Cambridge, MA and Oxford: Blackwell, 1994), pp. 104–41.

DiTomaso, Nancy, '"Sociological Reductionism" from Parsons to Althusser: Linking Action and Structure in Social Theory', *American Sociological Review*, 47(1) (February 1982), 14–28.

Docherty, Thomas, *After Theory: Postmodernism/Postmarxism* (New York and London: Routledge, 1990).

Dollimore, Jonathan, *Radical Tragedy: Religion, Ideology and Power in the Drama of Shakespeare and His Contemporaries*, 2nd edn (Hemel Hempstead: Harvester Wheatsheaf, 1989).

—, 'Shakespeare, Cultural Materialism and the New Historicism', in *Political Shakespeare: Essays in Cultural Materialism*, ed. Jonathan Dollimore and Alan Sinfield, 2nd edn (1985; Manchester: Manchester University Press, 1994), pp. 2–17.

—, *Radical Tragedy: Religion, Ideology and Power in the Drama of Shakespeare and His Contemporaries*, 3rd edn (Basingstoke: Palgrave Macmillan, 2004).

Dollimore, Jonathan and Alan Sinfield, 'Culture and Textuality: Debating Cultural Historicism', *Textual Practice*, 4(1) (1990), 91–100.

—, 'History and Ideology, Masculinity and Miscegenation: The Instance of *Henry V*', in *Faultlines: Cultural Materialism and the Politics of Dissident Reading* (Oxford: Clarendon Press, 1992), pp. 109–42.

— (eds), *Political Shakespeare: Essays in Cultural Materialism*, 2nd edn (Manchester: Manchester University Press, 1994).

Dreyfus, Herbert L. and Paul Rainbow, *Michel Foucault: Beyond Structuralism and Hermeneutics* (Chicago: University of Chicago Press, 1983).

Dutton, Richard, 'Postscript', in *New Historicism and Renaissance Drama*, ed. Richard Wilson and Richard Dutton (New York and London: Longman, 1992), pp. 219–26.

Dutton, Richard and Richard Wilson (eds), *New Historicism and Renaissance Drama* (New York and London: Longman, 1992).

Eagleton, Terry, 'Eliot and a Common Culture', in *Eliot in Perspective* (London: Macmillan, 1970).

—, *Criticism and Ideology* (London: Verso, 1978).

—, *Literary Theory: An Introduction* (Oxford: Blackwell, 1996).

—, 'Body Work' (1993), in *The Eagleton Reader*, ed. Stephen Regan (Oxford: Blackwell, 1998), pp. 157–62.

—, *After Theory* (London: Allen Lane, 2003).

Egan, Gabriel, *Shakespeare and Marx* (New York and Oxford: Oxford University Press, 2004).

Eliot, T. S., *Notes Towards a Definition of Culture* (London: Faber and Faber, 1948).

—, 'Tradition and the Individual Talent', in *Selected Essays* (London: Faber and Faber, 1999), pp. 13–22.

Emig, Rainer, 'Literary Criticism and Psychoanalytical Positions', in *The Cambridge History of Literary Crticism Volume IX: Twentieth-Century Historicial, Philosophical and Psychological Perspectives*, ed. Christina Knellwolf and Christopher Norris (New York and Cambridge: Cambridge University Press, 2001), pp. 175–92.

Empson, William, *Seven Types of Ambiguity* (London: Chatto & Windas, 1930).

Erikson, Peter, 'Rewriting the Renaissance, Rewriting Ourselves', *Shakespeare Quarterly*, 38(3) (Autumn 1987), 327–37.

Evans, Malcolm, 'Deconstructing Shakespeare's Comedies', in *Alternative Shakespeares*, ed. John Drakakis (New York and London: Methuen, 1985), pp. 69–96.

Felperin, Howard, *The Uses of the Canon: Elizabethan Literature and Contemporary Theory* (Oxford: Clarendon Press, 1990).

Fernia, Joseph V., *Gramsci's Political Thought: Hegemony, Consciousness, and the Revolutionary Process* (Oxford: Clarendon Press, 1987).

Fernie, Ewan, 'Shakespeare and the Prospect of Presentism', in *Shakespeare Survey 58: Writing About Shakespeare*, ed. Peter Holland (New York and Cambridge: Cambridge University Press, 2005), pp. 169–84.

—, 'The Last Act: Presentism, Spirituality and the Politics of *Hamlet*', in *Spiritual Shakespeares*, ed. Ewan Fernie (New York and London: Routledge, 2005), pp. 186–209.

Fernie, Ewan and Clare McManus, 'Materiality', in *Reconceiving the Renaissance: A Critical Reader* (New York and Oxford: Oxford University Press, 2005), pp. 278–81.

Fink, Bruce, *The Lacanian Subject: Between Language and Jouissance* (Princeton, NJ: Princeton University Press, 1995).

Fiske, John, 'British Cultural Studies and Television', in *Channels of Discourse: Television and Contemporary Criticism*, ed. Robert C. Allen (London: Methuen & Co, 1987).

Flesch, William, *Comeuppance: Costly Signalling, Altruistic Punishment, and Other Biological Components of Fiction* (Cambridge, MA and London: Harvard University Press, 2007).

Foucault, Michel, *Discipline and Punish: The Birth of the Prison*, trans. Alan Sheridan (New York and London: Penguin Books, 1991).

—, *The History of Sexuality, Volume 1: The Will to Knowledge* (New York and London: Penguin, 1998).

—, *Archaeology of Knowledge and The Discourse on Language*, trans. Alan Sheridan (New York and London: Routledge, 2002).

—, *The Order of Things: An Archaeology of the Human Sciences*, trans. Alan Sheridan (New York and London: Routledge, 2002).

Freedman, Michael, *Ideology: A Very Short Introduction* (New York and Oxford: Oxford University Press, 2003).

French, A. L., *Shakespeare and the Critics* (Cambridge: Cambridge University Press, 1972).

Gallagher, Catherine, 'Marxism and the New Historicism', in *The New Historicism*, ed. H. Aram Veeser (New York and London: Routledge, 1989), pp. 37–45.

—, *Nobody's Story: The Vanishing Acts of Women Writers in the Marketplace 1670–1820* (Oxford: Clarendon Press, 1994).

—, 'Counterhistory and The Anecdote', in *Practicing New Historicism* (Chicago, IL and London: University of Chicago Press, 2000), pp. 49–74.

Gallagher, Catherine and Stephen Greenblatt, *Practicing New Historicism* (Chicago, IL and London: University of Chicago Press, 2000).

Gearhart, Suzanne, 'The Taming of Michel Foucault: New Historicism, Psychoanalysis, and the Subversion of Power', *New Literary History*, 28(3) (Summer 1997), 457–80.

Geertz, Clifford, *The Interpretation of Cultures: Sketched Essays* (New York: Basic Books, 1973).

—, *Local Knowledge: Further Essays in Interpretative Anthropology* (New York: Basic Books, 1983).

Genette, Gerard, *Figures 1* (Paris: Editions du Seuil, 1966).

Gerratana, Valentino, 'Althusser and Stalinism', *New Left Review*, 101–2 (January–April 1977), 110–24.

Goldberg, Jonathan, *James I and the Politics of Literature* (Baltimore, MD and London: Johns Hopkins University Press, 1983).

—, *Sodometries: Renaissance Texts, Modern Sexualities* (Stanford, CA: Stanford University Press, 1992).

—, 'Dover Cliff and the Condition of Representation', in *Shakespeare's Hand* (Minneapolis, MN: University of Minnesota Press, 2003), pp. 132–48.

Gottshall, Jonathan and David Sloan Wilson (eds), *The Literary Animal: Evolution and the Nature of Narrative* (Evanston, IL: Northwestern University Press, 2005).

Gramsci, Antonio, *Il Risorgimentio* (Turin: Einaudi, 1949).

—, *Selections from the Prison Notebooks*, ed. Quintin Hoare and Geoffrey Nowell Smith, trans. Quintin Hoare and Geoffrey Nowell Smith (London: Lawrence and Wishart, 1973).

Greenblatt, Stephen, *Renaissance Self-Fashioning: From More to Shakespeare* (Chicago and London: University of Chicago Press, 1980).

—, 'Introduction', in *The Power of Forms in the English Renaissance* ed. Stephen Greenblatt (Norman, OK: Pilgrim Books, 1982), pp. 3–6.

—, *Shakespearean Negotiations: The Circulation of Social Energy in Renaissance England* (Oxford: Clarendon Press, 1988).

—, *Learning to Curse: Essays in Early Modern Culture* (New York and London: Routledge, 1990).

—, 'The Touch of the Real', in *Practicing New Historicism*, ed. Catherine Gallagher and Stephen Greenblatt (Chicago and London: University of Chicago Press, 2000), pp. 20–48.

Greimas, Julien Algirdas, *Modern Language Notes* (Paris: Le Seuil, 1971).

Hamilton, Paul, *Historicism* (New York and London: Routledge, 1996).

Hardy, Barbara, *Shakespeare's Story Tellers: Dramatic Narration* (London: Peter Owen, 1997).

Harpham, Geoffrey, 'Foucault and the New Historicism', *American Literary History*, 3(2) (Summer 1991), 360–75.

Hawkes, David, *Ideology* (New York and London: Routledge, 1996).

Hawkes, Terence, *Shakespeare in the Present* (New York and London: Routledge, 2002).

Hawthorn, Jeremy, *Cunning Passages: New Historicism, Cultural Materialism and Marxism in the Contemporary Literary Debate* (London: Arnold, 1996).

Higgins, John, 'Raymond Williams and the Problem of Ideology', *Boundary*, 2(1) (Autumn 1982), 145–54.

Hiscock, Andrew and Lisa Hopkins, 'Introduction', in *Teaching Shakespeare and Early Modern Dramatists*, ed. Andrew Hisckcok and Lisa Hopkins (New York and Basingstoke: Palgrave Macmillan, 2007), p. 13.

Holderness, Graham, *Shakespeare's History* (New York: St Martin's Press, 1985).

—, 'Radical Potentiality and Institutional Closure: Shakespeare in Film and Television', in *Shakespeare on Television: An Anthology of Essays and Reviews*, ed. J. C. Bulman and H. R. Coursen (Hanover and London: University of New England Press, 1988), pp. 206–25.

—, *Shakespeare Recycled: The Making of Historical Drama* (Hemel Hempstead: Harvester Wheatsheaf, 1992).

—, *Shakespeare: The Histories* (London: Macmillan, 2000).

Holland, Peter (ed.), *Shakespeare Survey 53: Shakespeare and Narrative* (Cambridge: Cambridge University Press, 2000).

Holloway, John, *Narrative and Structure: Exploratory Essays* (Cambridge: Cambridge University Press, 1979).

Howard, Jean E., 'Old Wine, New Bottles', *Shakespeare Quarterly*, 35(2) (Summer 1984), 234–7.

—, 'The New Historicism in Renaissance Studies', *English Literary Renaissance*, 16 (Winter 1986), 13–43.

Howard, Jean E. and Marion F. O'Connor (eds), *Shakespeare Reproduced: The Text in History and Ideology* (London: Methuen, 1987).

Howard, Jean E. and Phyllis Rackin, *Engendering a Nation: A Feminist Account of Shakespeare's History Plays* (New York and London: Routledge, 1997).

Jackson, Leonard, *The Poverty of Structuralism* (New York and London: Longman, 1993).

Jakobson, Roman, 'Closing Statement: Linguistics and Poetics', in *Style in Language*, ed. Thomas A. Sebeok (Cambridge: Cambridge University Press, 1960), pp. 350–77.

Jakobson, Roman and L. G. Jones, 'Shakespeare's Verbal Art in "Th'expense of Spirit"', in *Language in Literature*, ed. Krystyna Pomorska and Stephen Rudy (Boston, MA: Harvard University Press, 1987), pp. 198–215.

Jameson, Fredric, *The Prison-house of Language* (Princeton, NJ and Chichester: Princeton University Press, 1972).

—, 'Marxism and Historicism', *New Literary History*, 11(1) (1979), 41–73.

—, *The Political Unconscious: Narrative as a Socially Symbolic Act* (Ithaca, NY: Cornell University Press, 1981).

Jardine, Lisa, *Worldly Goods: A New History of the Renaissance* (London: Macmillan, 1996).

Jardine, Lisa and Jerry Brotton, *Global Interests: Renaissance Art between East and West* (London: Reaktion Books, 2000).

Jones, Ernest, *Hamlet and Oedipus* (New York: Norton, 1949).

Joughin, John J. and Simon Malpas (eds), *The New Aestheticism* (New York and Manchester: Manchester University Press, 2003).

Jowett, John, William Montgomery, Gary Taylor and Stanley Wells (eds), *William Shakespeare: The Complete Works*, 2nd edn (New York and Oxford: Oxford University Press, 2005).

Judt, Tony, *Marxism and the French Left: Studies on Labour and Politics in France, 1830–1981* (New York and London: New York University Press, 2011).

Kamps, Ivo (ed.), *Shakespeare Left and Right* (New York and London: Routledge, 1991).

Kastan, David Scott, *Shakespeare After Theory* (New York and London: Routledge, 1999).

Kermode, Frank, *Shakespeare's Language* (Harmondsworth: Penguin, 2000).

Knight, G. Wilson, *The Wheel of Fire: Interpretations of Shakespearean Tragedy*, 4th edn (New York and London: Routledge, 2001).

—, *The Imperial Theme: Further Interpretations of Shakespeare's Tragedy* (New York and London: Routledge, 2002).

Knights, L. C., *Explorations: Essays in Criticism mainly on the literature of the seventeenth century* (London: Chatto & Windas, 1946).

Kojeckey, Roger, *T.S. Eliot's Social Criticism* (London: Faber and Faber, 1971).

Kott, Jan, *Shakespeare Our Contemporary*, 2nd edn (London: Routledge, 1991).

Lacan, Jacques, 'The Mirror Stage as Formative of the Function of the I as revealed in Psychoanalytic Experience', in *Écrits: a Selection*, trans. Alan Sheridan (London: Tavistock, 1977), pp. 1–7.

Laclau, Ernesto and Chantal Mouffe, *Hegemony and Socialist Strategy: Towards a Radical Democratic Politics*, 2nd edn (New York and London: Verso, 2001).

Lavers, Annette, 'Deconstruction', in *The Cambridge History of Literary Criticism Volume 8: From formalism to poststructuralism*, ed. Ramen Selden (Cambridge: Cambridge University Press, 1995), pp. 166–96.

LeBihan, Jill and Keith Green, *Critical Theory & Practice: A Coursebook* (New York and London: Routledge, 1996).

Leitch, Vincent B., *Cultural Criticism, Literary Theory, Poststructuralism* (New York: Columbia University Press, 1992).

Lentricchia, Frank, 'Foucault's Legacy: A New Historicism?', in *The New Historicism*, ed. H. Aram Veeser (New York and London: Routledge, 1989), pp. 231–42.

Levin, Richard, 'The Poetics and Politics of Bardicide', *PMLA*, 150(3) (May 1990), 491–504.

—, 'Unthinkable Thoughts in the New Historicizing of English Renaissance Drama', *New Literary History*, 21(3) (Spring 1990), 433–47.

—, 'The Cultural Materialist Attack on Artistic Unity, and the Problem of Ideological Criticism', in *Ideological Approaches to Shakespeare*, ed. R. P. Merrix and N. Ranson (Lewiston, NY: Edwin Mellen Press, 1992), pp. 39–56.

—, 'The Old and the New Materialising of Shakespeare', in *The Shakespearean International Yearbook, Vol. 1: Where Are We Now in Shakespearean Studies?* ed. W. R. Elton and John M. Mucciolo (Brookfield, VT and Aldershot: Ashgate, 1999), pp. 87–107.

—, 'Selective Quotations and Selective Marxisms: A Response to Alan Sinfield and David Siar', *Early Modern Culture, issue 2* (updated 2001) http://emc.eserver.org/1-2/levin.html, accessed 18 March 2007.

Lewis, William S., *Louis Althusser and the Traditions of French Marxism* (Oxford: Lexington Books, 2005).

Liu, Alan, 'The Power of Formalism: The New Historicism', *ELH*, 56(4) (Winter 1989), 721–71.

Loomba, Ania, '"Delicious Traffick": Racial and Religious Difference on Early Modern Stages', in *Shakespeare and Race*, ed. Catherine Alexander and Stanley Wells (Cambridge: Cambridge University Press, 2000), pp. 203–24.

Lyotard, Jean-François, *The Postmodern Explained to Children: Correspondence 1982–85*, trans. Julian Pefanis and Morgan Thomas (London: Turnaround, 1992).

Macherey, Pierre, *A Theory of Literary Production*, trans. Geoffrey Wall (London: Routledge and Kegan Paul, 1978).

—, 'Introduction', in *In a Materialist Way: Selected Essays*, ed. Warren Montag, trans. Ted Stolze (London: Verso, 1998), pp. 1–48.

Machiavelli, Niccolò, *The Historical, Political, and Diplomatic Writings of Niccolò Machiavelli, Volume 2*, trans. Christian E. Detmold (Boston: J. R. Osgood and Company, 1882).

—, *The Prince*, trans. Geoffrey Bull, 4th edn (New York and London: Penguin, 2003).

Mackail, J. W., *The Approach to Shakespeare* (Oxford: Clarendon Press, 1930).

MacLean, Gerald, 'Introduction: Re-Orienting the Renaissance', in *Re-Orienting the Renaissance: Cultural Exchanges with the East*, ed. Gerald MacLean (Basingstoke: Palgrave Macmillan, 2005), pp. 1–28.

Mahood, M. M., *Shakespeare's Wordplay* (London: Methuen, 1957).

Man, Paul De, *Blindness and Insight: Essays in the Rhetoric of Contemporary Criticism* (Oxford: Routledge, 1996).

Mannheim, Karl, *Ideology and Utopia* (London: Kegan Paul & Co, 1936).

Marx, Karl, 'The Eighteenth Brumaire of Louis Bonaparte' (1869), in *Karl Marx: Selected Writings*, ed. David McLellan (New York and Oxford: Oxford University Press, 1977), pp. 300–25.

—, *Capital*, ed. David McLennan (New York and Oxford: Oxford University Press, 1995).

Marx, Karl and Friedrich Engels, *The Communist Manifesto*, ed. Gareth Stedman Jones, trans. Samuel Moore (New York and London: Penguin, 2002).

—, *The German Ideology*, ed. C. J. Arthur (London: Lawrence and Wishart, 2004).

Matar, Nabil, *Turks, Moors, and Englishmen in the Age of Discovery* (New York: Columbia University Press, 1999).

Maus, Katherine Eisaman, 'Richard II', in *The Norton Shakespeare*, ed. Stephen Greenblatt, Walter Cohen, Jean E. Howard and Katharine Eisman Maus (New York and London: W.W. Norton and Co, 1997), pp. 943–51.

McDonald, Russ, 'Preface', in *Shakespeare: An Anthology of Criticism and Theory 1945–2000*, ed. Russ McDonald (Malden, MA and Oxford: Blackwell, 2004), pp. x–xiii.

McGann, Jerome J., 'Introduction: A Reference Point', in *Historical Studies and Literary Criticism* ed. Jerome J. McGann (Madison, WI and London: University of Wisconsin Press, 1985), pp. 3–19.

—, *Social Values and Poetic Arts* (Cambridge, MA: Harvard University Press, 1988).

—, *The Beauty of Inflections: Literary Investigations in Historical Method and Theory*, revised edn (Oxford: Clarendon Press, 1988).

—, 'The Third World of Criticism', in *Rethinking Historicism*, ed. Marjorie Levinson, Marilyn Butler, Jerome J. McGann and Paul Hamilton (New York and Oxford: Basil Blackwell, 1989).

—, *Towards a Literature of Knowledge* (Oxford: Oxford University Press, 1989).

Miller, J. Hillis, *Reading Narrative* (Noman, OK: University of Oklahoma Press, 1998).

Montag, Warren, '"The Soul is the Prison of the Body": Althusser and Foucault 1970–1975', *Yale French Studies*, 88 (1995), 53–77.

Montrose, Louis, '"Eliza, Queen of Shepheardes," and the Pastoral of Power', *English Literary Renaissance*, 10 (Spring 1980), 153–82.

—, '"Shaping Fantasies": Figurations of Gender and Power in Elizabethan Culture', *Representations*, 2 (Spring 1983), 61–94.

—, 'Renaissance Literary Studies and the Subject of History', *English Literary Renaissance*, 16 (Winter 1986), 5–12.

—, 'Professing the Renaissance: The Poetics and Politics of Culture', in *The New Historicism*, ed. H. Aram Veeser (New York and London: Routledge, 1989), pp. 15–36.

—, *The Purpose of Playing: Shakespeare and the Cultural Politics of the Elizabethan Theatre* (Chicago, IL and London: The University of Chicago Press, 1996).

—, 'Introduction', in Pierre Macherey, *In a Materialist Way: Selected Essays*, ed. Warren Montag, trans. Ted Stolze (London: Verso, 1998), pp. 1–48.

Mousley, Andy, *Re-Humanising Shakespeare: Literary Humanism, Wisdom and Modernity* (Edinburgh: Edinburgh University Press, 2007).

Mulhern, Francis, 'Althusser in Literary Studies', in *Althusser: A Critical Reader*, ed. Gregory Elliott (Cambridge, MA and Oxford: Blackwell, 1994), pp. 159–76.

Mullaney, Stephen, 'After the New Historicism', in *Alternative Shakespeares, Volume 2*, ed. Terence Hawkes (New York and London: Routledge, 1996), pp. 17–37.

Nelson, Cary and Lawrence Grossberg (eds), *Marxism and the Interpretation of Culture* (Urbana and Chicago: University of Illinois Press, 1988).

Nichols, John (ed.), *The Progresses and Public Processions of Queen Elizabeth [To which are subjoined some of the Early Progresses of King James I]*, 4 vols (London, 1788–1821), vol. 1.

Nordlund, Marcus, *Shakespeare and the Nature of Love: Literature, Culture, Evolution* (Evanston, IL: Northwestern University Press, 2007).

Nuttall, A. D., 'The Argument about Shakespeare's Characters', *Critical Quarterly*, 7(2) (1965), 107–20.

—, *Shakespeare the Thinker* (New Haven, CT: Yale University Press, 2007).

Onega, Susana and José Ángel García Landa, *Narratology* (New York and London: Longman, 1996).

Orgel, Stephen, *The Illusion of Power: Political Theater in the English Renaissance* (Berkeley, CA: University of California Press, 1975).

—, *The Authentic Shakespeare and Other Problems of the Early Modern Stage* (New York and London: Routledge, 2002).

Orwell, George, *Nineteen Eighty-Four* (London: Penguin, 2003).

Palmer, D. J., *The rise of English studies: an account of the study of the English language and literature from its origins to the making of the Oxford English School* (Oxford: Oxford University Press for the University of Hull, 1965).

Parker, Patricia, *Shakespeare from the Margins: Language, Culture, Context* (Chicago and London: University of Chicago Press, 1996).

Parvini, Neema, *Shakespeare's History Plays: Rethinking Historicism* (Edinburgh: Edinburgh University Press, 2012).

Patterson, Annabel, *Shakespeare and the Popular Voice* (Oxford: Basil Blackwell, 1989).

Patterson, Lee, *Negotiating the Past: The Historical Understanding of Medieval Literature* (Madison, WI: University of Wisconsin Press, 1987).

—, 'Introduction: Critical Historicism and Medieval Studies', in *Literary Practice and Social Change in Britain, 1380–1530*, ed. Lee Patterson (Berkeley and Los Angeles: University of California Press, 1990), pp. 1–14.

—, *Chaucer and the Subject of History* (Madison, WI: University of Wisconsin Press, 1991).

Pechter, Edward, 'The New Historicism and its Discontents: Politicizing Renaissance Drama', *PMLA*, 102(3) (May 1987), 292–303.

—, 'Against "Ideology"', in *Shakespeare Left and Right*, ed. Ivo Kamps (New York and London: Routledge, 1991), pp. 79–98.

—, *What Was Shakespeare?: Renaissance Plays and Changing Critical Practice* (Ithaca, NY and London: Cornell University Press, 1995).

—, 'Misrepresentation, Ego, Nostalgia: Misreading "Misreading the Postcolonial Tempest"', *Early Modern Culture, issue 3* (updated 2003) http://emc.eserver.org/1-3/pechter_response.html, accessed 27 March 2007.

Pecora, Vincent P., 'The Limits of Local Knowledge', in *The New Historicism*, ed. H. Aram Veeser (New York and London: Routledge, 1989), pp. 243–76.

Pinker, Steven, *The Blank Slate: The Modern Denial of Human Behaviour* (New York and London: Penguin, 2002).

Porter, Carolyn, 'History and Literature: After New Historicism', *New Literary History*, 21(2) (Winter 1990), 252–72.

Poulantzas, Nicos, *State, Power, Socialism* (London: Verso, 1980).

Prior, Moody E., *The Drama of Power: Studies in Shakespeare's History Plays* (Evanston, IL: Northwestern University Press, 1973).

Propp, Vladimir, *Morphology of the Folktale*, trans. Laurence Scott (Austin, TX: University of Texas Press, 1968).

Rasmussen, David (ed.), *Renaissance Literature and Its Formal Engagements* (New York and Basingstoke: Palgrave, 2002).

Resch, Robert Paul, *Althusser and the Renewal of Marxist Social Theory* (Berkeley, CA: University of California Press, 1992).

Richards, I. A., *Principles of Literary Criticism* (New York and London: Routledge, 2001).

Ridler, Anne, 'Introduction', in *Shakespeare Criticism 1935–60*, ed. Anne Ridler (New York and London: Oxford University Press, 1963), pp. vii–xiii.

Rimmon-Kenan, Shlomith, *Narrative Fiction: Contemporary Poetics* (New York and London: Routledge, 1983).

Rosaldo Jr, Renato I., 'A Note on Geertz as a Cultural Essayist', *Representations*, 59, Special Issue: The Fate of "Culture": Geertz and Beyond (1997), 30–4.

Rossiter, A. P., *Angel with Horns: Fifteen Lectures on Shakespeare*, ed. Graham Storey (New York: Longman, 1989).

Ryan, Kiernan, 'Introduction', in *New Historicism and Cultural Materialism: A Reader*, ed. Kiernan Ryan (London: Arnold, 1996), pp. ix–xviii.

—, 'King Lear: A Retrospect, 1980–2000', in *Shakespeare Survey Volume 55: King Lear and its Afterlife*, ed. Peter Holland (Cambridge: Cambridge University Press, 2007), pp. 1–11.

Said, Edward W., *Culture and Imperialism* (New York: Knopf, 1993).

—, *Power, Politics and Culture* (New York and London: Bloomburg, 2004).

Sanders, Wilbur, *The Dramatist and the Received Idea: Studies in the Plays of Marlowe and Shakespeare* (Cambridge: Cambridge University Press, 1968).

Saul, Nigel, *Richard II* (New Haven, CT and London: Yale University Press, 1997).

Saussure, Ferdinand de, *Course in General Linguistics*, trans. Roy Harris (Peru, IL: Open Court, 2006).

Simpson, David, 'Literary Criticism and the Return to "History"', *Critical Inquiry*, 14(4) (Summer 1988), 721–47.

Sinfield, Alan, 'Power and Ideology: An Outline Theory and Sidney's *Arcadia*', *ELH*, 52(2) (Summer 1985), 259–77.

—, *Faultlines: Cultural Materialism and the Politics of Dissident Reading* (Oxford: Clarendon Press, 1992).

—, 'Counter-response to Richard Levin', *Early Modern Culture, issue 2* (updated 2001) http://emc.eserver.org/1-2/sinfield2.html, accessed 18 March 2007.

—, 'Selective Quotation', *Early Modern Culture, issue 2* (updated 2001) http://emc.eserver.org/1-2/sinfield.html, accessed 18 March 2007.

—, *Shakespeare, Authority, Sexuality: Unfinished Business in Cultural Materialism* (New York and London: Routledge, 2006).

Smith, Paul, *Discerning the Subject* (Minneapolis, MN: University of Minnesota Press, 1989).

Spargo, Tamsin, 'Introduction: Past, Present and Future Pasts', in *Reading the Past: Literature and History*, ed. Tamsin Spargo (London: Palgrave Macmillan, 2000), pp. 1–11.

Spurgeon, Caroline, *Shakespeare's Imagery and What It Tells Us* (Cambridge: Cambridge University Press, 2004).

Strohm, Paul, *Social Chaucer* (London and Cambridge, MA: Harvard University Press, 1989).

Taylor, Gary, *Reinventing Shakespeare: A Cultural History from the Restoration to the Present* (Oxford: Oxford University Press, 1990).

Taylor, Michael, *Shakespeare Criticism in the Twentieth Century* (Oxford: Oxford University Press, 2001).

Tennenhouse, Leonard, 'Representing Power: *Measure for Measure in its Time*', in *The Power of Forms in the English Renaissance*, ed. Stephen Greenblatt (Norman, OK: Pilgrim Books, 1982), pp. 139–56.

—, *Power on Display: The Politics of Shakespeare's Genres* (New York and London: Methuen, 1986).

Thompson, E. P., *The Poverty of Theory* (London: Merlin Press, 1978).

Tillyard, E. M. W., *Shakespeare's History Plays* (London: Chatto and Windus, 1944).

—, *The Muse Unchained; an Intimate Account of the Revolution in English Studies at Cambridge* (London: Bowes and Bowes, 1958).

—, *The Elizabethan World Picture* (London: Vintage, 1959).

Todorov, Tzvetan, *Litterature et Signification* (Paris: Larousse, 1967).

Veeser, H. Aram, 'Introduction', in *The New Historicism*, ed. H. Aram Veeser (New York and London: Routledge, 1989), pp. ix–xvi.

—, 'The New Historicism', in *The New Historicism Reader*, ed. H. Aram Veeser (New York and London: Routledge, 1994), pp. 1–34.

Vendler, Helen, *The Art of Shakespeare's Sonnets* (Boston, MA: Harvard University Press, 1997).

Vickers, Brian, *Appropriating Shakespeare: Contemporary Critical Quarrels* (New Haven, CT: Yale University Press, 1993).

Vitkus, Daniel, 'Turning Turk in *Othello*: the Conversion and Damnation of the Moor', *Shakespeare Quarterly*, 48 (1997), 145–76.

Wachowski, Andy and Larry Wachowski, (dir.) *The Matrix*, (Warner Bros. Pictures, 1999).

Wayne, Don E., 'Power, Politics, and the Shakespearean Text: Recent Criticism in England and the United States', in *Shakespeare Reproduced: The Text in History and Ideology*, ed. Jean E. Howard and Marion F. O'Connor (New York and London: Methuen, 1987), pp. 47–67.

Wells, Robin Headlam, *Shakespeare's Humanism* (Cambridge: Cambridge University Press, 2005).

White, Hayden, *Metahistory: The Historical Imagination in Nineteenth-Century Europe* (Baltimore, MD and London: Johns Hopkins University Press, 1973).

—, 'New Historicism: A Comment', in *The New Historicism*, ed. H. Aram Veeser (New York and London: Routledge, 1989), pp. 293–303.

Williams, Raymond, *Marxism and Literature* (Oxford: Oxford University Press, 1977).

—, *Problems in Materialism and Culture* (London: Verso, 1980).

Wilson, Rawdon, *Shakespearean Narrative* (Cranbury, NJ and London: Associated University Press, 1995).

Wilson, Richard, 'Introduction: Historicising New Historicism', in *New Historicism and Renaissance Drama*, ed. Richard Wilson and Richard Dutton (New York and London: Longman, 1992), pp. 1–18.

—, *Will Power: Essays on Shakespearean Authority* (Hemel Hempstead: Harvester Wheatsheaf, 1993).

Wilson, Scott, *Cultural Materialism: Theory and Practice* (Oxford: Blackwell, 1995).

Witteck, Stephen, 'A Brief History of Deconstruction in Shakespeare Criticism', *The Birmingham Journal of Literature and Language*, 1(1) (2008), 3–12.

Wolfson, Susan J., 'Reading for Form', *Modern Language Quarterly*, 61(1) (March 2000), 1–16.

Žižek, Slavoj, *The Sublime of Ideology* (New York and London: Verso Books, 1989).

—, 'Introduction', in *Mapping Ideology*, ed. Slavoj Žižek (New York and London: Verso Book, 1994), pp. 1–33.

INDEX